NICE PROMISES

Tim Sebastian

CHATTO & WINDUS

THE HOGARTH PRESS

LONDON

Published in 1985 by
Chatto & Windus · The Hogarth Press
40 William IV Street, London WC2N 4DF

British Library
Cataloguing in Publication Data

Sebastian, Tim
Nice promises.
1. Poland—Social conditions—1945–
I. Title
943.8'056   HN537.5

ISBN 0 7011 2705 8
ISBN 0 7011 3943 9 Pbk

Copyright © Tim Sebastian, 1985

Phototypeset by Wyvern Typesetting Limited, Bristol
Printed in Great Britain by
Redwood Burn Ltd
Trowbridge, Wiltshire

Contents

For Dee, Peter and Clare

Introduction

Even the dusk had the Polish colours. Red and white. The sun and the sky. The ferry glided towards the Baltic port, past the grey, numbered gunboats, tied up and idle. Passengers crowded on to the decks, hoping to see relatives. A few shouted and waved. Without them, the evening would have been soundless, the engines barely running, the sea flat, the seagulls out over the open water.

Later, as I crossed from the port to the town, groups of teenagers were out looking for fun. They laughed among themselves, running between the trees. The light from the streetlamps was too dim to make them out clearly. I found a hotel and a hot room. The mosquitoes found me. And the first of countless nights I was to spend in Poland passed by.

'Perhaps it'll look better when it's finished.' A western colleague glanced up at the square block of flats, fifteen stories high with plenty of rough concrete. 'Then again, perhaps it won't.'

He had a point. It didn't look much. But it was finished. I signed a contract for a flat on the twelfth floor later that afternoon. It was near the centre of Warsaw. The Moskwa cinema was within five minutes' walking distance. I didn't know it that day, but there was a prison and a military barracks a block away. They were to be the focus of considerable activity before my stay in Poland was over.

I moved into the flat in May 1979 as the BBC's first Eastern Europe correspondent. The block was designed on the Babel principle. The inmates were all foreign, and few if any had a common language. There were Ethiopians, Mexicans, Arabs – and some Japanese who didn't appear to understand anything.

The building was owned by the State accommodation agency, PUMA. It had borrowed the animal's name and cunning, but regrettably not its killer instinct. I was to complain frequently about this puma's unwillingness to hunt down the army of cockroaches which infested the building. In the end the battle proved fruitless. In any case, on long winter nights I found comfort in knowing I was not alone.

The porters would lock the main door at night. They slept on two old armchairs drawn together to make a bed. In the early hours they would shuffle sleepily to open the door, string-vested in summer, coated up in winter. I ended up apologizing for coming home so late.

At that time Poland was outwardly stable. Edward Gierek had led the Polish Communists for nearly ten years. He had pleased some people at home (fewer as time passed) and impressed others abroad. It did not seem a bad record.

He came to power in 1970 with a mandate to restore his party's credibility. Bloody riots in Gdansk had left dozens of people dead, a number of politicians disgraced and a population incensed by the brutal incompetence of its Government.

Gierek promised much and borrowed heavily from the West to finance the promises. But too much money went on short-term consumer products. There was too little left for capital investment. Gierek had not planned for the future. Inevitably, the economic damage caught up with him. The West's recession and the oil crisis did not help either. When he tried to raise prices in 1976, he encountered strikes and riots. He backed down.

For Gierek knew better than most what his countrymen could do to unpopular governments. They had shown in 1970 that if they could not change the administration through the ballot box, they might just achieve it out on the streets.

But little of this was visible in May 1979. Poles waited proudly for the arrival of 'their' Pope – John Paul II.

And that visit signalled a major resurgence of world interest in Poland. Metal boxes containing television equipment began arriving at Warsaw airport. American reporters threw dollars at their problems and offered to buy aircraft for cash when all the seats were full. The Western press brought its ambitions, insecurities and preconceptions and dropped them at Poland's door.

The TV teams would unpack, the reporters would apply their

Max Factor and then set off in pursuit of the unpronounceable. What had thirty-five years of Communism done for Poland, they asked. How did a normal Pole live?

There was much to learn. Not least the different set of social values, the enhanced importance of friendship and family ties, the new political creed. Communism assumed the duty of people to work together. Pluralism was unproductive. One Marxist banner and one Marxist movement were deemed sufficient to represent the Poles. But each day in Poland uncovered the exceptions. So much so that the rules ceased to fit, and while knowledge increased, understanding dissolved. Three years in Poland were to bring me an awareness of Polish complexities but little idea of how they fitted together.

It looked easy on paper. The Communist Party determined policy, the Government carried it out. Parliament (the Sejm) debated and defined new laws. The Party leader answered to the Party through the Central Committee. He answered to the people through Parliament . . . or television. It might have lasted indefinitely.

But when Edward Gierek appeared on Polish screens in 1980 to condemn the strikes and warn of national disaster, no one believed him. And neither the Central Committee nor the Parliament could help him. Poles had ceased to regard Gierek with simple, normal cynicism. In their eyes he had lost authority. His colleagues realized it before he did.

Behind the politics though, ordinary people had more mundane concerns. I was concerned about the supermarkets. The labels on tins and packets meant little. For a while it seemed that tripe was the only commodity on sale. Culinary disappointments multiplied. In contrast, my Polish brought a little amusement into a lot of lives. Perhaps that was a positive contribution. In between fits of laughter the Poles would remind me that the first ten years of the language were the worst.

Poland acquired Mr Stanislaw Kania as leader in September 1980, acquired him apparently in the early hours of the morning. No one seemed to feel much compulsion to react, least of all Kania himself. His acceptance speech took some time to filter out, though no one could imagine why. By this time, though, Western journalists were losing sleep over Solidarity. Camp-beds appeared in offices. Normally healthy reporters would be found slumped over their typewriters during the hours of daylight. Some became manic, others refused to wash. The Poles must have found the sight less than edifying.

The problem lay in the speed of events. If you slept at all you missed something. That meant wasting time in catching up. Poles, it seemed to us, never slept, never slowed down. We lost count of the strikes, the speeches and the negotiations. Suddenly another year had gone by and Poland had another leader: the first general to lead an Eastern bloc country.

In those days there was little free time to travel around Poland, and any outing from Warsaw was considered a reward. There was great rivalry between the cities. Gdansk thought it was cleverer than Warsaw, that it had a freer spirit and did the thinking for the entire nation. Katowice considered it worked hardest and earned the most foreign currency. Warsaw had little time for any other city, least of all Poznan. Warsaw people sometimes referred to Poznan inhabitants as 'potatoes'. They would tell of a partisan returning to Poznan from Warsaw in the early months of 1944.

'You know,' he told his friends, 'the people are going to mount an uprising in the summer.'

'My God,' said his less-than-bright friend, 'are the Germans really going to allow that?'

Inevitably, there was suspicion about those who came from distant towns and villages. It took time to develop trust, and no one had much of that. Foreigners though, were always well received. As one old lady told me, 'Whatever we've done to ourselves, we've never done anything to strangers.'

As a stranger I was given both friendship and advice unstintingly. I was told more stories than I could ever retell. I have checked the information I use as far as is possible, but there are bound to be mistakes and I accept responsibility for them. Facts are what you see with your own eyes. The rest is risky ground.

I have taken the risk in the belief that what people *thought* was true can also be significant. An accepted lie is just as influential as an accepted fact. And in Poland's jungle of rumour in the late seventies and early eighties half-truths and misapprehensions dictated countless actions and responses.

The title of this book, *Nice Promises*, derives from a Polish proverb: 'Nice promises and the fool is happy'. The irony was never lost on the Poles. So many nice promises were made by so many different people. So few were believed.

Undoubtedly Polish scepticism has enhanced the people's sense of humour. And for that as much as for their humanity, their determination and style – and for the lessons of a thousand days spent in their country – I thank them.

Tim Sebastian
London, 1984

ACKNOWLEDGEMENTS

Outside Poland, I should like to thank the following for their generous help and advice: Elizabeth Cooper, John Cochrane, Michael Davies, Robin Gedye, Ray Gowdridge, Brenda Griffiths, Alistair Harrison, Duncan Herbert, Larry Hodgson, Richard Jenkins, Anne McDermid, Kate McGovern, Wally Mears, John Miller, Ian Mitchell, Brian Mooney, Sheena Reilly, Rick Thompson, Lillian Thomsen, Peggy Watson, Patrick Worsnip.

Chronology

1970 December – Riots in the Baltic ports. Scores killed. Wladyslaw Gomulka toppled. Edward Gierek takes power.

1976 June – Riots and strikes over price rises. Gierek backs down.

1978 October – Polish pope elected and the atheist Government expresses its pride.

1979 June – Pope visits Poland. The country, people say, will never be the same again.

1980 July – Due to an 'unfortunate oversight', meat-price increases not announced until day after their introduction. Strikes coincide with Moscow Olympics.

August – Gdansk agreement signed, bringing Solidarity into being. Gierek falls ill, but no one waits for him to recover: Stanislaw Kania comes to power.

November – Joint Polish–Soviet manoeuvres.

December – Polish leaders summoned to Moscow.

1981 March – State radio announces that the nation's food supply will last only 12 days.

April – Visit of Kremlin ideologist Mikhail Suslov.

July – Emergency Communist Party congress. Kania voted in after show of support.

September – Walesa formally voted leader of Solidarity at its own congress in Gdansk.

October – Kania replaced as leader. General Jaruzelski comes to power.

December – Martial law declared.

1982 December – Martial law suspended.

1983 June – Pope visits Poland.

October – Lech Walesa awarded Nobel Prize.

Images of Martial Law

It was a waste of time. The telephone had been engaged all day. When it finally rang clear no one answered. There were long, single tones. You could count to ten between them. Why was no one there? The man put down the receiver and looked round his office. Friday, 11 December. It was freezing: the heating had been working well below capacity. Time to go home and wrap a blanket round his head, anything to get warm. He made for the door, and as he did so heard the sound of knocking on the other side. He stopped and listened. His instinct was to do nothing. If the caller were innocent he would go away. If he weren't, then that would be apparent soon enough. The knocking started again. The man opened the spyhole and peered out. A round grey shape stood there – identifiable only as human and probably civilian. He opened the door. An elderly woman in slippers, her hair swept back in a bun, stood shuffling from one foot to another, an expression of both penitence and aggression on her face. The woman said nothing – nothing intelligible – and pushed past him, heading for the bathroom.

'Look,' she croaked, gesturing towards the ceiling, 'look at that.' Water was dripping steadily through the ceiling, bouncing into the bath and on to the stone floor. Aggression first. 'It's not my fault,' she said, 'it's my son. He left the water on in the bath.' Then penitence. 'I can't afford to pay, I'll try to get someone to fix it for you or we'll do it ourselves.' He looked at her and muttered something vaguely sympathetic. He would have put an arm round her, but he realized his arm wasn't long enough. She seemed relieved and shuffled out of the flat, mumbling to herself. She might almost have been saying prayers.

The man went back to the desk and tried the phone again. Good God, he thought, there was someone there after all.

'I want to speak to Editor Bronowski, please.'

'Bronowski speaking,' said the voice. He sounded reasonably cheerful, but there was a note of caution. Well, that could mean anything. After all, Bronowski worked for the official news agency PAP, and God knew who listened to their telephones.

'I'd like to arrange an interview with the Trade Union Minister,' said the man. 'It's about all the strikes. Perhaps the Minister could tell me what he plans to do now that a general stoppage is likely to be called.'

'I'll try,' said Bronowski. 'I'll put in the request, but I'll tell you now that by Monday you won't want the interview.'

'Why, what do you mean?' asked the man quickly, but Bronowski had hung up. The line crackled a bit. Marvellous, thought the man, just me and the listeners left.

Late in the evening of 12 December 1981 a group of tired workers were wrapping up a meeting in the Lenin shipyard. The telephone rang. A girl went to answer it, listened for a second and replaced the receiver.

'Who was it?' someone asked.

'Don't know. Someone just said "Operation W" and hung up.'

'Anyone know anything about "Operation W"?' It was one of the group leaders speaking. A few people looked up through the cigarette smoke.

'Nope,' said one of them. 'No idea.' Who cared anyway? There had been so many codes to remember. About an hour later, however, they all found out what it meant.

That same night Warsaw was snow-bound. The sleet and the wind had been interminable. In daytime the slush turned streets into quagmires, at night they froze again, the darkness bringing a fresh covering of snow. At midnight Constitution Square looked miserable, lit up by the blue sulphur streetlamps. It was the Eastern Europe of the Cold War, of the spy novels. A few battered vans stood deserted. Tramlines and electric wires cut across the sky. In one corner, an unlit KLM sign and a Russian clockface. The clock's hands had been stopped for years at twenty minutes to four.

The night turned people into strangers. Sometimes the drunks stumbled into blocks of flats, searching for warmth. They lay beached on the stairs near the radiators, snoring and cursing. Vague, grey hulks to be stepped over or kicked, depending on whether the lights were working. The stillness was interrupted only briefly as a hotel cabaret ended and threw its patrons out on to the street. They overloaded the waiting taxis and spluttered off into the suburbs, the yellow headlamps picking a path through the car tracks in the ice. Polish Fiats, a cast-off Italian design, temperamental cars that had broken Italian hearts and later broke Polish ones. Even the newspapers called them outdated and inefficient. Why had the State chosen to make them? Everywhere you turned in Poland, it was the same question.

Later, looking back, it had seemed a normal December. Politically chaotic, with the economy disintegrating, but that was normal for Poland. The strangest pastime had been queuing for ice-cream in sub-zero temperatures. Then they invented the mushroom hotdog. Not bad either. Toasted rolls and cauldrons of watery mushrooms with cheese. When you took your gloves off to eat them one hand froze while the other burned: a small example of a very Polish dilemma. Dogs were another obsession, and pregnant women. The one was attributed to a long, hoped-for rise in meat supplies, the other to a climate of freedom inspired by Solidarity.

But the dogs and the pregnant women had gone home that night, back to the modern tenements and the acres of dormitory flats permanently unfinished. While they slept, the world outside changed around them.

There was at least one insomniac: K., in his early seventies, highly educated and a self-effacing member of the dissident group KOR. He lives in one of the grey blocks in the centre of Warsaw, a tribute to the economic hardship of the post-war years and the uniform designs that the State encouraged. K. rarely went out in winter because of his asthma.

At four o'clock that Sunday morning he turned on the BBC World Service and heard the first reports of a crackdown on the local Solidarity headquarters, not five miles from his flat. London, it seemed, was even closer to events than he was. Although the details were sketchy he went to bed knowing what it all meant, and knowing he would soon have visitors.

They came at seven o'clock. Apparently there is an unwritten convention, in force since the Stalinist period, which prevents the police calling between midnight and five in the morning. There were two of them knocking at the door, shaking the snow from their boots, and K. recognized them immediately. The same two who had come to search his flat at the height of the strikes the year before. Unlike many others, they at least had remained in stable employment. The meeting passed off with relatively polite form-alities. This time there was no search. K. and his wife stayed in their dressing-gowns, the security men in plain clothes producing a declaration and telling K. to sign it. It stipulated that he would cease all activity against the Polish State. He told them he had engaged in no such activity and refused to sign. They did not insist. They left after half an hour, warning him to be careful. There were others to see.

It had been a night full of horror, punctuated with irony. The wife of a prominent writer heard a 'frightful drilling noise' at her front door and reached for the telephone to call the police. It was at that moment that the police forced their way in. They had drilled the handle off rather than go through the formality of knocking. Some people were taken away in their pyjamas, bundled out into unmarked cars as the dawn came up and the snow-clouds appeared. Others were told to finish their breakfast, put on warm clothing and pack a suitcase. As usual, the whole operation had been carefully planned, scrappily executed, but highly effective. Practical Communism in the eighties.

The battle lines were established that first Sunday at about two o'clock in the afternoon. The crowds in Warsaw's Saviour Square had been visible from some distance. Only inside the Square itself could you see the riot police, the plastic shields clasped in front of them, the visors down, the white rubber truncheons displaying their special steel lining. They were just a few yards from the Solidarity building. The roads had been blocked off with armoured personnel carriers and police buses. This was one of a hundred similar scenes that took place that day around the country. The authorities gave them the clinical title of 'Pacification'.

As the riot police advanced, twelve abreast, they pushed the crowd before them. Pole against Pole in the fifth major confrontation since the war. The crowds became increasingly bitter; they whistled, jeered, yelled 'Gestapo'. Beside me a man muttered, 'Here comes the so-called People's Guard. Their mothers are all whores.' The hostility and tension was plainly visible on all faces, Polish faces that had never been indifferent to anything. People were shaking with anger. The conflict was finally out in the open, out of the offices and factories where it had festered for years. State institutions and departments had long before set to work against each other. Workers scorned management. Buyers didn't want to buy, sellers didn't want to sell. Bribes were what you gave to get what was yours before someone sold it. It had to end somewhere, and it did.

And yet few people had anticipated the events of that weekend. This time they had thought it would be different. For months even the cynics had begun to believe: atheists became agnostics. Christmas, it seemed, would last forever. One hope only half realized quickly led to another ten. After all, people had hungered for hope, and that made the shock of 13 December all the more powerful.

Black humour found its way into the shops well in time for Christmas. According to one story, a militia patrol shot dead an old man on the roadside, just five minutes before the night-time curfew came into force. 'Why did you do that?' asked a soldier. 'Oh, I know where he lived,' said the militia captain. 'He couldn't possibly have made it home in time.'

Some had other excuses for not getting home in those days. One evening, soon after the Emergency had been declared, riot police arrived in force at a small town hospital in the north and announced they were taking away the Chief Cardiac Surgeon (he had been a Solidarity organizer). As the police entered one of the wards the patients rose from their beds, some of them carrying their own drips, others barely able to stand, and formed a pathetic gaggle around the doctor. The police were faced with the option of forcing the patients aside or going away. This time they left.

They returned the next morning and ordered the hospital director to sack the man. He refused, and was summarily dismissed himself. His replacement duly signed the original order and told the doctor to leave the premises. As he did so, though, he provoked one of the more extraordinary sights of the entire crisis. Trailing behind him to the bus stop, through the cold and sludge, were some twenty patients, a few critically ill, wearing only dressing-gowns and slippers, some barely able to walk. This small crowd of casualties surrounded their doctor and waited with him at the bus stop until the bus took him away to the police station and internment. The purge had begun.

Regional administrators, local party officials, academics and journalists were at the top of the list for removal. Many were sacked or hived off to politically sterile occupations (though some have since been reinstated). There was hardly a single area of the State's administration or its economy that was unaffected.

H. was one of the first to be singled out. He had worked as a check-in clerk at one of the provincial airports. A few days after the declaration of martial law he was called to the local security office for a meeting with an official he had known for most of his working life. There was one other officer in the room. H. had never seen him before; in any case, there were none of the usual pleasantries. H. was simply told to surrender his airport pass. 'Presumably,' he said, 'this is a temporary measure for the emergency period.'

'No,' replied the officer he knew, 'it's for good.' And in an extraordinarily theatrical gesture the man pulled on a pair of white gloves and took the pass from H.

'Now send in your supervisor,' he added, as the interview ended.

It terminated four years of work at the airport, and H. wasn't the only one.

Later that first week a Polish Airlines plane was allowed to leave for London, the first flight to the West since the Emergency had begun. The aircraft had been due to leave mid-morning, but departed instead in the darkness of the late afternoon, some six hours behind schedule. Only later was it reported that each of the crew had been specially questioned and warned of severe penalties if they failed to return. By the time they took off they must have been terrified.

Others went nowhere except to the internment camps. There they accepted conditions calmly; sometimes the reaction came more from their families. But to a nation that lived through Auschwitz, countless invasions and occupations, even its own disillusions, mass internment was not a major trauma. A well-known actress arrived at one of the camps and said simply, 'I hope my make-up is all right.' The guards and inmates all turned out to welcome her. The only time she cried was when they released her, just before Christmas.

Internment was a haphazard weapon, but a powerful one. The more haphazard, the more it provoked doubt and disarray. People were taken in waves; some who expected to be picked up were left alone, while others, like the film director Andrzej Wajda, actually complained that the police were not after them. One Solidarity activist sought by the authorities for several weeks gave himself up and was told he was no longer wanted. Just as the Polish State found problems in running an economy, so the Government found it hard to stage an efficient clampdown. Sometimes they went looking for people who had been abroad for years. In one celebrated instance the army arrested a group of militiamen lying in wait for a suspect.

Trust was an early casualty in those days. Trust in friends and colleagues from work. Trust in the stranger you found idling on your staircase for no apparent reason, in your boss, even in the country you really believed was different from all the others.

If Solidarity had changed the mood of Poland and its people, so martial law forced many to revert to type. Those who had always supported the system became more anxious to show loyalty. A few formed 'initiative groups', which in many cases did little more than clear snow. But who in the neighbourhood could refuse just that little bit of patriotic assistance when the incentives were so clear? It would be too easy for someone to whisper that the citizen at Number Five had been awkward – or had 'failed to show a positive response'. So, clanging their spades, the citizens at Number Five, and Numbers Four and Six, went out into the snow with an elaborate display of enthusiasm and dug it. In just a few weeks these initiative groups plastered their posters all over Warsaw, in blocks of flats, even in bars. 'The days of anarchy are over,' they proclaimed. And when they were torn down there were plenty more to replace them.

Under such conditions of stress there was every incentive for employees to squeal on their colleagues. Anyway, some squealed their heads off. A woman who had been a local Solidarity organizer was summoned to her office and asked to explain her role in the union. Gaining fluency, she explained that her branch had included many dangerous extremists. She had therefore felt it necessary to exercise a restraining influence. She had tried to moderate their feelings, their outbursts and aggression. She had counselled against strikes, at all times seeking the path of negotiation.

She kept her job, but three of her closest colleagues lost theirs. And her husband, who had been interned, was released on the strength of her confession. Her friends judged her harshly, despite the impossible circumstances.

'She didn't have to tell,' said one of them. 'She used to be our friend. And do you know, before Solidarity she was a member of the Communist Party. She just wanted to win.'

Early in January 1982 two men had called for S. at his flat near the Vistula, but he had the good luck to be out. They told his wife they would come again, and they arrived one Saturday morning to take S. away for interrogation. He had had the foresight to pack a small bag with a change of clothing and some toiletries, but they didn't say whether he would need them. They drove in one of the unmarked Polski Fiats to the city's main jail on Rakowiecka Street – a building which carries the same stigma as the Lubyanka in Moscow.

S. was questioned largely by one man who told him he had

violated currency regulations. He could be liable for fines worth millions of zlotys. He recalled later that they had had precise details of meetings he had arranged over the previous six months – in particular, contacts with Westerners. All the time, they held out the possibility of internment, and S. says he was prepared for it. He tried hard not to show any nervousness, not to let his hand shake or his face twitch. He admits it wasn't easy. Occasionally the interrogator would get up and walk out of the room, saying he had to consult. 'Don't get excited,' he would tell S. reassuringly. 'Take it easy. I'll be back in a moment.'

At one point they asked S. to sign a declaration implying he had taken part in anti-State activities. He amended it. He says he was one witness that was determined not to be led so easily. Half-way through the questioning S. asked to be taken to the lavatory. He specifically wanted to be escorted, as he had no wish to wander alone through the endless corridors even had they allowed it. On his way, he said, only one thing caught his eye – a notice on the wall asking the finder of an electronic watch to return it to its owner. 'As if,' S. remarked, 'anyone in this place would be honest enough to do that.'

After seven hours of circular questioning S. had given little information, but he had the impression they knew what they wanted anyway. To his surprise the interrogator suddenly broke off in mid-sentence and declared: 'Well, we're not going to take you to internment camp after all – you're free to go.' S. sensed his good fortune. He told the officer, 'Don't look on this as a personal defeat. It's just the way I am. You should have known you'd get nothing from me.' The man didn't answer. S. wasn't given a lift home. He took his bag and wandered out in the street, where a soldier stopped him for an identity check. S. said later he nearly hugged the man.

It's impossible to know just how much the Government was monitoring day-to-day events at this time. And no one really knew who was doing the governing. As one observer put it, 'when you turn the place into a jungle, look out for what's in the trees.'

So it was that even senior members of the administration were excluded from the planning of martial law. They were as shocked as the millions they had governed. A leading member of the Council of State was woken by an army officer at two o'clock in the morning and told to sign the document legalizing the imposition of martial law. He expressed surprise and consternation, and the order was shouted back at him. 'Look here,' he told the officer, 'you can shout at me when I've signed it, but until I have you will talk to me with respect.'

It was clear that even after the military takeover senior members of the Government were treated with scant courtesy by the security services. At times they were overruled completely. One of General Jaruzelski's closest aides, Deputy Prime Minister Rakowski, had ordered the release of a prominent actress, but the order was apparently flouted. Rakowski is reported to have been approached by members of the suspended actors' union. Afterwards, he had immediately contacted the police in Poznan. The woman was promptly deposited on the pavement outside the police station, rearrested according to the time-honoured tradition and sent to a women's detention camp in the north-east. Rakowski was not informed, and some days later he received another visit from an actor who told him: 'You're either a liar or a bloody fool – which is it?' Rakowski said he was surprised and genuinely sorry. But it made no difference – the actress remained in detention.

News of such incidents helped cement a general feeling of despair. In those early days of martial law it seemed Poland was drifting. The chaos inside the administration was reflected on the streets. Occasional fights broke out between the army and the militia. Most demoralizing of all was the lack of communication. Telephones and telexes were cut, road-blocks set up on all the main highways. Only the trains were relatively free to run. Not unnaturally, rumours multiplied. According to one story a Solidarity leader in Torun had died on the operating table after a beating by the police. The rumour reached a senior member of the Politburo, who demanded information from the local militia. They denied the story. But the politician confided to a friend that the character of the denial made it difficult to believe. Who knew anything for certain? In this case the Solidarity leader lived.

There were some rural areas that didn't see a soldier for weeks. Workers simply barricaded themselves into local factories, drank illicit alcohol and sang patriotic songs – until the army arrived. They knew nothing of those who lived – or died – elsewhere.

Tremendous secrecy surrounded all civilian casualties, as most of them were taken to military hospitals. Ironically, the riot police were treated in civilian clinics. A surgeon in Gdansk reported that many officers had deliberately fallen to the ground feigning injury, so as not to obey orders. Some had said they were fed up and didn't want to be involved. Rumours persisted that they had been given drugs to increase aggression. But it was hard enough to treat either civilians or police. With all of them, the state of shock was aggravated by freezing cold and the stench of tear-gas. Doctors found it difficult to get near them.

More important, though, was the identity of the civilians brought in. Surgeons were required to report their names within an hour of treatment. But, knowing the consequences of revealing who had taken part in demonstrations, medical teams deliberately changed the names of those brought to them. Sometimes there were prominent Solidarity activists, well known to every-one. They were rushed through treatment and their wounds were patched. Sometimes, still half-senseless, they were given a new identity, a new address, and pushed out into the night.

Little concrete information emerged in those early days, particu-larly from the provinces. But the spirit of Christmas 1981 was obliterated. No one wished their friends a Happy Christmas, just a peaceful one. It says much about the Polish character that people in the port of Gdansk were able to continue their Christmas shopping as tear-gas canisters fell at their feet. Mothers pushed children in prams as young people rushed past them, blood streaming from their faces. An old man had a thunderflash thrown at him. He calmly picked it up and threw it into the road. Bystanders queuing for Christmas fare could barely be persuaded to leave their places as the ZOMO riot police battled in the street a block away. And yet some of them had seen it all before – ten years before. They all knew what it meant. Poles fighting Poles, just as they promised they never would, ever again.

There were, however, some surprises. Late in the evening of 24 December, as a family sat down for their Christmas meal in the city of Bydgoscz, a ZOMO riot policeman knocked at the door, a machine-gun in his hand, helmet and truncheon attached to his belt. To a simple provincial family he looked like a visitor from space. With some anxiety the father of the house asked him what he wanted. The policeman looked at the ground.

'I'm a long way from home,' he replied, 'and I would like to share your Christmas meal.'

Stunned and speechless, the family let him in. Not for nothing is there a free place at every Christmas Eve table throughout Poland. It is reserved for any stranger who may wish to join and share the twelve traditional dishes. Be they policeman or soldier, invader or friend, they have to be allowed entry. The family didn't regret their decision.

'We were a bit nervous when he let the children play with his gun,' said the mother. 'Otherwise, he was fine.'

Most people used to say they spent their lives in queues. Most exaggerated. But most of them had a point. And martial law brought a certain piquancy to queuing. In Warsaw a young girl told of a queue being suddenly surrounded by militiamen, who poured out of a van that had been touring the city centre. They immediately demanded identity cards and threatened to report anyone queuing during their working hours. The raids went on.

Money suffered under martial law, and that hurt the Poles. They found their privileged dollar accounts frozen and the authorities issuing only home-made dollar cheques instead. It was ironic that an Eastern bloc country resorted to printing its own version of a Western currency. A public admission of economic chaos. The process supported the old joke – why are Poland and the US so similar? Answer: because you can't buy anything for zlotys in either country. What made that even more ironic was the circulation of around 10,000 official banknotes, printed at source with the words *Wrona nie pokona* – 'The military will not humble us.' The notes became collector's items within days, and six people from the State mint are in prison for having the idea and carrying it out.

It was inevitable that when the military took over, Western aid dried up. The Poles never believed it could be otherwise. Few minded. They were puzzled, though, by the sudden deliveries of fraternal assistance from the other Eastern bloc countries. The juggernauts decked out with friendship posters trundled into the Capital's Victory Square to congratulate the people on saving Socialism. Some Poles were quick to point out that they had not been much in evidence a few months earlier, when the other countries had been throwing party tantrums about Solidarity – and even about their Polish comrades in power. How quickly the Eastern climate had changed. 'Friendship – from the working people of Berlin to the working people of Warsaw', declared the new posters.

I never saw an East German or Soviet aid parcel. But I was told that one variant consisted of three pieces of shortbread – one plain, one chocolate, one sugar-coated – a boiled sweet and a plastic toy watch. The report is interesting whether true or false. If true, because of the nature of the aid. If false, because many Poles (quality-conscious even in extreme hardship) would have objected to a consignment of Scotch smoked salmon if it had arrived without enough lemons in the same parcel. They may not have had luxuries, but they had a fair appreciation of them.

It was not just luxury they learned to forgo. Every day goods went missing. Vodka, regarded almost as an essential, fell under the rationing system. Everyone was entitled to a bottle a month. Children could exchange their coupons for chocolate or toothpaste – if there were any. The alcohol shortage did not prevent drunks appearing on the streets, just as the lack of petrol did not keep cars off the roads. In hundreds of flats all over Poland plastic buckets were hidden behind sofas or stored in cupboards, each containing home-distilled liquor. They called it 'Bimber'. It was made from berries and was disgusting. Most people said they used to shut their eyes, hold their nose and swallow. After a few gulps the effect would at least be alcoholic, if not fatal. Home-distilling operations became widespread among all classes. This from a nation that regularly sucked out petrol from other people's tanks when they ran out themselves, a practice seen at the roadside which often ended with the sucker spitting his guts out on to the tarmac.

But pleasures were not readily available and the home-made booze at least supplied a need. For many people began to escape into their own world during martial law. They tried to forget they were in Poland, stopped reading the newspapers, listening to the radio or watching television. One town made a great show of turning out on to the streets every night at seven-thirty just as the main television news went on the air. The police retaliated by checking identity cards. But soon everyone carried them, and the State could do little about it. Some people simply stood their television sets on window-sills, the screens facing outwards.

A university don described the mood in Poland soon after the start of martial law. Society, he said, divided into a small group who approved – he called them 'enthusiasts' – those who didn't, but who wanted to make the best of a bad job, those who were somewhere between passive resistance and terrorism – and the largest group, which went in for internal emigration. They did everything they could to leave the country – bar crossing a border. One student would fly frequently on internal flights and pray each time that the aircraft would be hijacked. 'If it didn't come in the first fifteen minutes,' she used to say, 'then you knew you'd had it. I'd have no hesitation about leaving if the plane went to the West. I wouldn't even look back,' she added.

She had taken a flight in March from the industrial city of Katowice to Warsaw. There was little in-flight service and much more in-flight surveillance. Two steel-helmeted riot police greeted passengers in the body of the plane. One told them where to sit and split up those in groups. The other rode shotgun in the cockpit. People were graded according to their hijacking potential. Old men and pregnant ladies got little more than a passing glance. Plastic-jacketed workers, frequent travellers on the low-cost flights, were carefully vetted. No one could leave their seat without permission. Flirting with a stewardess sometimes meant a document check and an interview at airport police headquarters at the other end.

One lady found herself sitting next to a riot policeman, who passed the time joking about his new-issue handcuffs.

'They could go round a bird's leg,' he told her proudly.

'Not round mine,' she ventured.

'Let's see,' he said, and closed the handcuff around her wrist – playfully, she thought. But the game went wrong. Despite their newness, the handcuffs couldn't be dislodged. Forcing them only tightened their grip. The policeman became agitated. He left his seat and started gesturing at people she took to be perfect strangers sitting in various parts of the plane. The strangers were none other than plain-clothes security men who came up one by one to try their keys on the handcuffs. By this time the joke was wearing thin and the flight-time running out. The lady in question was attracting unpleasant attention from fellow passengers and tried covering her hands with a newspaper. Eventually, she told the officer next to her, 'You're heading for trouble when we land. How are you going to explain to a senior officer that you were playing around with your handcuffs and got me into this mess?'

'That's your problem,' the officer replied. 'I have six witnesses here who will swear that you became rude and aggressive and had to be restrained. Make no mistake about it, it's your problem.'

They managed to remove the handcuffs just as the plane landed. But the policeman had made his point, all the same.

It is difficult to know how many people were sentenced for minor violations of martial law, many held simply so that their release could be seen as a concession. In this way the authorities could appear magnanimous during the dismantling of martial law. It was early on in the crisis when a member of parliament told me a Polish–Jewish parable to illustrate the authorities' strategy.

A family of five Jews, he said, lived in a Warsaw suburb, in a one-room flat. They never got a bigger apartment and finally they could stand the hardship no longer. The father went to the rabbi and told him of the family's distress.

'My son,' the rabbi said, 'go out and buy a goat, take it home and let it live with you.'

The bemused father did as he was told. A week later he returned to the rabbi. 'It was bad enough with the family,' he said, 'but the goat has made life intolerable.'

'Go and buy a goose as well,' said the rabbi, 'and take it home to live with you.'

Again the father did as he was told. But he was back in two days.

'Life,' he told the rabbi, 'is unbelievable hell. First us five, now the blasted goat and goose.'

'Go and sell the animals,' the rabbi told him, 'and then come back and see me.'

The father returned the next day, smiling broadly.

'Rabbi,' he said, 'life is so wonderful. Just the family together again – no goose and no goat. Thank you for all you have done.'

'And so it was,' said the MP, 'that on 13 December 1981 General Jaruzelski bought the Polish people a goat and a goose. And a year later he took them away.'

Even in the early days of martial law people began asking, 'Where are the ten million members who were unstoppable, where are the political certainties?' Some of them were back where they had always been – following the line of least resistance, back on the winning side.

If anything, the strong national and regional structure of the union had not prepared it for resistance – not had the unwieldy and poorly streamlined democracy that the men had built themselves. At the Warsaw steelworks several hundred employees met the crisis by holding a rally and trying to vote on a strike. This despite the fact that Solidarity instructions had been quite specific in the event of a State of Emergency: 'Strike and lock the factory gates.' Two people spoke initially. One said he had to go home because there was a baby to look after. The other did not want to strike, because he was a party member. It was a low-key beginning to a chaotic but momentous debate. They agreed to hold a referendum about the strike in all departments, and to meet again in an hour. Curiously, they believed they had time to dawdle through the democratic processes at exactly the moment democracy had been suspended. But telephones were cut and no one knew about the rest of the country. All the same, the slowness of the reaction was typical of Solidarity meetings throughout the previous eighteen months.

They reconvened, but no one had a clear idea of order. A Solidarity leader who voted against the strike was jeered and called a traitor and coward. In the disorder there were efforts to delay a decision until the next shift arrived. The manager shouted, 'Keep your minds cool and your hearts hot and just wait.' Someone yelled back, 'There is nothing to wait for.' In the end the strike became a reality, but no one seemed to lead it. Some departments tried to elect their own officials, but then gave up. People became scared and the majority drifted off home. Disheartened, aimless, the morning had brought the end of the dream.

As in other factories, the principal Solidarity leaders were arrested. But some strikes lasted longer, and not all of them ended in violence. On the industrial peninsular in Gdansk, factories had set up line-of-sight communications using semaphore. They had barricaded themselves in and constructed makeshift weapons – in one instance, a flame-thrower. The army had sent a man called Markowicz to talk to the workers. His name reminded them of the Polish word for carrot. He had been laughed out at his first attempt, and never came back. The strike, though, petered out after a couple of weeks, after the men saw the fruitlessness of the resistance and became anxious about their families.

The State continued to be challenged, though, both out in the open and underground. Judges, lawyers, even members of parliament scored their own victories. One woman MP used to visit General Jaruzelski every week and break down sobbing in his office. She refused to leave until he agreed to the release of those she petitioned for. A deputy prime minister used to break the censorship rules by posting letters for his friends on official visits to the West. And throughout the Emergency Warsaw still met in its network of coffee bars. The journalists met in theirs because the newspapers were suspended. Members of the Communist Party Central Committee met in others because they had nothing to do and believed their offices were bugged. While some State organs worked with their characteristic inefficiency, others developed lightening competence. So the edifice of martial law, prefabricated, custom-built, was shifted into position and secured.

The Government suspended all trade unions and party organizations. It therefore had no one to talk to but itself, and no incentive to talk to anyone else. Television newsreaders, now in uniform, scowled at the audiences or smiled pityingly. Many people, they were saying, had done wrong; but make no mistake, one of them added, 'Martial law is not a joke.'

Nor was it, and neither were its aftermath and its implications. As one Polish journalist commented in private: 'After years away visiting its Western lover, Poland and its economy have gone back to the Eastern wife. It hasn't been a triumphant return. The unfaithful husband has lost all his money, his health, reputation, everything.'

The Government had little to tell a people who, it was forced to admit, had long ago given up listening seriously. There was little point deceiving them, except in petty ways – and that more through error than design. But since so few people read the official newspapers, the newspaper kiosks began to practise a new trick. They were to hide most of the copies under the counter, so that no one should see the State's propaganda, lying there unread and unwanted, spattered by the rain.

The New Boys

Inside the hall of the Gdansk shipyard the atmosphere had been stifling. Freezing outside, clammy inside, it hadn't helped to improve tempers. For months the men had been arguing with the Government, and now they were arguing amongst themselves. The cigarette smoke was everywhere. Exhausted figures lay halfway under tables or slumped in chairs. The windows had long since misted over and condensation ran down on to the sills. People had been shouting at each other for what seemed like hours, and outside in the darkness workers in blue overalls and yellow helmets pressed their heads against the glass, trying to see inside and hear what was said.

Even if they could have heard what was happening, it would hardly have riveted them. The speeches were about as exciting as the half-eaten sandwiches on the tables, the bottles of mineral water in plastic crates, the hard chairs and the hard floors.

One man wanted to escape, an old man with a walking-stick and monocle. Grey and shambling, he wore a suit and a bowtie, incongruous among the workers. He spoke more slowly than all the others and seemed to come from a different world. Outside in the night drizzle he hurried towards the main gate of the yard.

'I didn't want to come tonight,' he muttered, 'but they would have called me a traitor. They argue, but they don't know what they want. It's all chaos. Walesa has become so unpredictable.'

It hadn't taken long for the doubts and the in-fighting to begin. Perhaps that was inevitable. To take on the system, Solidarity had been obliged to use the system's methods, it had picked up its weaknesses as well. The elderly man was Lech Badkowski, a writer and a specialist in history. His jokes, though, were right up to date. In his facetious way he used to ask his English acquaintances, 'When will the Russians come to Piccadilly?' Badkowski had a slight lisp, but otherwise he showed no weakness. He was part of the older, intellectual ingredient on which Solidarity was to rely so heavily. He held the rank of union spokesman, though he didn't hold it for long. He was outmanoeuvred in a corridor coup. His effective demotion had coincided with his own disillusionment. Not that he hadn't enjoyed the post; he seemed able to make himself understood to a variety of people, even the Japanese correspondents who didn't appear to understand anyone. Badkowski surrounded himself with female assistants and posters, both of which became major attractions for the visitors. The women acted as interpreters, studiously answered questions and smiled winningly when the effort of explaining conflicting policy statements became too great.

For a while it all looked like business as usual. Outside Solidarity headquarters there wasn't even a police car. The biggest obstacle was the puddle of rain that gathered on the stone floor just inside the main doorway, but you learned to jump that.

When the authorities finally cornered Solidarity, the animal was exhausted, psychologically spent. Solidarity had been born tired; you only had to look at the faces of the workers, the many who slouched to the factories, sick of fighting, and the many more still on a high after days of sleeplessness. One Solidarity official used to complain, 'We can't do everything. They all come to us wanting something. How can we cope?' But they did keep coming. And yet Lech Walesa still lived on an everyday Gdansk housing estate with a wage of less than a hundred pounds a month. The union officials all smoked and drank, at a rate at which some officials predicted their physical extinction by the year 2000. They swore in public and queued in stores and they believed with all the certainty of children that it would never, ever happen to them.

Shortly before martial law, the new union spokesman, already in his forties, but with the engaging smile of a three-year-old, had professed himself certain that the army would never turn against his union.

'That's what you think,' said his questioner.

'That's what I know,' he replied.

And he walked out of his office past the daily bedlam of union activity, the corridors and the staircases full of young utopians, photos and posters depicting union triumph, the queues for badges, key-rings, hats, T-shirts and seaside souvenirs for use during the sunshine, and he still didn't believe it. I used to tell him jokingly that one day I would have to send him food parcels in prison. I would feed him through the bars and smuggle in a file. He may have remembered that, or he may not. When they took him away he must have had other things on his mind.

Solidarity broke a special tradition in Eastern Europe, the one that says you have to be an intellectual to dissent. In the early days of the strikes in 1980 the workers had proved the exception. A tram worker, a giant of a man in his fifties, his face worn into lines, had told quietly of the desperation and the solid resolve of his colleagues. Holding out his enormous, chapped hands, he said it was a disgrace to have no meat in their soup. Something had to be done.

'How can you have a soup without meat?' he asked. 'We Poles don't want to live like animals.' He said it so quietly you had to lean forward to hear him. He sat bent in his wooden chair, his grey crewcut etched out against the light. 'The authorities tried to bring the army in,' he said, 'to work the trams.' From somewhere deep down he laughed, throwing back his head. 'They wouldn't have been able to work that old rubbish,' he said. 'They couldn't get it to move. It's only us who can do that.'

It was the quiet anger that had so misled the Government, especially in the shipyards. A young worker searched for his schoolboy English to announce: 'Our patience is finished, we want the Government to listen to us.' He was tired in the shipyard. Everyone was tired, some a little scared. So to pass the time a few of them took refuge in organization for its own sake. Some made sandwiches from food no one thought they had. Others made stamps and stamp pads to commemorate the days of the strikes. Even then the workers had their eye on history. Some of the stamps said simply, 'Flats for everyone', a cry that had been lost on the wind years before. There were press cards for all the tired foreign journalists. And one day an enormous film unit arrived, 'The Polish Documentary Company', much loved by everyone because it continually made films that were never allowed to be shown. It had filmed everything, and had attended all the dramatic events in the post-war years of People's Poland. It knew where to find news being made.

In those early days of change the workers were at least as undemocratic as the system they tried to alter. They held negotiations in factions, in groups of three or four, in warehouses, in corridors, between managers and local officials. Government representatives are believed to have entered the shipyard with hardly anyone knowing. As with all revolutions, deception and secrecy were bywords. Outside the yard, police even asked the foreigners what was happening.

'We're traffic cops,' one of them announced sarcastically. 'In fact,' he laughed, 'we're all traffic police these days. That's all any of us are.'

In Warsaw, the leadership waited anxiously for a message from the party chairman, Edward Gierek, then on his yearly outing to the Soviet Union. The trip all but coincided with the Moscow Olympics. His message arrived in Warsaw in the end, but according to a Government minister at the time it was not what they had expected.

'I want a full report,' his message began.

'Good,' they all thought. Action will follow.

'A full report,' the message went on, 'about why Poland did not win more medals at the games.'

It was hardly surprising that a few thousand workers ran rings around a government unable even to admit the existence of an imminent crisis.

The characters of those who forced their way to the top of the movement were very different. They weren't all the nice boys that the West wanted to paint them. Some were tough, uncompromising and yet unsure of the power at their disposal. Many alternated between ridiculous overconfidence and terrible fear about the future. In an interview Walesa himself once said, 'History may judge us badly. People may decide that we went about things in the worst possible way, not the best.'

But Walesa was not alone even at the beginning. His advisers drifted to the shipyard like wise men drawn to Bethlehem. At the beginning there were only two of them, lawyers who stopped off at a roadside café somewhere between Warsaw and Gdansk and came up with the name 'Solidarity'. The inspiration arose from a conviction that the system could be changed by its own methods. Lawyers could use the law against the State that had written it. Neither trials nor witnesses need be bent. Even in the early days, those lawyers believed they could fight through the courts and win. For a time, they were proved right.

Walesa often appeared surrounded by his assistants. Some were old, learned, humble; others staunch, tough, the generation that had been looking for a fight, disillusioned with the state that had promised a flat and a car for everyone and come up with neither. There was Wladyslaw Sila Nowicki – white-haired, quiet, but with a logic so timeless that he could silence a crowd of angry workers simply by the strength of his arguments. He was the lawyer, the thinker, the man who so often pleaded for a moderate, gradual approach, rather than a battering-ram through the wall of Party headquarters.

There were others. Tadeusz Mazowiecki, tall, thin, always ashen-faced, always looking ill, a journalist and a Catholic adviser. Some nights he could be found eating quietly in the fish restaurants of Gdansk. During the day he would be arguing earnestly in corridors, whispering in Walesa's ear. Walesa once told an assembled union meeting, 'It's Tadeusz's birthday.' So they all sang 'May He Live a Hundred Years'. He looked highly embarrassed. With him much of the time was a man called Bronislaw Geremek, another adviser who had an extremely attractive red-haired girlfriend with a child. He was bearded, and possessed a rare touch of flamboyance: tweed sports jackets, Hush Puppies and a red string tie with the Yves Saint Laurent logo. Solidarity embraced all styles. Mazowiecki and Geremek were a part of the union's intellectual cement, and the one most feared by the authorities. At the time of the crisis a deputy prime minister told his staff privately: 'The one thing a communist country cannot support is an alliance between workers and intellectuals.' But that is what it faced, and that is what it had to fight.

Many Solidarity men started from the premise that the meek

would never inherit the communist earth. They used to laugh at Westerners who said they were moving too quickly. 'It's like riding a bicycle,' one of the union's Warsaw officials said. 'Sometimes it's more dangerous to go slowly than to go fast.'

They did go fast. A few days after the union was founded the new machine took up residence in a disused hotel on the main road between Gdansk and Sopot. 'We got the union,' said one official, 'but we didn't know what to do with it. We weren't prepared, organizationally or emotionally.' He smiled as if remembering something. 'But we were learning,' he added, 'as we were marching on.'

In the meantime, inside the union building, young workers had washed their faces and exchanged the overalls and helmets for leather jackets and the aloof expression of bureaucrats. High above street level they carried sheaves of files out of one echoing room into another, fobbed off the gaggle of press men, talked and fell asleep in endless meetings and queued with the rest of the town's inhabitants at the shop selling waffles just outside the main door. It was as if a tide of thirty-five years' distress and frustration had been directed through those flimsy doors. People passed through the headquarters as if it were a station. Some came just to wander, others to talk; others just hunted souvenirs. Still more wanted to find out what was going on and take the information home.

But the 1981 summer ended and the Baltic port of Gdansk was locked into another East European winter. The union sent its representatives out through the country trying to make the peasants stop drinking and talk politics instead. To make workers think further than the number of lavatories at their disposal. To make millions of people think for themselves after giving up for so long. The effect was to bring strikes and unrest to many towns throughout Poland and what one minister called 'So many fires breaking out that we haven't enough firemen to extinguish them.'

It is impossible to overestimate the importance of Lech Walesa in beginning Solidarity's revolution. No one else had his popularity. No one else was instantly commercial. No one else could talk their way into and out of trouble with quite such ease.

He didn't always talk sense. Only when Polish translators worked at his speeches did they find phrases which had little or no meaning, contradictions and, said some intellectuals snobbishly, grammatical errors. Walesa could be coarse. He was the only Solidarity leader to use a four-letter word at the union's congress. Sorely tried by the turgid, interminable speeches and the bickering in the corridors, who could have blamed him? But the day afterwards the union's own press used just a letter and a dash to mark Walesa's lapse.

For eighteen months he walked on quicksand, buoyant and for all the world supremely confident. He seemed to have time for everything and nothing. At workers' meetings his tongue was often sharper than his intellect.

'Forget the preamble,' he told one man. 'Give us your name and get on with it. We haven't got all day.'

In another meeting he actually left the podium and went to the back of the hall. Either he was looking for sport or he was perfectly serious. No one knew. He soon found what he was seeking, though: two translators, one working for the Soviet news agency Tass, the other for *The New York Times*. Walesa prodded them awake.

'Strike, or no strike?' he asked the Tass man.

'No strike,' came the answer.

'Strike, or no strike?' he asked the *New York Times* assistant.

'No strike,' the man affirmed.

Walesa went back to the podium and took up the microphone.

'I don't know what you think,' he told the astonished crowd of workers, 'but I've just spoken to two men and they don't want a strike, and that's my view too.'

Walesa smoked incessantly. His pipe became a stylized hallmark. He was often puffing on it during interviews, scraping at it in the rare moments of quiet. But there was only one time I saw him at peace. It was two o'clock in the morning. He had just finished a marathon session of talks at the Council of Ministers in Warsaw. With his friends and colleagues he headed for the Catholic Club to tell the press his version of what he had done. Suddenly, in the middle of it, the power failed. The monologue ended abruptly and the entire room, with its complement of hacks and hangers-on, became dark and silent. Outside, the traffic had died away. For thousands of miles in all directions everyone was asleep, except in this one room. In the darkness, Walesa had his hands over his face. He seemed to be praying. But when the lights went on again, he was back to normal. He grinned aimlessly at a Japanese correspondent who grinned back and bowed.

'Tee-hee,' giggled the man, and bowed again.

'Tee-hee,' replied Walesa, and bowed as well.

Everyone collapsed laughing.

In the summer of 1981 I asked him, 'Are you worried about Soviet tanks massing on the border?'

'I don't see any tanks,' he replied curtly.

Vintage Walesa? Or was it just a bad day? With Walesa, you never knew. There was always the flip retort, the quick escape. After all, he was a man who had spent his life trying to avoid the People's Police.

'What do you think is your biggest failing?'

'I simply haven't got enough time.'

'Was there ever an attempt on your life?'

'Not until now. But I only get three hours sleep a night and that's murder, isn't it?'

Inevitably, Walesa was different things to different people, but for almost everyone who came across him he was a novelty. He filled a gap in Poland's public life. He was the antithesis of the Communist politicians. He refused to wear a tie except when he went to the Vatican. He spoke poor Polish, cut off his inflections, jumbled his words, a sin indeed in culture-conscious modern Poland. Only once did he read from a script, and it was a disaster. Even Solidarity people said so. One young girl didn't know whether to laugh or cry. 'No, really,' she said, 'it was absolutely dreadful.'

Was Walesa honest when he spoke publicly? Sometimes he gave the impression of not being so. It was not so much a desire to cheat as simply learning the art of manipulation. That meant covering his cards, perhaps obsessively, and it also meant that a conversation with him could either be entertaining or useless. The man remains enigmatic and private.

The authorities found him difficult to deal with. They tried ordering, flattering, even ignoring Lech Walesa, but they failed to make him their man, and they never got the measure of him. The Polish State paid him his greatest compliment by admitting, tacitly, how emotive his name had become. During the early weeks of martial law, the Andrzej Wajda film of Solidarity, 'Man of Iron', was playing in Paris. A Polish émigré who saw the film sent a postcard to his friends in Warsaw telling them of his reactions. At one point he wrote simply, 'Bravo, Lech Walesa'. The military censor who read all letters and postcards coming into the country crossed that out in black ink.

Walesa was interned for a year under emergency regulation. During that time his wife visited him by a highly complicated route. She drove first to the Interior Ministry in Warsaw and then changed cars, doing so again several times after that. The (unsuccessful) idea was to throw off people who followed and, of course, to unsettle her.

'My husband,' she said at the time, 'tells me everything will be all right.' That was typical Walesa: straight off the shelf, conman, hustler, smiler, fixer, amateur dramatist; all that, but not a pessimist. In any case, what was he supposed to tell his wife? During his absence the family managed, but it was a sad little group. Walesa's assistant, Mietek, hung around the flat in green cords, sports jacket and tie, helping out. He wasn't liked by some of the Solidarity people. They thought he was a non-entity, and called him 'Zero'. Walesa's wife, Danuta, said the girls were well enough, but the boys needed their father's hand.

There were only one or two people outside the flat, who studiously avoided looking at visitors: not a heavy police presence. The Walesa family were offered the chance to leave the country, but they turned it down. Like the whole labour problem, the Solidarity movement and the country's desire for change, the Walesa family consistently refused to go away.

It was Mrs Walesa who ruled the household. If her husband brought home unexpected guests, he made them wait outside until she agreed to let them in. She used to scold him: 'What do you leave them there for?' she shouted at him once. 'Bring them in, where do you think you are?' She took no part in union affairs, and with seven children she had little time for herself. At home she was quiet and shy, a slightly dumpy woman with short black hair and no make-up. In public, though, she would be transformed. Her clothes were good, if not stylish. Many Poles thought her pretty. Hard to believe, though, that this quiet, subdued, very ordinary woman is married to one of the most famous men in the world. It is all very traditional: he is simply the man of the family. He smacks the children, and they will miss him when he's away. But it was always like that with Solidarity. Its leaders were always different from what they seemed. So chaotic and disorganized, in many ways so amateur. Mrs Walesa is probably an appropriate symbol. Like the others she never looked the part for a revolution, least of all one that would end the way it did.

The criticism of Walesa was that he used his popularity to steamroller negotiations inside the union. As Janek, the young union spokesman put it, 'Even if his decisions were not accepted by his colleagues, he always felt he had enough popularity to go out and put his case to the workers, and that they would back him. And much as they hated it, his colleagues knew that that was right.' Inside the union it became clear they could not topple Walesa, but they could try to isolate him and vote against his friends. They could surround him with people hostile to his style of leadership, people who would block his plans in their early stages, who would work on him, feed him alternative ideas like narcotics: uppers one day, downers the next. The attempts were largely unsuccessful. Walesa's native cunning made him highly unpredictable.

The State could never forgive Walesa for what he did to them. He spoke to ministers in a way they had never been spoken to in their lives. Invariably they were disorientated, and had to seek further instructions from Warsaw. But Solidarity never relieved the pressure. Ministers were hauled back to the negotiating table, nervous and suspicious, time and time again. In one confrontation in the south of the country, Walesa took the microphone and told the minister, 'Don't mess around with me, this is not a serious conversation. I can involve the whole country in strikes if that's what you want. I repeat, this is not a serious conversation. What happens now is your decision.' For a time Solidarity won most of the battles.

For as one strike ended another would begin. In every tiny village all over the country, the union took over a house or a couple of rooms, sometimes just a floor, and made them the starting-point for the revolution. They produced coloured badges and flags. They printed lists of demands, found factories that still had paper and hijacked the supplies for their own publications. Piles of newsprint would be stacked in hallways and on staircases at a time when State newspapers were complaining of a shortage. A competitive economy had suddenly come into being.

Into its offices the union channelled typewriters and telex machines. Each unit set up its local news service, a daily bulletin that many printed for distributing themselves or for telexing to Warsaw. At times the information was dubious, if not purposely misleading. In one instance unionists reported a strike in a major city. Questioned more closely, they revealed it was a strike by students.

'How many students?' they were asked.

'About five,' they replied.

'How long had they been striking?'

'Oh, just during their lunch-breaks.'

Some of the banner headlines from the regions were similarly unreliable. But the information service continued day and night. It was common to be telephoned at two o'clock in the morning to be given the latest news of negotiations. Solidarity men took it for granted that you would be waiting for the call, and they were hurt and mystified if you suggested the story could have waited. Each region had its priorities and its pride, and believed every event to be of vital importance to the outside world. Every village, however tiny, was suddenly on the world map.

There was a favourite anecdote to support this view.

A man from the tiny southern village of Ustrzyki Dolne decided he would pay a visit to Yokohama in Japan, but he didn't know how to get there. He went to his nearest city, and they told him to make his way to Warsaw; maybe someone there had heard of Yokohama. He arrived in Warsaw, and was advised to try Moscow. Undaunted, he set out for the Soviet capital. The Russians pointed him east, and he made his way to Vladivostok, hoping for some directions from there. Eventually he reached his destination, stayed a week and decided to go home. Entering a Japanese travel agency he asked for a single ticket to Ustrzyki Dolne. 'Certainly, sir,' they told him, 'coming right up.' The joke illustrated a point of view that was obsessively 'Polocentric', and which the crisis had accentuated. Many Poles felt the world owed them more attention.

The leaders of Solidarity never really looked like leaders in the traditional sense. They needed crowds to make them shine. Listening to their off-the-cuff comments, it was sometimes hard to take them seriously. On the day of their first television programme they arrived at the studios in Gdansk looking as though they were out for a stag night. They had brought their studied disorder with them. Dressed in jeans and leather jackets, they arrived noisily in a car with headlights on, sounding its horn.

'Where are the girls, then?' asked Walesa, as he looked around the studio set. 'What about some more comfortable chairs?'

They didn't seem to realize that their presence in the most sacred of all Communist bastions, the TV station, was making history. Or perhaps they did, and were determined not to be overawed. In fact, publicity became a constant preoccupation for them. They learned its power and they learned how to use it. Janek, the union spokesman for much of its life, was a master of the one-liner, the quick fifteen-second TV cut, the pithy retort that would force his face into television bulletins round the world. Something like: 'We're strong, and this time we've proved it,' or 'Never mind the Russians, Poland has always been a brick too hot to handle.' The comments rolled off the tongue. The union said the things everyone wanted to hear, Poles and Westerners alike.

Janek was wiry and articulate, the angry young man of the union – angry and intelligent, behind him were science degrees, foreign travel, even a few years at a British university. Had he been in the

West he would have gone straight to the top. In the East, as things turned out, he would make it by a more circuitous route.

It was early on in its life that Solidarity began to worry about its public image. I remember Lech Walesa leaning out of his car window, late one night, to be told that a Western agency was reporting a failure in his talks with the Government. It had been snowing, and it was bitterly cold. 'What the hell did they say that for?' he shouted, and then, in apparent contradiction, 'Where did they get that?' He put his head back inside the car and started a furious argument with his assistants. If this was a revolution, it all looked pretty haphazard.

Solidarity paid close attention to what the West said about it, sometimes reacting hysterically to articles and broadcasts. On one occasion the union's Warsaw branch demanded the retraction of an American report that it considered overtly hostile. Its author had quoted a group of workers as saying that even with Solidarity there was still no toothpaste in the shops, and what was the union going to do about that? The Warsaw branch might never have heard of the report if State television had not broadcast its substance in its main evening bulletin. The union reacted like a stuck pig, and demanded that the correspondent refute the story. He declined, and Solidarity threatened to turn off the entire water supply to the capital. The Western press was fine when it criticised the Government, but hadn't it forgotten where its sympathies were supposed to lie? It was only when the row got as far as Janek that it was stopped. Solidarity activists were told to back off. Others would decide when and where to pick the quarrels.

During that period Poles were encouraged to wear their emotions on their sleeve. The public debating platform created by the union brought suppressed feelings to the surface. Somehow it seemed natural that in 1981, just four months after the union's creation, a group of teenagers should gather outside the cathedral in Warsaw just after Christmas Eve mass to shout 'Russians go home.' Not only that, but they got away with it, and the militia, with their headquarters a block away, made no move to interfere. In just four short months Solidarity had stretched the boundaries of acceptable behaviour in Poland. In the coming months they were breached many times over, and finally broken.

But the union was far from surefooted. It blundered into quarrels it had no need to fight. In his own, rather innocent way, Janek admitted that once they had got Solidarity they were not sure what to do with it. Most people had left the shipyards wanting a bath and some food, not another battle.

'We had to organize these people,' he said. 'It wasn't just factory workers, there were metal-workers, miners, actors, bakers, everyone. All of them were looking to us.'

Many union officials seemed to have dual personalities: quiet and unassuming on a social level, but hard and ambitious when it came to union politics. For most of them knew they had precious little time to learn how to play the system they wanted to change. Their first and only Congress, staged in the summer of 1981, proved that if nothing else.

It was the only time that the union was able to throw itself a party, and it showed up the organization for what it was. At one end of the scale sharp, incisive, backed by subtle and imaginative intelligence – at another level, blunt and almost pathetically immature. There were those who belonged to a right-wing lunatic fringe, part of the 'hang 'em all from the lamp-post' brigade. They would occasionally telephone police stations to say they had planted a bomb in Communist Party headquarters. The moderates, not just the police, had a hard time fighting them off.

The Congress did not set out to ape the authorities. It simply borrowed some ideas from the State and rejected others. The name 'Congress' sounded familiar. But there was a difference between the red slogans of the Party and Solidarity's baby playing in a field, which featured on the union posters. The baby was one of the Walesa children. The idea had been that the child would grow up with the union, but that was not to be. Then there was the venue, the Olivia Sports Hall on the outskirts of Gdansk. Like the authorities, they chose a place that was different: a strange, ship-like building with a sloping roof, impressive only for its size. There were the subcommittees and the voting rules no one seemed to understand or follow. There were the plenary sessions and the daily news conferences and, like the Party, they tried to hold the serious rows in private.

For the Congress contained little public debate. It was more a question of applause, shouting and complaints about over-long speeches. It was difficult not to see the event as simply an elaborate attempt to give the union legitimacy. After all, no one had actually voted Lech Walesa into power, so it was decided that he should fight for his position. He won the vote, but not before the members had cut him down to mortal size and given him just a working majority. But it did not change his position with ordinary people.

For his own part Walesa acted out the elder statesman (he joked that he now had as many medals as a Soviet general). Much of the Congress he chose not to attend at all. At times, though, he would saunter in, dressed in jeans and T-shirt, sit in the front row and chat to his colleagues. If he had had a bar in front of him he would have put his feet on it. But somehow everyone knew all along where the authority really lay, and speakers would automatically defer to him, if not by name, then with a nod of the head.

Many of the delegates talked well, many badly. At one point an old soldier rose to pledge loyalty and tell the young men how he admired them. He was the oldest of the pre-war generals, well into his eighties, but his message was timeless.

'Lies and deceit,' he told them, 'are as old as the world, but truth is eternally young. If you are the soldiers of truth, I am convinced you will be victorious.' He had stood on the platform, stiff and shaking with emotion. There were few dry eyes in the hall, even among the tough guys that led that union.

On a later occasion two Government ministers were jeered and told to take their message to a more sympathetic audience. State television was ordered for the first time at any congress to go away and not come back. Its team went off to its van and sat morosely in the car-park. It seemed as though most of Poland's undergraduate language students were attending. Multilingual bouncers stood at the door and sandwich makers conjured food from thin air. And outside the police and army patrolled in open jeeps, wearing steel helmets and carrying guns, all of them strangely divorced from the people inside the building. They might have been in two different countries, neither of them Poland.

The fact of the Congress was the most memorable thing about it; it brought colour and spontaneity to Gdansk. The Congress drew people like a fairground: they used to drop by on their way home from work, stand outside and listen to the speeches on loudspeakers. They traded posters and badges, some so rare they were bought for hard currency. Two of the most popular slogans read simply, 'Soviet tanks, no thanks', and 'I love the Soviet Union.' At weekends, the crowds were attracted by the flags and the other crowds. To be there was like tasting forbidden fruit. People were conscious of taking part in an event unthinkable elsewhere in Eastern Europe. No one got up on a soapbox and started his own monologue. No one needed to. There were plenty of speeches coming out of the building to suit all tastes: extreme, very extreme and downright anarchist. The editor of the local Solidarity bulletin was even replaced for being fanatically anti-Government.

Inside the gates a lobby system grew up. Journalists button-holed the union's personalities, clustering round them in little groups, discussing the fine print of resolutions and the policies they never could or would put into practise. The conversations were all so earnest, the talk of free elections, public accountability, more democracy. The building echoed with it. The building is all that survived.

By any standards it was an odd spectacle. Two years before-hand the same people had been lost in a vast political no man's land. The majority stood somewhere between open dissent and total withdrawal, but, standing in the basketball changing-rooms or the spectator's galleries, these new officials might have been political activists all their lives. They took over the administrative offices, gave themselves titles, ordered in foreign journalists and demanded explanations for some of their stories. Some were rude, others charming. They worked long hours into the night, churning out the union's newspapers, discussing the problems of the world over endless cups of coffee. But after three weeks of talking, the nine hundred delegates had issued only one direct appeal to the Polish people. 'Help us', they said, 'to go on talking. Give us accommodation and feed us because our own provisions have run out.' The situation was desperate, but had an air of tragicomedy: nine hundred delegates billeted around the city *en famille*, and only one serious topic of conversation – when was the marathon Congress finally going to end? It was a sad comment on all the idealism, but for too long the delegates had been obsessed with details and triviality. As one of their own spokesmen put it, they had turned the event into an orgy of debate and argument. No one had worked out the broad concepts and the broad designs.

The meeting finally ground to a halt because the food did run out, and anyway the sports hall was needed again. The main conference centre was going to be an ice-rink again. 'There'll be real skating now,' said one commentator, 'instead of just a lot of people sliding around on their bottoms.' At any rate, the delegates folded up their posters, climbed into the ramshackle buses, tied on the flags and streamers and drove back home across Poland. As they pulled out of the car-park they could see a sign scrawled across the main road that said simply, 'Television Lies'. No one bothered to contradict it; none of the police even rubbed it out. It might as well have advertised Coca Cola. On the whole, the delegates seemed pretty pleased with the outcome. They felt confident about the future. But almost before they got home, the carefree summer was over. Solidarity had three months left to live.

The State, of course, attacked the union much of the time, but ordinary Poles began to luxuriate in the joy of public criticism themselves. Solidarity, said a hotel receptionist, had done nothing to improve telephones or telexes. There was no more food in the shops than before. Worse still, and this only came out later, Solidarity supervisors had gone into shops and started to marshal queues. 'Gone in,' said one woman, 'and tried to tell us who could buy what.' Perhaps the most common cry of all was simply, 'We want a bit of peace. When is there going to be some peace?' In just eighteen months Solidarity had come down from the clouds and become a piece of Polish furniture. It was still immensely popular, but it no longer possessed divine authority.

Under Solidarity, Poland was in a constant state of flux, of transition. There was activity where before there had been none. This was especially true of the provinces, the hundreds of small, grey, unremarkable towns and villages spread over the country. Wherever there was industry or agriculture there had been Communist Party activists, youth leaders, small pools in which fish could grow big and from which they could move into bigger pools. But now there was something else as well, union buildings where the State found itself facing a constant challenge. It did not happen overnight. The constant cry of the union officials in Gdansk was that the regions kept referring upwards. Local members were unsure about important decisions in their area. Who were they to pick on, would they get central backing from Gdansk, what was Solidarity policy? The result was chaos. Some branches picked on all officials, irrespective of merit. Only in the major cities and factories did they have a clear idea of what to do. By the end of the union's life they were doing their best to force out local administrators and factory managers. Pointedly, they would leave a wheelbarrow outside the door of the man in question. It meant that if he didn't leave voluntarily, he would be carried out in it.

The union began to act almost as a political party. Lech Walesa, sometime worker, sometime striker, now a leader of millions, began a series of campaign tours. They began undramatically in Warsaw, where, surrounded by aides and accompanied by a bodyguard, he went out to try to find a pair of shoes. Symbolically and practically, he was now ready for the fight.

His first stop was at a factory club on the outskirts of the southern city of Czestochowa, where the red-and-white Polish flags were flying in welcome in the sunshine. The only sign of authority was a lone police car at a discreet distance down the street. Walesa began with a pep-talk with plenty of staccato syllables. The new order was in, he said, and the old one out. It was the standard warm-up in those days, the type of thing the crowds expected to hear. Then to lunch in a factory canteen – no sign of any management. Walesa was seated in the middle of a long table. Someone made a painful speech of welcome. He looked embarrassed. The food was the best they could offer.

There were meat and potatoes, enough for him and his retinue. At the door downstairs, bouncers kept out the unwanted and the uninvited. The timid and the curious waited in the cold. That afternoon he treated the city to a sight it had never seen before. He toured the centre in a van sporting Solidarity posters – in front of it a police motorcycle escort, behind it a white Mercedes. On the streets people turned and looked in amazement. Some waved from the trams, a few passers-by smiled and shook their heads in disbelief. In a country where only the politicians in power campaign, it was, to say the least, extraordinary. Later that day Walesa was out on the city's football pitch, sprinting boyishly for the microphone. One more display of unstoppable optimism. The workers thought he was the best thing they had seen for a long time, but he didn't think much of them. He said the turnout could have been better, told them to get better organized, to stop relying on advice from the union headquarters, and they took it all without a murmur. From the top of the stadium you could see the workers getting off buses, hurrying in lines through the industrial land-scape. Behind them were the chimneys and the power stations and the grey, provincial city of Czestochowa. It was not the prettiest place for a campaign tour, but it had seen history. No one went home that night saying they had heard it all before.

As the union grew older, however, the disputes inside it developed, becoming bitter and time-consuming. Members admitted that the sessions lasted three or four times longer than necessary. They quarrelled about a word or phrase in a statement, and people used to get up in the middle and walk out for fresh air. On one occasion delegates had to mount a search for the Warsaw branch chairman. He had been on the point of going home, having apparently lost interest in the entire business.

At the height of its power Solidarity believed itself unstoppable. Its activists walked with a swagger. In some cases they were formed into a town militia. In one instance they divided the town between themselves and the police, in an effort to keep order. They dressed in plain clothes and wore red armbands. Another first in Eastern Europe: an independent army formed to keep order on the streets. I remember one group of unionists arriving at the Victoria Intercontinental in the capital's Victory Square. They took one look at the fur-coated array of prostitutes, at the darkened recesses of the nightclub where the business of the night was often transacted, and declared: 'When we come to power, we're going to get rid of all this.'

As a union Solidarity devoted much time and effort to its external relations, and was criticized for it. The men, some said, should have done more to help on the factory floor. But the foreign affairs of Solidarity involved some extraordinary contacts, many of which have still not come to light and may never do so. Rumours persisted that Lech Walesa had met the Russians in secret ·at their instigation. There was talk of a secret meeting across the Polish border inside the Soviet Union. A Polish photographer once told of a strange drive with Walesa where they headed for the Soviet frontier but never seemed to arrive. They turned off the main road on to a side track and had talks with some officials, who appeared to be Russian. The story is poorly documented and unlikely to be true, but some kind of direct contact with the Russians cannot be entirely ruled out. For their part they must have decided that Solidarity was hostile, and it would have been characteristic for them to want to meet that hostility face to face. I once asked the union spokesman if he could give me a categoric assurance that no such encounter had ever taken place. He could not. All he said was, 'I don't know of any. If there was a meeting, it was so secret that even I didn't know about it.'

Other unusual contacts did take place. It's clear there were meetings with Hungarian trade unionists, some official, some secret. Solidarity was even offered support by the IRA. The letter, as far as is known, never got a reply, and was kept in a secret cache in the port of Gdansk. Soviet dissidents from the Ukraine are also thought to have had direct links with the union. Czechs and Slovaks added to the ever expanding book of contacts. Solidarity began to find out more than was healthy for it to know. Money came in from abroad, foreign machinery began to be seen in union offices. Suddenly it seemed there was a state within a state, conducting its own policies at home and abroad. It went round sticking leaflets on people's cars, putting up posters in blocks of flats, slogans on trams and buses and factory gates. The new messages were shouted down at passers-by from office blocks in Gdansk. At airports people were showing Solidarity badges and having an easier time through customs. Solidarity had money too, millions of zlotys in its own funds. The State seemed powerless to intervene. In the newspaper offices and in radio and television, Solidarity branches were formed. In their public pronouncements they were unusually frank. At one stage the head of the union branch at Warsaw Television felt secure enough to say, 'Never in the history of broadcasting has there been an organization as stupid as this one.' He was among the first to be interned under the Emergency Rules of 1981.

The union's broadcasters put up counter-slogans on the walls and advertised their own strikes in the nerve-centre controlling the State's propaganda. And that is why, in the autumn of 1981, a section of the Army Communication Corps moved into Warsaw's Television Centre. They took over the offices where Western television networks had been satelliting their material and they recorded everything, all the plays, the news bulletins, the pop programmes and the potted ideology. They made their own programmes as well, and no one, if you can believe it, realized why they were doing all this until much later. By then, once again, it was too late.

Taking from Caesar

Mikhail used to visit at any hour that suited him, but he preferred to come at dusk. In winter it was during those few minutes, perhaps no more than twenty, when the East European sun just touches the darkness. He would come in without introductions or pleasantries, a grey, podgy, anonymous shape that had spent years blending in with the crowds. With him a shabby briefcase, sometimes just a plastic bag, and in it a sheaf of papers and carbon copies, some so faint and worn they were barely legible. A thin smile and a nod, and he would sit down.

'I want to show you these,' he would say. 'Vitally important. And there's an appeal here too.' There was always an appeal direct to the Polish government, sometimes to one or two outside the country. Mikhail would hand over the papers and wait while you read them. He lived in a world dominated, he felt, by injustice. In the West he would have been dismissed as a crank, a tedious fool to be first humoured and then shown the door. In Poland the State had made him into something far more substantial: a dissident.

He never had much hair – a short crop at the sides, the crown bare – but one day he arrived with none at all, and I knew he had been in gaol. I was not surprised, though, for Mikhail courted trouble. No protest was too small for him; he went to all of them. If there were speakers, he was one of them. But he had little time for group dissension. He declined to associate with Solidarity or any of the groups that preceded it or outlasted it. He was a loner, picking his own way through the crowded rush-hour streets of the capital.

There is no doubt that he felt himself to be special. He had lived in Warsaw throughout the Second World War, and I suppose anyone who had done that has a right to feel special. He had survived the Nazi occupation, he knew which bomb had fallen where, who had been shot on which street. The bullet-holes still etched into many of the capital's buildings all meant something to him. He often acted as if the war had happened yesterday, a trait he shared with so many of his countrymen. But the years since the war had not been gentle with him. I learned later he had a heart complaint, and that meant his spells in prison were short. No one wanted him to die there. There were enough martyrs as it was; Poland, it seemed sometimes, bred them like racehorses. Despite setbacks Mikhail went on with his one-man crusade, until one day he disappeared and didn't come back. He was one of thousands who were packed into the internment camps in the early months of 1982. He was eventually released, but I didn't see him again. Military rule broke many contacts, and his was just one of them.

Mikhail had his independence, but he wasn't alone. He belonged to that tiny international minority of dissidents present under all regimes. He never gave up, and neither did they. Once a dissident, you are set apart from the rest of society. It is a lifetime's commitment, and it brings with it a lifetime of trouble.

A Polish journalist once spoke of the huge gulf between the State and the opposition. 'Perhaps,' he said, 'you don't understand these things, but we wake up every morning and face a moral decision. Do we support the status quo or oppose it? Do we acquiesce? Will our conscience leave us alone? Is today going to be better than yesterday? In the West,' he added, 'you don't look at life in the same way.'

The Polish view of resistance has been refined over centuries of hardship and deprivation. To resist and go underground is a national characteristic. It is passed on by parents from their wartime memories, and is even learned indirectly in the schools. One man, Piotrusz Kowalski, who had grown up in Warsaw, never forgot the message of his childhood. His father had given him a makeshift printing-press. He had taken it to school and made the cardinal error of showing it to his friends. Someone talked. The result was a classroom inquiry and the confiscation of the printing-press as a dangerous object whose use could be harmful to the State. The boy turned into a man who knew that printing-presses either belong to the State or to the underground resistance. There could be nothing in between.

For the Poles this is simply day-to-day conditioning. It explains why some refuse to talk openly in their own homes, why they pull the telephone plug out of the wall, whisper in the kitchen or turn on the bath-taps and suggest a stroll around the block, even in the rain, for a conversation. There were those who changed cars several times on their way to a rendezvous, those, like Mikhail, with their pockets full of manuscripts and their minds on distant principles. There were Polish officials who never understood the Western interest in dissidents, but many of them did. After all, Poles prided themselves on their window to the West. When one secretary from the Foreign Ministry asked a foreign correspondent why he bothered with members of the underground, he was told simply, 'Because you bother with them yourselves.' The official, who had spent a great many years in the West, smiled at the journalist and said simply, 'I will pass on your views.'

In Krakow, the police once asked a young dissident a similar question.

'Why do you give interviews to foreign journalists?' they inquired.

'Because the Polish journalists ignore me,' she replied.

Her name was Halina, and she never stopped smiling, despite frequent interviews at police headquarters. She was interested in everyone and knew much that the authorities did not. She lived in a rambling old house that seemed to contain several families, but may have held only one. The rooms were full of books and had polished wooden floors. Visitors were required to put their feet on dusters and skate across the floor, trying not to fall over. There is a similar procedure in many public libraries in Poland. Small comfort; you emerge uncoupling the dusters from your soles and feeling more than a little ridiculous.

Halina never minded what she said. She would say it on tape or in front of the camera, and in the late seventies she got away with it. At that time Poland had less than a handful of political prisoners, and as long as the dissidents stopped short of terrorism or public incitement they were simply picked up, questioned and left to get on with it. Like Halina, many dabbled in underground activities at university. In some towns it was hard to avoid coming across a dissident leaflet. Plenty of students simply read them and passed them on, and there the involvement ended. But Halina continued amassing a store of information and recollections.

Lively, blonde and vivacious, she spoke excellent English and stood out from her circle of jean-clad student activists. All of them knew the West – they had travelled there – but none of them ever dreamed that they would leave Poland. It was possible, they thought, to fight some parts of the system and love others, fight some people and love others. No one ever said anything unpatriotic about the country, but they knew it for what it was. Their attitude was – it's difficult, but interesting.

They all knew the underground code, they knew where dissidents held meetings, who were the go-betweens, how they used to come to safe houses via different routes and at different times, how they left after dark. They were not the only ones, either, climbing over fences, sliding through muddy gardens and parks. The underground culture was known by large numbers of people throughout the country, even if they were not involved in it.

The habits and reflexes of opposition went back to the days of the Nazi occupation and well before. They had been a daily fact of life under Stalinism, but then came relaxation and by the time Solidarity arrived the underground had almost surfaced. That was as far as it was to get. In the space of twenty-four hours the imposition of martial law in December 1981 took it back nearly three decades and forced it deep under cover. Once again the underground became common property. Its numbers multiplied many times, its messages appealed to ordinary people to be patriotic and help the movement. Poles were told, for instance, to put candles in their windows on the thirteenth of every month to mark the date of the military crackdown. Few ever complied. They were told to wear black armbands, to carry extra shopping-bags so as to confuse police searching for underground leaflets. The opposition, they were told, was everywhere.

It was surprising who had contacts with the resistance and who tried to make such contacts. Early in 1982 a top Government official apparently attempted to set up a meeting with the Solidarity resistance. According to those involved he contacted a staff reporter on a weekly newspaper, *Polityka*, and asked him to act as go-between. This initial approach was made outside the official's own office, as he was convinced the security services had bugged it. He said he was prepared to meet the fugitives alone, at a place of their choosing. He would guarantee safe conduct.

The journalist made the contact for him, assured the opposition leaders that it was genuine and waited for final instructions. They never came. The official is said to have referred the plan to the Party leader, General Jaruzelski, who rejected it. He believed, apparently, that if the meeting had taken place and the news of it later leaked, the effect would have been explosive. The Russians, already exasperated, might have finally lost patience with the fraternal government that inexplicably talked to its dissidents and offered guarantees of safety at secret meetings. Not that the security police were behind in their attempts to track down vanished opposition leaders, but they didn't win all the battles.

The resistance in at least one major city had its own police informant who passed on vital information. On one occasion the security services came within five minutes of arresting a leading underground activist, but thanks to a tip-off from inside police headquarters the man left his house through a back window as detectives went in the front door. The informant was also able to say which telephones were being monitored and what the police did or didn't know. Only the underground failures ever got publicity; little was known about the dozens who were able to evade police detection for many months, who were passed down elaborate escape lines, who perfected disguises and who could laugh at official attempts to catch them.

The underground knew exactly who they could trust. They cashed in that trust the moment the military takeover began. One Solidarity leader hid in the basement of a building on the outskirts of Gdansk. He was careful; he didn't go out, didn't meet any friends and only left when he went to the railway station in disguise to catch a train to Warsaw. Others were less careful. One senior Solidarity activist actually had to be arrested by his own friends and held for his own protection under guard. He was locked in a room in the suburbs of Gdansk and only released when his colleagues agreed to go with him. It was said that he had little idea of subterfuge, that he would frequently drink and talk a great deal. The underground had rigid rules and detained him as much for their own safety as for his.

There is no doubt, though, that the opposition was penetrated by informers just as Solidarity had been. The sporadic arrests of middle-ranking dissidents pointed both to betrayal and to the efficiency of the secret police. Had they wished it, they could have probably caught more. But official philosophy cautioned against this. Catching them would only drive the others deeper underground. Give them enough space to move, however, and they would eventually start making mistakes.

Ingrid had a talent for escape. That was surprising, for she had striking looks, long blonde hair, and was very thin (she claimed this was the result of a heart disorder; she was one of those Poles who imagine that illness lends a certain prestige).

Anyway, Ingrid had a great heart. I remember knocking at her door one Sunday morning, hearing muted scuffling on the lino and seeing her disembodied face peering into the hallway. 'My God,' she said, adding superfluously, 'it's you.' As I walked through the door a young man emerged, pulling on his jeans and grinning at me. I made an excuse and offered to leave, but Polish hospitality had taken over and the coffee was already warming up. Leaving her boyfriend at the kitchen table Ingrid pulled me into the living-room to show me the latest pamphlets from the local underground cell. She had spent the night with her boyfriend, but she was not sure about his politics. So he remained sitting at the kitchen table just a few yards away, eating his breakfast. I wondered if he knew what we were doing.

Ingrid had wanted to give an interview to the foreign press, but as with Communist officials such matters were tightly controlled. She first had to seek permission from the underground authorities. That involved a day trip through the city to lose any followers, and a hurried encounter in a block of flats. But the idea of the interview was rejected.

'They're so scared and disorganized,' she said, 'at the moment they'd rather not talk at all. Maybe later.'

Ingrid had once attended a meeting in one of the big hotels used by Western tourists, but she unwittingly brought a 'tail' with her. She herself came on foot, entered reception and disappeared upstairs to one of the rooms. Some fifteen seconds behind her, a four-door Polski Fiat saloon drew into the forecourt with three occupants. One stayed at the street entrance, another in the car, the third disappeared into the hotel. She left later with a Western journalist, but the men made no move to follow. It looked certain they already knew where she was going.

From an official point of view Ingrid and those like her were the outcasts of society. They were painted as pathetic counter-revolutionaries, troublemakers pandering to Western imperialism. But the treatment they received often depended on who they were and what kind of families they came from. One dissenting speech did not necessarily spell political or social oblivion, particularly if your father was a member of parliament or high up in the Communist Party. Sometimes schoolfriends grew up on opposite sides of the fence. The abrasive dissident Jacek Kuron, for instance, had once taught at Warsaw University, and knew a number of senior Party figures by their first names. On one occasion in 1981 he even debated publicly with a Communist Party lecturer who had attended the same classes. Stefan Bratkowski, head of the journalists' union and expelled from the Communist Party, also had colleagues in high places. A Government spokesman once queried the report of a speech by Bratkowski and commented, 'I know old Stefan, I've known him for years. He may say things like that, but he doesn't actually mean them. He just blusters a bit.' That is how close the two sides were, groups of intellectuals who had trained in the same place but who had gone their separate ways. Sometimes the old connections had their uses.

No less a person than the head of the Institute for Marxist-Leninist Theory in Warsaw was given the job of contacting the underground soon after the start of martial law. Far from having to hide in the sewers or risk pneumonia from a night-time rendezvous, all he did was ring up one of his old students and ask her to come round. While most of the world was convinced that no one was talking to anyone and that the Polish crisis amounted to a complete breakdown in relations between union and Govern-ment, the situation was very different. A teacher was talking to his dissident pupil. Each knew which side the other was on. Groups of intellectuals and some former Solidarity advisers were talking to the State. There was no black or white any more, and if there was no one knew which was which. There were some who would hunt with hounds and then run with foxes. Grey people, determined only to be winners.

Towards the end of the seventies the dissidents drew some benefit from the revival of interest in Polish affairs. By 1978 there was a Polish Pope in the Vatican, a tough talker in his own right, and the opposition at home felt encouraged. It was possible to meet dissidents publicly and go to a restaurant for lunch with them. People would go to their flats openly or film them walking down the street. True, they might be detained the next day, but they were soon back in business again. When the police came to detain Adam Michnik, one of the leading figures in the opposi-tion, they would address him by his Christian name. 'Come on, Adam,' they would say, 'let's go. Another forty-eight hours and you'll be back home.'

According to popular legend he had been held for questioning some forty times in the space of ten years. It was just part of his trade, which he conducted from a jumble of a flat just around the corner from the Czechoslovak embassy. A heavy, black official car sat near by for most of the day. It seemed a dark flat, but that may have been due to the heavy curtains, often closed. There were piles of newspapers and books scattered around the living-room, the standard hallmarks of the underground politicians of Eastern Europe. Michnik used to take his message to the Poles as well as to the Western press. His supporters would often arrange semi-secret meetings in blocks of flats or social clubs. He would hold court for an hour, and then there would be questions. It came closer to public debate than almost anything else on offer in the country. One gathering took place in a local leisure centre in a Warsaw suburb. The basement walls were covered with tigerskin wallpaper. There was a cross, and a picture of John Paul II.

Strings of beads were hung across the doorway. It was a curious mixture of incongruous objects and incongruous people, house-wives, pensioners and a few young firebrands looking more like motorcycle kids than political revolutionaries. This was the politi-cal activity of the late seventies: unofficial, but tolerated. These were the people who printed the alternative election leaflets, sometimes showering them out of high blocks of flats when parliamentary deputies were going through the voting ritual. One of the posters mockingly listed its own parody of electoral prom-ises – 'Flats by the year 3000,' it said. 'Water in the television and water in the sausage.'

Slogans like these only reflected general cynicism. They didn't need to inspire it. Before the coming of Solidarity no one expected much in the way of change. Dissidents often argued more with themselves than with the State. Occasionally Western corre-spondents would be barred from attending a dissident news conference, but there was no greater excitement than that. The State had reached an uneasy accommodation with its critics, watching them constantly, harassing them intermittently. Poland would never be completely quiet, but dissent had become manageable.

Sometimes the understanding was apparent, not just in ordi-nary life, but in prison life as well. A lawyer gaoled for two years during the seventies said he used to advise both inmates and wardens on their legal affairs. Prison guards would ensure that he was not disturbed during his afternoon siesta. He became for a while 'Capo' of the prisoners, respected and fawned on by the governor himself. He was one of the few lawyers the State ever brought to court. These days he lives in a remote country village in the north, close to his family. He has put away his files and his law books and he now makes the best 'Woodcutter's' sausage in Poland. The secret, he said, was real meat, properly smoked. He grinned with pride when I told him how good it tasted. He still has strong views about politics. 'You English,' he said, 'you don't understand the Russians. I've been to England,' he added. 'I quite liked it. I liked the tea.'

There were plenty in the opposition who never gave up, though.

Jacek Kuron, balding, thick-set like a bulldog, was to remain a formidable opponent of the State despite continuing police arrests. He had a sharp, rasping voice that cut through meetings and arguments. Often he succeeded merely by shouting louder than anyone else. Like Michnik he knew prison well, but he learned to enjoy life outside it. Although he had his own flat in Zoliborz, a fashionable Warsaw suburb, it was more like a commune. There was constant movement. Workers and fellow-dissidents visited constantly. They eyed each other with suspicion. Some had come to talk, others to listen. They sat on the floor, drank tea if available and tried to get their host's attention. Tried, because the interruptions were endless. The carefully monitored telephone seldom stopped ringing.

Kuron was not one of the realists in the opposition. Even when interned under martial law, he continued writing theses suggesting that the system could be reformed and the Russians could accept it. Never mind the fact that the events which had put him into detention tended to prove the reverse. In part he lived on his memories, those of a crowd puller. Under Solidarity's aegis he had drawn the students into the lecture halls in scores. The open-necked shirt, the woollen singlet, the cords, all had an air of studied disorder. His appearance spoke eloquently for the movement he represented.

The evidence is that he got on badly with Lech Walesa. In the chaotic days when Solidarity was an infant, he travelled to Gdansk to make sure that one of the adviser's jobs in the union went to him. He annoyed people by pushing his way into the union offices and answering telephone calls that weren't for him. Kuron had plenty of opponents. There were those in the union who wanted respectability in their hierarchy, and it was they who asked, 'Why appoint a dissident? It will only give the Government ammunition. Then they can say that we are all anti-socialists and all dissidents.' How true the prediction turned out to be. Under intense pressure the union did appoint Kuron, and the State did accuse it of plotting treason. It was the obvious outcome.

Kuron was one more figure who talked his way to the top. A practised talker, an educated man, a committed opponent of the

State, he had all the credentials and used them. In an organization like Solidarity, which had come from nowhere, he impressed people enough to win their support. He had the *gravitas* and the political dexterity that they were just beginning to learn. Towards the end of the union's life he seemed proud of his achievement. He would not give interviews without demanding a bottle of Scotch as payment. He would not acknowledge you if he met you in the street, but he would cadge a lift if you were going his way. It would be difficult to describe him as a pleasant man, but he had sincere convictions and never stopped fighting for them, which is why the State in turn could never leave him alone. And he was not unknown in Poland. People had heard of him because his family had owned both land and reputation before the war; they also knew him from foreign radio broadcasts.

There was nothing secretive about listening to such programmes. In fact, Poles would openly tune radios to the BBC or Radio Free Europe while standing in a shop debating whether to buy a new set. There were families that would cluster round to hear at least one of the main nightly broadcasts in Polish. Government officials used to admit openly to listening to the transmissions from the West. Many Poles would know the names of broadcasters and Western correspondents based in Warsaw. Some of the journalists were so famous they were asked to sign autographs in State offices and universities. There was interest in those who looked in on Poland from the West, although there was plenty of criticism as well. A BBC programme which had featured a discussion on sex became a major talking-point in Warsaw for days afterwards. 'How could they use such words?' people asked. 'I thought it tasteless and disgraceful,' complained a housewife. 'I was surprised at the BBC.' The reaction sounded more reminiscent of Tunbridge Wells than a Warsaw suburb, but the Poles had their conservative streak. They expected to be treated as serious people. That meant telling them about Poland and politics. They could handle sex for themselves.

Throughout the seventies and early eighties, the underground movement recruited where it could. Friends or relatives of activists were sometimes asked if they would help out by storing dissident leaflets and helping with the printing or distribution of them. Many assisted, but plenty had reservations. 'I have my children in the house,' said a mother. 'I don't want anything to happen to them.'

There was no stigma in refusing. The level of resistance varied enormously. Put ten Poles in a room, and you might emerge with eleven opinions, all of them passionately held. Few people were what they seemed. An old lady from Gdansk recalled how the police had entered her apartment soon after martial law, saying they had come to search it. As they went through her meagre possessions, she sat calmly, saying little. She was not afraid of them, and ordered them to treat her with the respect she deserved as a lady and a Pole. The officers were apparently dumbstruck, stopped their search, made their apologies and even tried to kiss her hand as they ushered themselves out of her flat. One of them asked her, 'Dear lady, would you first state for us that you are satisfied with the search? It's customary in these cases.'

'What have I to be satisfied about?' she asked, incredulous. 'You're experts, aren't you? You seem to know your job.'

But it was a transitory victory. 'The worst thing,' she said later, 'was that Pole was doing it to Pole.' Gripping the hands of a friend with her gnarled fingers, she whispered, her eyes full of tears, 'Don't let it get to you, young one, don't let it get to you.'

I remember visiting a handful of survivors from Auschwitz. We sat rather awkwardly in a modern tea-room just off the market square in Krakow.

'What do you recall from the times in the camps?' I asked. The answer came as a shock.

'The good times,' they replied, and seeing my surprise went on: 'How do you think we could have lived through the constant horror without having good times, without celebrating Christmas, playing with the children, acting plays, staging concerts, while all the time Germans were handing out death in the gas chambers? There had to be good times.'

The logic was indisputable, the sentiment extraordinary. But it helped to explain how the Poles went on to look at all their many crises. Both officially and in private, they tended to blame others for their misfortunes. The State encouraged it. Pre-war history justified it. Many, however, counselled against such attitudes. As one university teacher in Warsaw put it, 'When you look at our situation, don't be too quick to see a foreign hand behind it. We have the government we deserve.'

Sometimes the Poles sought to bypass their system, rather than resist or confront it. They discovered that the rules were not as important as the people paid to enforce them. Teachers, for instance, charged with instilling Communist values, would sometimes avoid slavish adherence to the Party line. How else could a pupil at Warsaw university write a thesis suggesting the Soviet military were similar to the American? Not only did he write it, but it was marked high in the class ratings. At times the teachers felt obliged to lead double lives. There were several dozen who subscribed to the so-called 'Flying University', a system of unofficial lectures held in private flats. Here, the professors would impart the uncensored truth as they saw it. It was an alternative culture, available privately in the evenings. The subjects belonged mainly to the arts, history being the most popular. The Second World War was the major preoccupation. Students had often been given one version by their parents and another by the State textbooks. Sometimes the meetings were disrupted. Students might be prevented from entering a flat; occasionally their names were taken as they left.

Early in 1981 the teachers felt obliged to meet the Western press. A group of them assembled in the ornate flat of a nonagenarian economist, just opposite the city's main gaol. His rooms were full of Chinese furniture. The setting could hardly have been stranger. They were all old men, and they talked purposefully but with little resentment. They were not out to overthrow the system, they simply felt it their duty to offer things the State did not. But their arguments were unavoidably critical. 'Why not tell the truth?' asked the science lecturer. 'How can the truth hurt good people? The truth can only be harmful to bad men.' It was said with the innocence of a child, or that of a man who has spent his life defending children's principles: 'right' and 'wrong', 'good' and 'bad'. The lecturers wore dark grey suits and had an air of formal respectability about them. In the West they would have been taken for bankers or consultant surgeons. Here they were dissidents, playing around with that sacred East European commodity 'information'. Taking from Caesar the monopoly Caesar most definitely considered his.

Despite the ornaments in the flat, the vases, the elaborate lampshades and the draped curtains, most of the journalists managed to get out without breaking anything. Cameras bore down on Ming-style pots, but missed them. Priceless plates were handled, but not dropped. With evident relief, the lecturers ushered their guests out into the familiar stone corridors, where the doors were uniform grey and the smell of cabbage a permanent fixture.

I went to see one of the lecturers a few weeks later. He had a thick, rasping cough.

'How long have you been in Poland?' he enquired.

'More than a year,' I replied.

'Good,' he said, 'now the anatomical make-up of your body is more Polish than English.'

For all his knowledge he took little care of his own body. Once, when the temperature fell way below zero, he wandered out into the icy streets to sit on a park bench and give an interview. Part of the reason might have been that the grandfather clock in his living-room ticked so loudly it was hard to hear what he was saying. But that day as he sat outside, his voice competing against the wind, small snowflakes gathered on his grey hat. He looked cold and tired. A few people passed by, buttoned up against the winter, not interested enough even to stop and stare. He went on talking all the time, with tremendous detail and precision. It was important to him that the West understood. While the traffic laboured on into the city and the cars slithered and skidded in the tracks in the ice, an old man was practising dissent.

He belonged to the class of people who didn't like talking in their own homes. Of course, it was hard to know just how far the official hand could reach. But it certainly went further than many people imagined, particularly as far as the telephone was concerned. An attractive blonde in her late twenties told of her surprise at discovering that her calls were being monitored. She had just told a friend she couldn't meet for coffee when a male voice chimed in, 'Why don't you meet me instead?'

'No,' she replied, 'I won't. And who are you, anyway?'

'A friend,' he insisted, 'I listen to your conversations.' He told her he wanted company, and, what's more, that he had enjoyed her conversations.

During the strikes of August 1980 I had tried repeatedly to call a member of the dissident group KOR (Workers Defence Committee) to obtain information. I would give my name, establish contact, and the line would be cut. The process would be repeated. It was enough to give my name and the line would be broken. I tried some twenty times and the result was the same. Both my listeners and I were bored by then. A simple telephone call had become far too much trouble.

But it was not only inside Poland that the authorities kept track of their people. One Warsaw resident found that out when he visited a friend in England in the late fifties. The man was apparently treated like a rare bird when he got to Britain. He was billeted in a country house in the south of England. People there hardly knew where Poland was, and believed that Communism was more like an infectious illness than a political persuasion. So remarkable was the man's arrival that he was invited to talk at the local village hall. He did so in his near-fluent English, but had the bad luck to be reported by a local newspaper. Somehow the article, pointing up some of his more unflattering comments about Poland, reached the Polish embassy in London and was signalled to Warsaw. The man was met on his return by people he had never seen before, but who seemed to know him remarkably well. Some two weeks later he was in prison. He had more than a year in detention to reflect on the dangers of the English countryside and the efficiency of his country's security service.

Resistance in Poland cut across the generations and began at an early age. It would be hard to imagine a teenager in Britain or America talking about setting up partisan units in the forests in the event of outside invasion. But that is exactly what a teenager in Warsaw told his astonished father towards the end of 1981.

'I'm sorry, Dad,' he said, 'but if you won't come with us, you'll be a traitor and we won't bother with you anymore.' The father, a well-known journalist, told the story with a mixture of pride and hurt, a very Polish response. 'He was serious, you know. He meant it,' he said. 'Typical young man, first sign of trouble and it's back to the forests.'

For the most part committed dissenters joined the dozens of secret organizations that printed, cajoled, discussed and debated. Some wrote reports and submitted them to the highest State officials, others were local, obscure and unrealistic. The police played cat-and-mouse with them. If the groups smuggled in printing equipment, detectives would swoop and confiscate it. That was regarded as a major setback, but there were always more printers than the authorities knew about, and more hideouts. Ironically, the presses were scattered in abundance through the provinces, where people were unable or unwilling to use them. In Warsaw, where the underground needed them desperately, they were in very short supply. As part of the subterfuge, some groups smuggled texts out to the West, had them reprinted and then brought them back into Poland to disguise their origin.

The organization of the groups was rather like an octopus: there was a small centre with very long 'legs', i.e. chains of contacts, leading to it, which meant that members in the regions never knew who the central controllers were. They simply received instructions by letter or dropped message. If they were caught they could not implicate anyone else. Information was given out on a strictly need-to-know basis. There was the constant fear of detection, however, and one region would invariably distrust another. Suspicion was unbelievably intense. Sometimes the underground in Gdansk would refer to counterparts in Warsaw as 'plugs' (i.e. informers), simply because they had not been arrested. The logic implied that if you were free you had to be working for the police.

Invariably, if one member of the group was detained, those who had worked with him or her were also cut out of the organization. The process was completely ruthless. It took no account of friendship or personality. On one occasion the leader of an underground printing-house cut himself out of his own group because he thought he was being followed. He once recounted how the group had hijacked a consignment of paper from a factory, but something had gone badly wrong. It seemed there had been a leak, and the police had known in advance. Instead of swooping on the dissidents they had placed a minute electronic transmitter in the paper, hoping it would lead them to the hideout and the gang. But the underground knew about the device. They simply drove the paper out into the country and left it in a disused barn until they were sure the transmitter batteries had run down. To them that was easier than hunting through a van load of paper for something they might in any case miss. Some six months after stealing the paper, the consignment was picked up and distributed.

The organization of the underground publishers was sophisticated far beyond Western expectations. By the late seventies one printing-house had some hundred titles on its books, with many thousands of stencilled copies in circulation. Money was borrowed from the main dissident organization, KOR, money to buy paper and pay for an entire commercial network. Illegal and haphazard, the whole process was none the less run on strict business principles.

'Where did we get the paper?' asked one of the organizers, smiling at such a simple question. 'We found out where paper shipments were going and we bought them or stole them. Delivery was so unreliable that no one knew what was happening to any of the things going around Poland, never mind paper. Then we'd find a house, a different one each time, and we'd be in business.' The man, bearded and in his early thirties, chuckled to himself at the beauty and simplicity of it all. There was more, too. He leaned back in his chair and sipped a cup of coffee. 'The paper shipments would sometimes be broken up into fifteen or twenty loads,' he said. 'It meant the police could never get all of it, only a part. We used to meet once a month. People submitted manuscripts and we got specialists to give opinions on them and consider whether these were good books. They had to be good books.' He looked up to make sure I had understood. We had a network of salesmen who knew very little. Some were picked up and held for forty-eight hours, some were released.'

'What happened to the others?'

'They would perhaps find difficulty getting a passport, that's all. The authorities weren't that interested in them.'

'How much were they paid?'

'Well, in Warsaw the seller got ten per cent of what he sold, outside Warsaw twenty per cent, and then there were the printers. They would go to a house, shut themselves in and print for a week, eating and sleeping where they worked. Then they would take a month off and print somewhere else for another week. We had to take terrible precautions. The printers wouldn't get rich, but they wouldn't do badly – anywhere between five and eight thousand zlotys a month. Over the national average.'

The man looked out of the window. He was safe now, but there were old habits that stuck, habits like sticking two mirrors on the car windscreen – one for the driver, one for the look-out. 'Things have changed under Solidarity,' he said. 'There was a huge need for books. We started producing libraries for factories. We had a man in the Ursus tractor factory outside Warsaw. He didn't have a single book at home, hardly knew what a book was, but he looked after them all so carefully and knew where each title could be found. Factories used to sign orders with us as if we were legal and official. Incidentally, I think these books or most of them survived even martial law. The authorities got some of them, but the people got most. They still have them.'

The ingenuity of such groups was unlimited, but they were only a part of the whole. Far from being a grey, silent monolith, Eastern Europe was alive with such organizations. The underground contacts were strongest, it seemed, between Poland and Hungary. Intellectuals from Hungary came to Poland to learn about printing techniques. The Poles held classes in private flats. A few Russians came as well. Underground leaflets were sometimes smuggled by long-distance lorry drivers who would travel through Poland from the Soviet Union, bound for East Germany. The traditions of resistance and dissidence were developed and refined. Political imagination received fresh, if limited, stimulus.

Nice Promises

During the Solidarity period dissidents even discussed supporting the Communist Party. Could this, they thought, be the chance for grand dialogue? They decided quite quickly that it could not. To begin with, they said, the Party had all but collapsed. Secondly, the spectacle of dissidents supporting Communists would have been so offensive to the rest of Eastern Europe it might have resulted in Soviet intervention. One intellectual in the underground was asked what he would most like to see. 'The strengthening of the Communist Party,' he replied, ironically. 'Only then will we both have a challenge.'

But the challenge had always been there for the dissidents, and with the advent of Solidarity it came out into the open. Among its more extraordinary appearances was a public sale of underground literature at Warsaw's grand polytechnic, close to the city's Constitution Square. There were ugly caricatures of the then Soviet leader Mr Brezhnev – one showed him with an impudent little elf called Poland sitting on his shoulder, laughing at him. There was literature that never had and never could be publicly distributed anywhere else in the Eastern bloc; the later works of Alexander Solzhenitsyn, for instance. There were stands and kiosks emblazoned with the names of hitherto underground publishers. As one of the organizers put it with mock naivety, 'All the material here was printed in accordance with the Constitution of the Polish People's Republic. The only thing was that it didn't pass through the censor, that final arbiter of good political and cultural taste.' With sentiments like that being expressed by a student in his early twenties, it appeared that the Polish revolution was well on the way.

It was odd, though, how normal it all seemed. The inhabitants of Warsaw queued outside the gates of the Polytechnic as though waiting for a cinema to open. They browsed through the anti-State literature as though used to it all their lives – some clearly had been. Only the fact that many began reading their purchases the instant they bought them gave away the excitement. The exhibits sold out within the first few hours. No one could quite believe they had got away with it. As for the authorities, it must have become apparent by then, even if they had ignored it previously, that the control of the printed word had slipped away from them. The police had earlier called on the Rector and told him to prevent the exhibition, warning him that it was subversive. He had been polite and noncommital, and the sale had gone ahead unheeded.

Many people kept mementoes from that period. Solidarity posters or badges, T-shirts, the union statutes. They hid them all as the underground code dictated. There was, it seemed, always someone plotting. Someone travelling to give information. There was always intrigue. Many involved in it had been wartime child couriers, the seven- and eight-year-olds who had run through the city sewers carrying messages for the Resistance. How could children like that grow into anything but adults like these, tough, resourceful and completely irrepressible?

During the Christmas festivities of 1981 there were four people in a cell in Warsaw's Rakowiecka Gaol who enacted a time-honoured prison ritual. They had saved their bread ration for some days and had collected sugar and matches. On Christmas Eve they melted a piece of chocolate from a visitor's parcel, soaked it through the bread and added some sugar that almost tasted like icing. After the guards had been in around six o'clock and removed the prisoners' day clothes, they cut their Christmas cake and thought how good it tasted. There were four equal shares, and they ate ravenously. The cake was gone in seconds. The occasion belonged to the good times.

One of the men who had been in that cell got out a few months later. He told of life with his compatriots – a hijacker and two former Government officials. They could buy food once a month, matches and cigarettes, but only six packs. The cell had contained just a sink and a lavatory, night clothes were long johns and a shirt that was changed every fortnight. They had two blankets and sheets. The interrogation, he said, had been uninspired. The defence lawyer was only allowed in the day before his trial. No one who was convicted could go back to his old cell.

There was half an hour's exercise a day, and they never saw anyone from other cells. At meal-times they would pass an aluminium bowl through the cell door and two other prisoners would fill it up. They were given pens and papers, but no toothbrushes or toothpaste. The man had been asked what his parents' social status was. 'What's that?' he asked.

'Their job,' came the reply.

'My father's a cleaner,' he told them. They wrote down 'worker'.

The man still remembers his Christmas cake. He says he will always remember it. But more than that, he recalls his feelings on going to bed that Christmas Eve.

'You know,' he said, 'despite all the difficulties, we all went to bed thanking God and really believing that we lived in a wonderful country.'

Party Rule

They chose Chopin for the music. The scene was a garden full of bushes and trees. There may even have been a lake, but the picture is old now and few people can remember. Standing in the middle of this Communist arcadia were a man and a woman smiling benevolently for the cameras. Poland's first man and his first lady. Physically a big man, he wore a dark suit. His hair was thick but closely cropped. His wife had a long dress on. It was impossible to make out the colours, for those were still days of black-and-white television. Her dress was elaborate rather than elegant, her hair piled up in layers – not beautiful, not even tasteful, but in the early seventies still an impressive sight.

They were the Gierek family. Wife a model Socialist, husband General Secretary of the Polish United Workers' Party. A loyal ally of Moscow, a family man and a former coalminer. A dream for the propaganda people. For nearly ten years Gierek had most of it his own way. He was blissfully happy. The rumours said he enjoyed reading the sporting newspaper and the wiretap reports on his closest colleagues, and they read those on him. After all, everyone had to be careful. Each year he went dutifully to the Soviet Union along with the other East European leaders for talks with the Russians, and each year, it seemed, he came back with his credentials approved and his image intact.

But had Gierek been able to look into the 1980s he might have acted differently. He might, for instance, have foreseen a macabre cocktail party in the bitterly cold winter of 1981. The party was at his villa just outside Warsaw, but he didn't live there any more. He had been summarily packed off to obscurity in his home city of Katowice. There had been a few generous comments about his career, but many more that were ungenerous.

Outside his house the snow had been cleared away by the security men, and scores of Western cars were parked in the drive and on the forecourt. Such a thing had never happened before. After all, the aim of building a house so far from the main road, with so many twisting byways and cart-tracks leading to it, was to keep people away, not invite them by the dozen. But tonight was different. This was a New Year's party for the foreign diplomats and journalists and for all the loyal staff who had once shaken Gierek's hand at so many airports and meetings, who had refilled his glass and taken his photograph, and who were even now preparing a case against him together with a list of his crimes and deficiencies.

Although he was absent that night, Edward Gierek's career had turned full circle. The hospitality was superb, the company predictable, and it was not until most guests had drunk far more than the local militia would normally allow them to drive home with that the point of the party became evident. No one saw who began the excursion. Suddenly little groups of guests were being ushered upstairs to take a look at the former master's bedroom. His bed, his bathroom cabinet, the 'his and hers' basins and, downstairs, the small cinema where he watched private films before specially invited audiences. Gierek's disgrace was complete, his tastelessness on show to the world. To allow the foreign press in was like allowing in a herd of cattle. Who could ever live there again?

There were rumours that the entire episode had been filmed and recorded secretly for later analysis. Who had said what to whom, who had chatted too long to the pretty Hungarian diplomat, who had talked to the man from Tass, who out of the Eastern pack had made unusual contact with the Westerners? Such things might have proved interesting if the security services had found themselves with a wet afternoon and no one to play with, but it was unlikely they bothered on this occasion, and it was never proved one way or the other.

Gierek's priority on taking power in 1970 had been to elbow out his predecessor, Wladyslaw Gomulka. Political assassinations were ritual affairs. There was no mechanism for a smooth transfer of power, neither in Gierek's time nor in any other. Sometimes people were fired because of rumours started by their opponents.

Often these were slurs and slanders without substance. Nonetheless, within a closed elite, rumours gathered credence with the telling. They were evidence of suspicion, and that was enough to end many careers.

When ousted, Gomulka had to learn to live his own twilight existence – somewhere between disgrace and rehabilitation. For he never formally achieved either. Years after his dismissal he was sighted walking his dog near the Parliament building in Warsaw. He approached a young lady pushing a pram, and, in a display of exaggerated paternalism, leaned over to coo at the dormant baby.

'I say, don't you think the child's a bit too hot?' he asked the mother.

'My God,' she said later, recounting the story, 'ten years out of politics and he's still interfering.'

The human stories of the politicians, the jokes, some rude, some pointed, served to bring politics down to earth. They acted as the people's safety valve. They humanized that second-oldest profession in the world and made it acceptable at the dinner tables, the bars and the restaurants of the entire nation. Few Poles ever seemed to want to discuss anything else, and in the early eighties it was easy to see why. The mortality rate in the Communist Party had risen sharply. The blood that normally spilled out of sight in the corridors was running publicly on the streets. Men and women went to meetings of the Central Committee not knowing whether they would leave with their jobs and reputations intact. For the majority there was no elegant retreat. They either died in office or were thrown out.

In Poland as in all the Eastern bloc countries there was only one political party that counted, but its members came with varying political complexions. Some brought doubts and had little interest in Marx or Lenin. However, they often found that the red card still set them apart from their friends, and sometimes from their families as well.

Barbara, a twenty-five-year-old, said her mother had been horrified when she joined the Party. 'She was absolutely furious,' she said. 'So were many of my friends.' Her father had been more realistic, 'OK,' he told her, 'maybe you can do something, change things, criticize.'

'But with my friends it was different,' she said. 'There was always the stigma.'

After a three-year probation period Barbara became a full Party member, but being Polish that didn't prevent her having a dissident boyfriend. She even used to help him type out his unofficial pamphlets without seeing any conflict of interest. He called her his 'red spider'. Barbara had begun work in the State television service, another decision that brought her unpopularity. 'My mother,' she said, 'used to tell me how people would pass the television building in trams and look down scornfully at those who got on at that stop.' At the height of Solidarity's influence the scorn changed to hatred, and some television workers were spat at when they left the building.

Barbara had joined the Party without giving a direct commitment to Communism. 'I was required to sign a declaration saying I supported the programme of the United Workers' Party. Nowhere did I have to say I was a Communist. There were no privileges at that level. I went in so as to get involved, and I stayed because leaving could have jeopardized my career even if joining hadn't helped it. Frequently in the meetings we found we were there to listen rather than to discuss our own ideas. One man who quoted Marx and Lenin to reprove the Party was severely reprimanded and accused of sowing confusion. Only once did we discuss the Solidarity issue, but no one knew what decisions to take or which way to go.'

And that was why the Polish Communist Party had been unique. It disintegrated from within, splitting into factions to the point where some Eastern bloc countries suggested it should be scrapped and rebuilt. Martial law, it seemed, had been introduced as much to deal with the Party's malaise as to smash the grip of Solidarity. It failed to do even that, at least for a time. I remember asking one Party member just how long after 13 December 1981 the squabbling inside the Party had resumed. He smiled ruefully. 'Around about the fourteenth,' he replied.

If people like Barbara joined the Party to change things, there were others who genuinely believed in Communism for its own sake. Albert, in his fifties, ruddy-faced with grey, wiry hair, was one of them. He worked for a State export company, but looked more like a Dickensian schoolteacher. He had a great sense of humour, and even liked a political joke or two when no one who mattered was listening. He entered into office bonhomie and joked about who was going out with whom, yet Albert was one of the truly committed. And if you had been through what he had and were still in the Party, then that was commitment indeed.

Albert kept his distance, despite the affable air. It was only those who worked directly for him who filled in the personal details. He had finished the war on what he took to be the right side – the Communist army which took over political power in 1948. Albert thought he would be all right, but he was wrong. His politics worked against him. For some reason, never disclosed, he fell under suspicion. The price of that was to be carted off to the Soviet Union and held in a labour camp. But he refused to believe he was finished. According to Warsaw legend he wrote a personal letter to Stalin and was eventually reprieved in the early fifties. Back in Poland he began work on a project of enormous symbolic significance. It was the building of a giant steelworks in one of the most traditional, conservative areas of Poland – Krakow. The idea which fired him and all the others was that of converting the masses. Thousands of young Marxist revolutionaries poured into what they saw as the centre of middle-class reaction. Not only were they supposed to build the steel plant, they were also to integrate with the bourgeois families, marry their daughters, talk round their fathers and sow, once and for all, the permanent roots of Communism.

It did not really work, either for Albert or for the majority of the others. Yes, the steelworks were built, but the families kept their daughters and for that reason, perhaps, Albert never married. He moved to Warsaw, lived alone and spent the sixties and seventies mellowing. When Solidarity burst upon his office he was struck first by scepticism, then fear. His Communist doctrine had taught him that nothing should move that quickly. There were channels to be gone through, there were proper procedures, the Party would see to it. Albert clucked over his wayward assistants like an agitated hen. He tried to joke about Solidarity, hoping it would go away.

His guilt, or so the State judged it later, was in not condemning his colleagues the way others had done. At any rate, the Party authorities threw him out soon after martial law was declared, and he was also suspended from his job. Friends who went to visit him said the shock had changed him beyond all recognition. He used to spend the day sitting in a chair beside the front door, his coat and scarf folded, ready for the summons. His gloves lay on his lap.

With Albert you could bridge the personal gap, but the political differences remained unassailable, locked away with the convictions and conditioning of his youth. He had genuine warmth and wanted to be liked, was self-effacing and hated ceremony. Once he tried to cut bureaucratic corners and commissioned some reports from his staff about their contacts with foreigners, but tore them up without reading them: a rare contradiction in that society. But talk to Albert about politics and his eyes narrowed. There was no other political system except Communism that he wanted to live in. In public his Party could do no wrong. Charges about Soviet action in Afghanistan were countered with examples of American involvement in Vietnam. We could have argued all day, but Albert didn't like to be unfriendly. He always agreed to differ and shook my hand graciously when I left. 'Mr Tim,' he used to say, 'come back and see us again.' For a while he would go to parties, but as the eighties wore on he gave them up. Even his own birthday would have been ignored without the vigilance of his secretary. It was she who arranged a cold little gathering at his office one working Saturday, she who invited the guests, and he who was profoundly embarrassed by the whole affair.

Albert's door was always open, but that was his choice and it made him vulnerable. Others were told to open their doors. They were licensed to talk to foreigners and give interviews. Sometimes they could ply you with information, steer you towards a story or a source. The important thing was to leave you with the impression that you had been given some exclusive information. Alone among your hapless colleagues you had been chosen to take home the scoop of the year. Some of those scoops were handed out at the top of a dull, grey, Communist Party building that overlooked a park close to many of Warsaw's foreign embassies. You took the lift but the stairs were quicker, and right at the top was the inner sanctum and Professor Andrzej's smiling businesslike welcome. Sartorially he was an odd mixture, part elegance and part disarray. Too many good Party meals had made it hard for the shirt to restrain the stomach. A wide tie, a dark suit and fluency in English completed the public image. He was convincing.

'We could all leave and become émigrés,' he once told me. 'I could have defected dozens of times, but it was more challenging to stay and contribute.'

He headed an institute that had far more facilities and information than it would ever acknowledge in public. It dealt sometimes with public opinion research, a study considered rare in Eastern Europe. And yet the professor was reported to have computers at his disposal which could in a matter of hours assess the public reaction to any specific Government move. Even so, the authorities insisted on introducing unpopular measures.

The professor had begun his Party life with much ambition and skill. He had understood quickly that there was no direct route to the top – all the senior positions seemed filled for the foreseeable future – but there was another way. He allied himself to a rising star who was much nearer the summit, supported him, and rose with him. He never stepped too much into the limelight, staying close enough to take some of the praise but far enough away to disappear if things went wrong.

And he survived his benefactor. His office became a sorting-house for Party gossip. Western journalists used to troop in and out, the phone would ring constantly. There would be talk of high-ranking personalities, and with it all a liberal dose of the professor's vanity. 'Let me show you the latest interview one of your American colleagues did with me,' he would say. In a society which banned public advertising the professor had made something of an art out of self-promotion. I told him once that I thought his Party's record was disastrous. He was completely unperturbed. 'It does look that way,' he replied, 'but there are many things the Communist Party can be proud of. Look,' he continued, 'think of the way it was after the war. Poland was in ruins. American money went to Germany. We had nothing.' Then came the punchline. 'We have at least made good our biological losses.'

'Is the Party taking credit for the fact that Poles go to bed with each other?' I asked. The professor seemed not to hear.

The national Party organization was often beset by rivalry. Different regions supported different factions. At one time Poland was ruled by the Katanga group, so named because the leaders came from a rich mining and mineral region. Then there were the cliques formed in 1968 and 1970 – and the so-called 'Moscow men', who have survived longest. Party rule varied enormously from one city to another. A journalist from the south told how people in his region used to stand up when the local Party leader entered the room. Later, he moved to Gdansk and found himself the object of great amusement when he got to his feet at his first Party meeting there.

In Warsaw you seldom caught sight of the people with real power. You saw only ministers and Party leaders. But who put them there? And who helped dismiss them? Who ran the Party's own civil service? You could see their lights burning late in the offices of the Central Committee, but for safety's sake these figures stayed out of sight. Solidarity could never touch them. They were the watchdogs, the men who decided the vital agendas for meetings and which men shook which hands. They ran the system because they knew it better than anyone else. They had constructed it. They were called 'the apparatus'.

Little was known about such people, but they survived purges and could use them to strengthen their own position. The apparatus had close links with the security services. They provoked the type of rumour that could finish a Party member's career. There is evidence that even when some of them were publicly sacked they still kept their offices and their salaries.

Perhaps no one would have thought much about 'the apparatus' if it had not been for the political struggles of 1981. So many known politicians were being sacked and disgraced that it was hard to see how the system held together. The mistake made by Poles and foreigners alike was to look only at what changed in

Poland during that period, not at what stayed the same. There was only one answer to the question, 'How is the system able to survive this concerted attack?' The apparatus.

The Polish Communists never went in for mass conversions. Indeed, they never sought to enlist great numbers. Party membership was a privilege, and it had to be earned. But it was sometimes the key to a whole range of other favours denied to ordinary people. Many of them were never mentioned, either by those who gave or those who received. It was taken for granted that for a Party leader and his closest colleagues every larder was open, every store unlocked, every industry waiting only for the opportunity to serve. If a senior official visited a car factory he might well be offered one of the vehicles, not, of course, straight from the production line, but delivered quietly a few days later. If he wanted his flat renovated then the Ministry of the Interior had a special department for that. The very senior officials would have their food delivered. Others could collect their orders from special shops.

Dotted around Poland were magic villages well away from main roads and sometimes guarded by a perimeter fence. No one visited by accident, and those that came to pry were turned away. Local residents would sometimes give such places special names, like 'Bermuda'. One farmer told me how a local Party official had built a country house for his son. He had pointed towards a wood. 'There's a clearing in there,' he said. 'It's a wooden bungalow, several bedrooms, all built with the best of everything. How can there be a shortage of building materials when things like that go on?' The man had found the gift highly amusing, for the boy had been just twelve years old.

Even in disgrace, life could be very pleasant for the Party's upper stratas. Piotr Jaroszewicz, former Prime Minister and once described as the most hated man in Poland, was at one time rumoured to have been held at a mountain chalet in the south of the country. Not a great hardship for him, and certainly not for his family. His son, a former racing-driver who had diversified into highly non-Communist business ventures, still drove his red E-type Jaguar around the capital, servicing it at one of Warsaw's most expensive garages.

The military lived in style, too. Houses were sometimes attached to bases and guarded round the clock. Food and furniture would come from the West. Families lacked nothing. Queuing was not a feature of their lives.

The privileges were too numerous to list. Few people knew about all of them, and it was only when Solidarity began to attack the Party in public that the majority came to light. Suddenly the special clinics, the cars, the boats and the foreign travel became public issues. The union began to demand the sharing of such concessions. It started to dictate what could or could not be sold in special shops. Party men who had grown up to believe they could live forever in luxury became fearful. Who, some asked, will bring us our films and our entertainment? What about our special petrol allocations?

One Party worker from Krakow used to tell me how his position had brought him nothing but work and worry. Years later when he was kicked out, he confessed it had also brought him a car, access to special food-supplies and a leap up the housing queue. 'If my criticism becomes too great,' he told me, 'then I will be asked to leave the Party.' It did, and he was, but not before he had resigned of his own free will. The letter sacking him arrived a few days after that. The Party had wanted the final word.

His name was Jan. His wife had been in the Party as well, but it did not seem likely that his children would follow them. He had known too much about the inner workings of the Government for his resignation not to matter. A few weeks before Edward Gierek was sacked I had gone south to see him, and I asked who the next leader might be. It had been clear for days that Gierek would be ousted. Jan smiled and talked of a man called Stanislaw Kania.

'Who's Kania?' I asked.

'A former police chief in Lodz.'

'Thank you,' I replied, and left taking no notice of his words, convinced that such an outsider had no chance. A few nights later in an apparent last-minute power struggle, after fierce factional in-fighting, Kania emerged as the final compromise candidate. At least, that was the story that filtered through to the Western observers. But the Party faithful like Jan had known who it would be, because they had planned it weeks before.

In his time Jan had been a progressive. Inside the Party, he had been more prepared to argue with the dogma than many of his colleagues. He had once argued with a dissident, who said he wanted freedom of the press. Jan said, why not? The dissident said he wanted free travel and free publishing. Again Jan told him, why not? The dissident said he wanted more democracy. Jan suggested free elections. At each turn Jan outbid the man, to the astonishment of the few who were watching. Jan's mistake was in thinking the Party could embrace such new ideas and still remain an East European communist party. Soon after the advent of martial law, he realized his error.

He didn't just fall from grace, however. He jumped. Jan began to have contacts with the underground – not that his track record helped much there. He wanted to publish articles abroad. He seemed suddenly seized by the need to speak out, and because Poland is the land of the unexpected he seemed to get away with it. He didn't lose his car or his flat, though he didn't get much work. But he stayed out of jail.

The last time I saw him, he still had plenty of ideas. He sat in his small flat on a Krakow housing estate, a daughter on one knee, a thin elfin smile on his face, expounding yet one more scheme for the future. Just across from the tiny study his wife worked in the kitchen, bottling fruit and vegetables to cushion her family against the mounting economic crisis. When the jars were full she hid them behind the books in the living-room.

The turning-point in Jan's political career had arrived before martial law. It was on a hot day in April 1981, in the central town of Torun. On the face of it the meeting seemed like one more exploration into dogma and dialectics. But it was not that. The delegates had dropped the jargon for the sake of unashamed criticism of their own party. Watched by Party faithful and leered at by Western journalists, delegate after delegate professed himself disillusioned with Party rule. A dissident faction was opening up inside the Communist Party and holding a public reception to tell the world about it.

They took the name 'Horizontalists', for they believed that power should no longer devolve vertically from top to bottom. They mostly wore suits and ties, were businesslike but excited. None more so than a lady in high heels with a squeaky voice and the gift of not needing to breathe while speaking. She kept up her high pitched squeak for well over half an hour. A few among the audience laughed and shook their heads in amazement as she came down from the podium.

No one had actually announced the meeting in advance, but the news had been leaked into the Warsaw grapevine and the press knew about it. Some of the delegates, though, had been summoned at the last minute by telex. At lunch-time they strolled around in the sunshine talking of the next meeting, scheduled, they said, for Gdansk at the end of the year. They did not know that quite another event was being scheduled for Gdansk that coming winter: the internment of the Solidarity leadership. But then that only shows how far they had lost touch with the Party authorities, and the authorities with them. It was not just the fact that this local Party unit had a leader who had been expelled by the central Party administration. Measured against all the other irregularities, that was of small account. But the people actually believed they could inject radical change into the Party structure, without the Russians so much as shaking a caviare spoon at them. They believed they could show some support for Solidarity, not realizing that, if they did, Moscow would have no choice but to attack them and the union at the same time.

Back in Warsaw, one of the movement's sympathizers, a journalist, criticized the West for making too much fuss about the day's events. It was just a meeting, she said, why build it into a sensation? But her views were to change. The moment the authorities opened the borders after martial law was imposed, she passed through them and did not return.

Since that day in April nothing has been heard of the 'Horizontalists' either. Only behind the scenes in the corridors of the Central Committee was the story of their demise pieced together. Immediately after the Torun meeting, the Party's inner cabinet – the Politburo – had refused point-blank to allow the same thing to happen again. The leaders of the movement were summoned to the Central Committee building in Warsaw. They refused to go. Such disobedience was rare. Instead, they suggested a meeting at a factory in the city of Lodz. The Politburo turned that down. In the end, after unprecedented wrangling inside the Party, four meetings were held in Warsaw and both groups attended. By this time the Party hierarchy was sick with worry about the 'Horizontal' movement. It insisted there could be no sequel to Torun unless the whole Party attended. Any suggestions of a split had to be contained. These were tense, panicky days, when everyone began suddenly to talk about Soviet intervention. It was not merely theory, either. The day after the fourth meeting in Warsaw a letter arrived from Moscow which warned the whole Party that it had gone too far. The Russians suggested that if they could not even maintain superficial unity, then someone else would have to do it for them. The letter forced everyone to go to ground, and the 'Horizontal' movement died. As far as the State was concerned, it had never existed.

In the early days of the 1980 crisis Poland divided clearly into optimists and pessimists. Since every conversation led automatically to the crisis and every argument to a conclusion, people had to make two assessments. Did Poland have a future? Many thought not. And what was the future going to be? As the days went by, the optimists stood out as a noisy minority.

Poland's journalists belonged in both camps. For they knew more than they could write about, and had learned to sit on all kinds of uncomfortable fences. Nowhere was this more true than in the weekly *Polityka*, where the staff could argue from a position of knowledge and write from a position of impotence. For the chief editor was a deputy prime minister and member of the Communist Party's Central Committee: Mieczyslaw Rakowski. A short man, with short grey hair and a square jaw, his mastery of English was gradually exhausted as the crisis intensified. His position ensured certain privileges for his staff, but meant that they were always carefully watched. Whatever enemies Rakowski acquired were visited on them as well. He retained their loyalty, however, despite the fact that his personal popularity in the country oscillated dramatically. Rakowski, some said, bought their loyalty. Poles believed he secured passports for his staff and their relatives and gave their children access to the best schools and the best doctors. Generally, it was said, he made their lives easier and ensured they could jump queues.

But the accusations didn't stop the Poles buying his newspaper and admitting freely that it was the best in the country. Rakowski was allowed to operate a system of self-censorship, and though he was frequently derided he often won grudging respect. Like so many of his colleagues, he was one of the capital's high-profile charmers. He had been to England and attended house parties in the country. He had his close circle of Western friends, including some among the British press. If you met him in a restaurant, and it would have to be a good one, he exuded Polish gallantry, dashing around the table to kiss women's hands and bowing briefly to the men.

Some say Rakowski survived by bending with the prevailing wind. Others said he never gave up fighting, and won all his major battles. The truth, as always, seemed to lie somewhere in between. Rakowski certainly had to fight, sometimes against powerful odds. One of his sons decided to remain in the West, a fact that would have spelled automatic disgrace in any other Eastern bloc country. 'I consider it my personal tragedy,' he once told a press conference of Western journalists. 'It's a painful, private matter.' The press seemed to agree, but Rakowski's critics did not. There were mutterings in the Warsaw Party branch that if he could not keep his children in order he wasn't fit to be in government. Rakowski rode that out. He also rode out a request by the Soviet ambassador to suppress articles about Moscow's trade relations with Poland. And he lived through a direct Soviet attack on his paper, which said it was Communist only on the front page.

Rakowski seemed to have powerful friends, but his position remained precarious. Soon after martial law he travelled to West Germany for talks with Helmut Schmidt, the then Chancellor. During that visit his staff were called in by the security services and were told they would have to submit to the same political vetting as everyone else. Until then Rakowski had said he would handle the vetting himself. In fact, it never took place. But the security services had given Rakowski a warning, and when he returned from Germany he had time to consider how unsafe his seat could have become in his absence.

Whatever the country said about Rakowski, his colleagues apparently went on trusting him. In the early days of martial law he gathered the senior journalists in his office together to tell them what was going on. He was asked how many people had died. 'I swear to you on the head of my sons,' he replied, 'that no more than nine people have been killed.' The staff believed him. After all, he had held the newspaper together. And when everything else was falling apart and a man could still swear in front of a group of witnesses, then you had to give him the benefit of the doubt.

During that chaotic period a man on Rakowski's staff tried to leave the country. He had been promised a passport to do research in Western Europe, but under martial law such trips became impossible. Nonetheless, the man was called to the passport office by telephone and told that his papers were ready. He went the same afternoon, and to his surprise was informed that the documents were not available. He should go home and make further inquiries. It was at this point that he received a visit from a captain in the security services. It was a friendly encounter. Why did he wish to go abroad? Who were his contacts and how long would he be staying? The man answered politely and the official left. Soon afterwards came another summons to the passport office.

'I'm not sure what it is about your documents,' a clerk told him on arrival, 'but they keep changing their minds. Here they are,' she said, 'and if I were you I'd go quickly before something else happens.' The man left the country the same day and did not return. All the signs pointed to intense departmental rivalry over his case, with different ministries making different decisions. In that kind of power struggle there were few certainties.

Long before the military takeover the State had sometimes used its own journalists to cultivate the Western press, and it was the same afterwards. That may explain why, in the early days of 1982, when the telephones throughout Poland were cut and everyone was suspected of informing, I received a verbal message to call on a senior Polish correspondent. He lived in a fashionable suburb of the city. The snow-ploughs had not made it that far, and the narrow roads were treacherous. It was dark and bitterly cold when I arrived. I exchanged a few pleasantries with his wife, and then he suggested a walk. There could be only one reason to go for a walk in those temperatures, and it had nothing to do with health. He thought his house was bugged, or wanted me to think that was the case. Either way, we trudged out into the new snow and headed for a small area of parkland.

'You know, it's been planned for weeks,' he told me. 'All the martial law decrees, all the street notices, the special passes. Everything was printed in advance in the Soviet Union. They had told us clearly that if we didn't organize a clampdown, then they'd do it for us.'

That was his message, and it was one heard frequently from Party officials at all levels. The man walked me back to my car. He was a smooth performer, and spoke fluent English. He had acquitted himself well. He had not asked too many questions about what I thought. He simply wanted me to understand the Party line. He had once told me that no one in Poland wanted to overthrow the system. All they wanted was pure socialism. The kind they had read about and been taught in the schools. Now he seemed happy that order had been restored.

The other Eastern European parties found Poland's style of socialism difficult to accept. They had watched the Poles do more foreign travelling than anyone else in the bloc, receive millions of dollars from relatives in the United States and keep them in private accounts – and they didn't like it. Little by little, the fraternal parties fell out of love with each other. The tension was inevitably concentrated on Poland's borders. In 1981 Polish tourists travelling to East Germany by train or car complained of systematic harassment by German border guards. Goods they had bought in the West were confiscated, particularly shoes, which the East Germans knew were virtually unavailable in Poland. On the Czech border the story was similar. Early in 1981 a Polish tourist and his family were returning home by car and were stopped at the

Czech frontier. They too had bought shoes, and were ordered without explanation to hand them over to the Czech customs. They refused to do this, and a shouting match developed. So loud was the noise that the Polish border guard came over to ask what was happening. The tourist told them his story. The Pole then turned angrily on his Czech counterpart. 'I have one of your lot passing through my post,' he told him. 'The tyres on his car were bought in Poland. Unless you return the shoes which these tourists have bought, I shall take the tyres from the car. The man can drive home to Prague without them.' The Czech gave in and the two families crossed the border, their purchases intact, watched carefully from both sides, as if a major East–West spy swap was in progress.

As Solidarity grew stronger, the pressure from the other Eastern bloc parties increased, and Warsaw instructed its ambassadors in Prague and East Berlin to make formal protests about the treatment of Polish citizens. On a visit to the Polish embassy in East Berlin I remember asking an official how bad relations between the two capitals had become. His eyes gestured to the ceiling as if to suggest this was not a private discussion, and he smiled.

'We are both trying to ensure that they don't get any worse,' he said.

Some of his colleagues in the Polish military mission were reported to be less tactful. They had told the East Germans to their faces what they thought of them. Diplomatic tension was rising.

Few people were surprised at the rapid decline in relations between Warsaw and East Berlin. Historically, they had reasons enough to dislike each other. The border between them had been no more reliable than a geological fault, and over the years rows had broken out from time to time. The most telling is said to have occurred during East Germany's thirtieth-anniversary celebrations. All the Eastern bloc leaders attended, including Leonid Brezhnev, who sat on a high chair during the ceremonial march-past while all the others stood. East Berlin was literally infested with security men.

The Polish delegation was led by Edward Gierek, and with him were a handful of colleagues from the Politburo. The celebrations went well until a private meeting between the Poles and the East Germans. There were polite greetings and congratulations. Normally it never went further than that. But the East German leader, Erich Honecker, is then reported to have presented the Polish delegation with a German Army dagger reminiscent of the kind used during the war. 'You see,' he told the Poles, 'we're back on top. We're somebody again.' The allusion, whether intentional or not, could not have appeared more tactless. Some of the Poles simply turned on their heel and faced the other way. It was all Gierek could do to prevent them returning instantly to Warsaw.

There was, however, worse to follow. During the Solidarity era Polish journalists would find their newspapers confiscated by East German customs. The papers were no longer put on sale at all. And in retaliation the Warsaw-based correspondents from both East Germany and Czechoslovakia were called to the Polish Foreign Ministry to receive a reprimand. In the words of an official, they had wrongly assessed the situation in Poland. The Polish message was quite specific, but it had little effect. After all, much of what was attributed to those correspondents was said to have been written by their superiors back home.

For the most part, the East European journalists were amiable and hard-working. Not that very much of what they wrote appeared publicly in the newspapers or agencies they worked for. But they covered everything, wrote down every detail, charted the vicissitudes of the Solidarity campaign in a way that would have had Western reporters weeping with boredom. They had their excitements as well, though. At one point during the crisis Tass reported that workers had taken over a factory in the southern town of Kielce and were holding the managers hostage. Polish officials denied the story instantly. At a press conference the Communist head of the Journalists' Association was asked what he thought of the report. He looked quickly round the room for maximum effect.

'I think the same as you do about it,' he replied, as the cheers and laughter exploded around him. As they left the building the

Eastern bloc journalists were teased playfully. 'Where did you think up that story?' one of them was asked. 'Don't look at us,' he replied, clearly embarrassed, 'we didn't write it.'

By the time Poland announced its State of Emergency the Communist Party had been living through its own crisis for months. In some factories workers had placed baskets at the shop-floor exit so that the men could throw in their Party cards as they left. Such was the disillusionment among tens of thousands of ordinary members. One writer who gave up offering articles to the State press in the end admitted, 'I couldn't bear to look at myself in the mirror while shaving.' His wife, a lifelong Party member, resigned, bitterly disappointed by the actions of her Communist colleagues. She said there was nothing else she could do to influence Polish politics, nor did she want to.

Many fought with their consciences, though. Those who had joined the Party for no better reason than because their parents had handed down membership began to suffer. 'We had to stay,' said one of them. 'We can't hand it all over to the militants. Someone has to fight from within.' Zbishek was one of those. He had joined a State newspaper in the provinces, believing he had a mission. He was an enormous bear of a man. A gentle giant who spoke of the Party with tears in his eyes. He had joined because his father was a member; his faith had been imbibed with his mother's milk. But the events of the early eighties left him bewildered and uncomprehending. Why was it not possible for the workers to have what they want? Why could we not talk sensibly about the situation as it really was? I had a soft spot for him, because to Zbishek even a drink in a bar was a formal occasion. Every time he went anywhere he would dress up in the same brown suit and wide tie with blue-and-white patterns. He had nothing else to wear. He took every failure of the Party as a personal defeat, and some were indeed laid at his door. During the period of martial law he was relegated to writing stories about the weather and doing film reviews. His superiors no longer trusted him with politics, but he was in good company.

For by that time Poland's former politicians had long since lost the trust of the State and the people. The liberal Solidarity climate had gradually exposed the group closest to the former leader, Edward Gierek, and the new administration had added to the exposures. It was a delicate operation. Collective leadership meant collective responsibility. And if the propaganda was not handled carefully, anyone who had held office in the old government, from Defence Minister to the tea boy, was in danger of being implicated. That was why none of the major leaders was ever brought to trial. They all knew too much about each other. Quietly, and without official press comment, the man charged with the State's own investigation into its forebears was dismissed. But the disgrace of former politicians was achieved in other ways, sometimes at the hand of the public itself.

The city of Katowice is known for two things. Coal production, and the slow anger of its workforce. When coal production fell, however, the anger rose. When a group of miners encountered their former local Party boss out for a walk just outside the city early in 1981, they could not let the event pass without a show of feelings. According to the story later confirmed by officials in private, Zdzislaw Grudzien was surrounded by men who jeered him, held him to the ground, removed his clothes and smacked his bottom while holding him over a log. Laughing, they walked off with his clothes and threw them away. No one is sure how he got home. For some time afterwards he was disinclined to put his head out of doors, but eventually he and his wife moved to Warsaw where their connections with the Interior Ministry secured them a flat, refurbished by official craftsmen, at the Ministry's own expense. Their problems, it seemed, were over. They would have remained so had it not been for the new-found investigative zeal of the Warsaw daily newspaper, *Zycie Warszawy*. Like many State institutions it had been partially liberated by the advent of Solidarity. Reporters who would not have previously dared to comment on a Communist official set out to hound Grudzien and to find out, as if they didn't know, how he had managed to jump the Warsaw housing queue. A reporter rang his doorbell, but he was out. He left his card warning that he would be back again to get some answers. But Grudzien died of natural causes before he could give any, and the story was dropped. The cynics said it would have been dropped in any case, for Grudzien still had friends. Somehow the story would have been blocked well before publication.

At least for a time, then, the Polish Communist Party accommodated many different kinds of support. There were thousands of passive members, people who never bothered to attend meetings and had simply failed to go through the formalities of resignation. In the end, though, they were all tested. For the upheavals of Solidarity and martial law laid bare a generation of Party members. Even the most reticent crawled out of the political woodwork and gave an opinion on something. Some would have preferred not to. And one member of parliament admitted that it was a great relief no longer to have to get up in Parliament and talk in florid terms about freedom and passports for everyone, fearing that one day he might have to fight for his seat. With few exceptions, they could all settle back into their old ways.

All this must have been strange to visiting Communist delegations, especially those from the Soviet Union. And when at the height of the troubles the Kremlin's ideological referee Mikhail Suslov called hurriedly on the Warsaw government, there were signs of considerable nervousness among Polish officials. On the surface it went well enough. A phalanx of black Chaika saloons headed into central Warsaw from the airport, their lights on, the way cleared by police. It was already afternoon, and talks began immediately. By early evening the talking was still going on. At around eight o'clock Soviet aides nervously approached the Polish officials and asked in whispers about the arrangements for dinner. 'But we thought you were handling that at the embassy,' they were told. The Russians became angry and terrified. 'You're the hosts,' they implored. 'You should have done something about it.' No one is sure what Mr Suslov himself thought of it all. He returned that night to the Soviet embassy without an official dinner, and left early the next morning. All the rumours portrayed Mr Suslov as a strictly orthodox Marxist, who from his slight figure did not seem over-interested in food. Nevertheless, he must have had cause to wonder what sort of a Communist party it was that could receive him in such a sloppy fashion.

Officially Speaking

Sooner or later anyone who was anyone went there. It was not the best restaurant, nor the most expensive. The décor was plain, the service slow. In fact, there was a much better place just across the road. But Warsaw society insisted on patronizing the so-called Writers' Club. For a while it had been transferred to a street corner near the Solidarity headquarters, waiting for its original premises to be redecorated. When it finally returned to them it was hard to see what had changed. The staircase was the same stone, the grey door loose-fitting and peeling, the food lukewarm. And yet the old habitués trooped in by the dozen. The rich and famous enjoyed it because people fawned on them. The poor and famous enjoyed it because it was cheap. Foreign journalists enjoyed it because they ran into ministers who would normally run away from them. And if the bills were too small to be worth claiming, then so be it.

At half-past one during almost any weekday lunch-time it was crowded. A balding man with glasses used to sit in the corner. He would bring his 'guests' there daily, but it was they who paid. When he was not looking round to see who had come in he would lean across the table and whisper confidences in bad French or bad English. He worked for a monthly paper and, it seemed, did know what was going on in the Communist Party. He never told anyone, though. A sleek, well-groomed official from the Foreign Ministry was often there, who would send his beer back saying it was too cold. A doorman demanded membership cards from people who never had them. Some tired waitresses tried to smile and not be abrupt when reciting the list of dishes they could not provide.

Everyone went there far too often, and the conversation became predictable. The greatest certainty was that nothing of consequence would ever be imparted to anyone there. People used to walk round the block to do that. Officials came mainly to sell a rarified kind of optimism, not much in evidence as the crisis of the eighties' wore on. Sometimes, former officials went in there simply to sharpen a hatred or two. There was a one-time Government minister who occasionally wrote for the official newspapers.

'I'm suspect now,' he once said. 'They only trust me with the anniversaries.'

One sensation at least was recorded at the club: the unexpected arrival of President Carter's National Security Adviser, Zbigniew Brzezinski, who slipped away from an official visit to drink beetroot soup with a few old friends. They had laughed loudly and drunk much, and Brzezinski left the club with his friends shouting after him, 'Don't give in. You be tough with those Russians.'

One went to the club to fill in the gaps in the grapevine. To learn which faction was on the way up, who was talking to whom, who had been abroad, who had a new flat and how many square metres it occupied (one of the most crucial questions of all). Another popular meeting-place featured live stage performances. Pietczak's cabaret was famous in Poland. You had to have influence even to get a seat. For it consisted of a semi-risqué programme of skits, songs and jokes. Politicians were often the target. And some of them used to join the audience to demonstrate their liberalism. A former secret police chief was often to be found there with his wife, both laughing uproariously at the kinds of jokes that had once put people in prison. Occasionally the audience and even some of the actors would glance nervously in their direction just to make sure they were still smiling. The show acted as a safety-valve, as did those permitted in other parts of Eastern Europe. It was hoped that the clientele would return home with a warm feeling that they had tested the system and that freedom of speech was, after all, alive in Poland.

But the cabaret, like other institutions, became dangerous. Its director, Pietczak, wrote a song called 'Let Poland Be Poland' that became a second national anthem. The workers used to sing it as a victory song when their strikes ended. It quickly assumed the status of a political challenge. When the cabaret reopened some months after the start of martial law, the song had disappeared from the programme. Pietczak said he no longer wanted to sing it, even among his friends. He had plenty of requests for it, but turned them all down.

Unlike other East European politicians, the Poles enjoyed being seen around town. Senior officials were invariably treated like kings, but like kings with a fatal disease. You gave them enormous respect, but tried not to get too close. Waiting on a minister was all very well if he was satisfied, but the penalties for inadvertently spilling his soup or standing on his foot must have seemed awesome. On one occasion I watched a restaurant manager hurry out of his office to greet an official. He was sweating profusely, uttering all kinds of respectful greetings, offering him titles he didn't have and dishes the restaurant didn't have either. Amongst all this, the official behaved with distant charm, brushing away the nervous lackeys like flies. He left half of the food on his plate and then embarrassed the staff by insisting on paying for it. It was much more effective than official walkabouts, for it caused maximum panic among ordinary people and brought the politician some concrete evidence of his power.

If a minister announced a visit in advance, local officials would arrange a crowd of well-wishers to attend. If it was a senior figure, then food supplies would have been improved in the local shops some days in advance. Nobody wanted the minister to be accosted or barracked by the frustrated proletariat complaining about shortages of toothpaste. Eventually, in 1981, even the official press became sick of the staged walkabouts. One paper wrote, 'We have had plenty of this sort of thing in the old days. Let the politicians see what life is really like.'

Even before then, though, there had been a joke about ministers and the way they saw ordinary life. One of them, as the story goes, rose to make a public statement, a warning about the impending winter. Not surprisingly, since he did so at the end of October and the weather had turned cold. But that year the minister had some special advice.

'It's going to be a hard winter,' he said, 'so you'll all have to follow my advice carefully. Put straw up against the windows, fill up any old cracks with clothes and top that off with newspapers.'

The point of the joke was the man was the Minister for Energy, and the tragedy was that he actually said it. As one student put it, 'This man got up to tell us we were returning to the sixteenth century. No heating, no lighting, no anything at all.'

But ministers seldom had to see much of ordinary life unless they wanted to. If they were not in their special residences, they might be drinking malt whisky or playing tennis with the foreign ambassadors, though it wasn't always clear whether they had more enjoyment in accepting or turning down such invitations. Polish officials liked to party, and if nothing else their presence at a function ensured that other guests were able to park near by. By and large, they were approachable at receptions. They were smooth, sophisticated performers. Undisturbed by loaded questions, and as sharp as any Western politician having to deal with Parliamentary debate. To keep their job even in a one-party system, such men had to be permanently on the alert. Especially during the crisis of 1980, when officials were being axed nightly.

There were only rare glimpses below the surface of official life. In 1981 General Jaruzelski gave the first official television interview ever given by a Polish prime minister. The interview was held over for more than six months. Then one small excerpt was transmitted. The chief of propaganda in the Central Committee apparently said the interview showed Jaruzelski in a silly, unflattering light, and was therefore unacceptable. Jaruzelski had shown surprise when the television reporter told him it was the first interview of its kind. 'Really?' he asked. 'Is that so?' He had apparently seemed pleased to talk to someone outside politics. The two had chatted about his home and family. The reporter said his wife had been charming, and although the General seemed stiff and embarrassed on occasions, she thought that might have had more to do with the steel belt he wore for a slipped disc than congenital shyness.

On the whole, the rumours of Jaruzelski's diffidence seemed to have been put around in a misguided official attempt to humanize the man. But who has ever become leader of an East European Communist party, been a four-star General trained by the Russians and handled the country's worst political crisis since the war by being shy? Jaruzelski was not shy.

Unlike his wife he had no talent for foreign languages. She apparently spoke German and taught it. Nor, it seems, did he have the sense of the unusual that characterized his teenage daughter. According to the father of one of her schoolfriends, Miss Jaruzelski had on one occasion been seen to browse through unofficial leaflets printed by Solidarity. In fairness, so many were on the streets in 1980 that it was hard to avoid them. At the time, though, she told her friend, 'My father would kill me if he found me with these.' Miss Jaruzelski had other surprises to offer. Soon after martial law, when all private telephones were cut, her friend was woken one morning by the sound of her telephone ringing. She listened for several minutes in disbelief before answering it. When she picked up the receiver, the General's daughter came on the line to ask simply if she could borrow a book. She said nothing about the telephone or how she had got it to work. The friend was too stunned to say anything except yes, and replaced the receiver. Minutes later she picked it up again to try her luck, but the line was dead.

For years the Polish authorities had used the media as a blunt instrument for propaganda, and yet there were always surprises. Polish journalists often asked ministers such searching questions that the censors had to cut out the queries, rather than the responses. In 1980 a newspaper interviewer had collared the minister concerned with fixing prices. The text of that interview had gone before the censor, and the blue pencil had scrawled liberally across it. Nonetheless, the minister still appeared vague and incompetent.

Question: 'You failed to stop prices rising last year, didn't you?'
Answer: 'Yes, I know. Prices went up very steeply.'
Question: 'But there must be certain rules. Things aren't out of control are they?'
Answer: 'We certainly aren't helpless.'
Question: 'But people are taking no notice of you.'
Answer: 'That is true.'

Many Polish journalists found they had to lead both restricted and double lives. One reporter found that the Journalists' Association had awarded her a prize for an article that the censor had refused to publish. 'Where else but Poland could such a thing happen?' she asked. 'The only people who had read the article were the censors and the prize committee. Nobody else in Poland even knows I wrote the thing.'

During the Solidarity period, however, many restrictions were lifted without warning or announcement. Editors often had little idea about what they could or could not publish. And in that climate a newspaper in Krakow set a dangerous precedent. When the police were accused of beating up Solidarity activists in a northern city, the editor sent his own reporter to assess the situation. Alone among the national and regional press he then printed the reporter's story side by side with the version offered by the State. The readers loved it. The State said nothing. And the paper, which had long been known as outspoken, became famous again overnight.

The editor was sacked immediately after the imposition of martial law, but not before he had commissioned an unusual poll. Famous people were asked to recommend a book for Lech Walesa to read. For rumour had it that Walesa had never actually read a book. The President of the Journalists' Association had the best answer. He suggested a Polish–Russian dictionary. Poles throughout the country laughed about that for a long time.

The new media mood was felt most quickly in the regional radio stations. For a time they enjoyed unprecedented autonomy. In the north, Gdansk Radio broadcast, sometimes live, the historic negotiations in the Lenin shipyard between the Government and Lech Walesa. One throw-away line of Walesa's seemed to have stuck in the audience's mind. 'What about the political prisoners?' he had shouted across to the Government minister. The question must surely have made broadcasting history in Communist Eastern Europe, and have staggered people across the border in the Soviet Union who were able to pick up the transmission.

But no one person controlled the media in Poland. The Government and the Communist Party had their own separate watchdogs and spokesmen. And towards the end of 1981 it was clear that they were talking less and less to each other. Not only would contradictory articles appear in the newspapers, but at times there were contradictions in the same article. On one occasion a report on agriculture contained the phrase 'private farming is against the principles of Socialism'. That would not have raised many eyebrows in Moscow, but in Poland, where eighty per cent of farming was in private hands, it was unprecedented and extraordinary. Who had authorized such a comment? Why was it never explained? Why did the rest of the article accept the principle of private farming? How many different hands were fighting for control of the press?

Ironically, the most effective form of censorship during that period was no censorship at all. As one reporter explained it, 'It was like having a balcony with no railings. You were so scared, you never went near the edge, and the authorities' control was that much more effective.'

Control of the foreign press usually came from the Communist Party press agency, Interpress. Its story is a remarkable one of survival and volte-face. Few other organizations could have made a living out of selling the public image of a Government at a time when it had no policies and no cohesion. In the summer of 1980 it wheeled ministers into news conferences in their shirt-sleeves to exude calm and tell the world the strikes were over. Some of them were sacked soon after their appearances. And on one ironic occasion the Interpress director himself summoned the resident Western correspondents and told them plainly, 'Free trade unions are unacceptable in a Socialist State.' Some months later he had to choke back his words and introduce Lech Walesa to the same audience, in the same room, as the head of Eastern Europe's first free trade union movement. The director was lucky enough to have been born with a red face, so it wasn't clear whether he was blushing or not. However, seventeen months later he collected the final victory for himself. He brought in the Government spokesman, a martial law commissar and General Jaruzelski's personal adviser, now in uniform, to announce the 'state of war', the suspension of the trade union and a neat little package of other restrictions.

The offices of Interpress kept several glass cases which normally contained a sampling of their publications, but which were turned to a different purpose during martial law. Inside one of them had been placed a selection of old bits of wire, a few plastic radio cases, a camera, some transistors and batteries. Under each object was a label naming the previous owner. All items, it was said, had been used by Western agents for purpose of espionage. These exhibits preceded a series of films, first shown privately at Interpress and then broadcast on the State television. Each dealt with the discovery of Western agents, in most cases diplomats, who were filmed apparently without their knowledge during interrogation. All those involved had already been ordered to leave the country. The title of the series was *Who's Who*, the same title Solidarity had used for a biography of its own officials. It was no coincidence. One aim of the films had apparently been to shake up the Western community and to frighten any who might have been involved in 'incompatible activities'. It was hardly subtle, and was probably ineffectual. But it gave the Westerners themselves an opportunity to see who was who and what was Interpress.

Most of the staff had a pleasant social manner. Far from keeping their distance from foreigners, they cultivated them. They always attended parties, from formal receptions to small private dinners. They kept to the traditions, never arriving without a box of chocolates or a bunch of flowers. In their headquarters there was a coffee bar. Westerners were encouraged to come in and discuss their plans. Interpress could help. Its connections could secure interviews with ministers, theatre tickets, even organized trips. They once took a group of journalists on a visit to a military barracks just outside the capital. Tank and infantry units staged exercises on marshland. They captured a bridge, and there was plenty of noise accompanied by colourful flashes. But the equipment was clearly old, and that gave rise to some embarrassment.

'Haven't you got anything newer?' someone asked.

'Of course we have,' said an officer, 'but we can't show it.'

Then came the political lecture. All this, said one of the commanders, is defensive. Someone in the crowd muttered 'obsolete'. The Warsaw Pact is a defensive organization, he added, open to anyone. He turned to a British reporter. 'Even your country could join,' he smiled. 'Our troops are not trained to take an aggressive posture.'

The officials had done their best to make it a nice day out. A look at the barracks, lunch in the mess and meat for everyone. And then a shooting competition: the nearest most of us will have come to bearing arms in a Warsaw Pact country. Everyone's score was compared, but honour remained in the family. The winner was a Czechoslovakian correspondent. It would have been uncharitable to say he had done it before, but everyone said it all the same.

There was no doubt that Interpress had access to important information, because it sometimes let it slip. In the early days of martial law, one of the organization's temporary staff had described how he had found out in advance what was going to happen.

'I saw papers,' he said, 'and I didn't believe what they were telling me. It was too momentous, too extraordinary. I didn't know everything, but what I saw was enough.'

In general, interviews with State officials yielded little that was not in the official press. If you asked a minister how the food economy was progressing, he might first blame the bad winter, compare this year's figures favourably with last year's, and attribute the remaining problems to Western interference. Rarely would he actually admit that the food economy was a disaster. But there was another way of going about such interviews. On one occasion I confronted a senior official with the 'worst of all worlds' scenario.

'Your economy is shattered and there's no way out,' I told him. The man looked stunned.

'You're right,' he said, without thinking. 'It's a pretty dismal picture.'

The interviews did not all follow a pattern. One official at the Ministry of Foreign Trade had a liability with him in the room, and one he could not control: his secretary. Every time he answered a question, she would contradict. Public transport, he would say, has improved greatly in the last five years. The number of buses has risen by at least sixteen per cent.

'That's what you think,' interjected the secretary. 'When was the last time you travelled by bus? The queues, the people, the waste of time. It's chronic,' she added, 'quite chronic.'

The man smiled. He had clearly encountered this sort of behaviour before.

'My secretary,' he said, 'is a little excitable. She doesn't take all the factors into account.'

Most people thought the story of their antics was far-fetched, but it gathered credibility as more reporters were dispatched to the ministry and had the same experience.

But there were Government buildings where the doors remained firmly shut. Even when the Council of Ministers came to be used for industrial negotiations, the door was closed. Onlookers and journalists remained outside for hours, sometimes in freezing temperatures, as the negotiations took their course. One night, though, the authorities took pity. It was around one o'clock, and the temperatures had been falling since late afternoon. People had waited outside the building, anxious to know if there had been any progress. Cars passing by would slow down and let the drivers see what was happening. One of the reporters finally banged on the main door. 'For God's sake,' he shouted melodramatically, 'do you want us all to die out here?' Nervously, the doorman let us into the hallway. There were no chairs. We sat on the staircase and, as the hours went by, a few laid down to sleep. That was more than petty officialdom could stand. 'Get up!' one of the doormen shouted. It was only three o'clock in the morning. 'Get up! Where do you think you are?' As with all Governments the press was welcome when it was useful, and not otherwise. Only one person seemed to be smiling that morning, and he was the New China News Agency correspondent. But then, he smiled at everything. At four o'clock he asked innocently, 'What do you think of Mrs Thatcher?' At five o'clock he wanted to consider the prospects of Soviet intervention. At six o'clock came the sweetener, the offer of a Chinese meal at the Chinese embassy. An offer that, unfortunately, he seemed to have forgotten by breakfast time.

Sometimes, though, and only in the hours of daylight, Government trade officials would take you out for a meal. One of them who lived in the south always wore a shapeless tweed hat that he had bought in England. At other times he wore a tweed suit and woollen tie. The accent was mainly Oxford, with only tinges of Warsaw. Surprisingly, he never talked much about England, although he knew it well. His acquaintances belonged to Richmond Polo Club and he had friends with country houses. Although we used each other's Christian names, this remained a formal relationship. Eduard was a fastidious man and observed all the courtesies, holding doors open for you and apologizing profusely for being late. He tried to treat his colleagues like members of a gentlemen's club. He once spoke of his office partner as a 'decent chap and a good friend'.

Eduard must have had good friends in the right places, for he never panicked, never showed the slightest sign of nervousness even in the worst days of the crisis. But he always knew which way the wind was blowing. Sometimes he would criticize the Government, at other times he could be more understanding.

'Give them time,' he would say. 'There are tremendous difficulties.'

Eduard fitted in well with the Westerners he met, unlike Olgierd, his Warsaw-based colleague. Olgierd started turning up at too many Western parties, trying to date Western women and getting just that bit too drunk. Olgierd became greedy. He asked foreigners to give him unrationed petrol. Some agreed. He became greedier, and more unpopular, in the process.

Eduard once told me that it was the foreign businessmen they really cared about. I expressed surprise that they kept coming back to Poland and dropping seemingly inexhaustible piles of money on the country. 'That's easy,' he replied. 'We send them out near the Russian border. They can shoot bison and boar to their hearts' content. Then we bring them back to Warsaw, and they have their pick of the women.' Small wonder that they kept returning and rattling the change in their trouser pockets.

It was always a surprise how much officials felt able to say privately. Invariably they said more than their counterparts in the rest of Eastern Europe. When the Soviet Union invaded Afghanistan, the Polish press reported it late and gave it little space. Through official leaks Warsaw let it be known it was unhappy not to have been told by the Russians in advance. On disarmament the Poles stressed their own initiatives, not just those of Moscow. And on one occasion they were able to host a surprising meeting between Brezhnev and Giscard d'Estaing. In their own inimitable way, they had tried to keep the meeting secret in advance and failed. Journalists were rung up on a Friday night by the Foreign Ministry and told, 'We strongly advise you not to leave town.'

'That sounds like an unpleasant warning,' one reporter replied.

'It's not meant that way,' said the Ministry official, 'but there's no more we can tell you. Something's going to happen.'

The reason for the phone call was clear enough. Warsaw was becoming anxious that the Western press might go away for the weekend, leaving no one to cover its moment of glory. So it was left to an Interpress official to leak the names of the visitors at a cocktail party. Where else? The only other question was where they would meet. There were few possibilities in the capital. Someone rang up the Palace at Wilanow. The caretaker answered the phone and told the caller they were closed and expected foreign visitors. That sealed it.

Polish officials would often obscure the most trivial fact and release the more important one. In that they differed markedly from their East European neighbours, who kept everything secret, no matter how insignificant. The Poles would allow Western visitors into a nuclear research centre, but would prevent them taking pictures of bridges featured in official postcards. They would allow court proceedings to be filmed, but began to worry about shopping queues. They were haphazard and unpredictable.

Inevitably, there were functions that remained closed to outsiders. No outsider ever made it into a meeting of the Politburo or the Communist Party Central Committee, a squat, grey slab with square arches wide enough, so rumour had it, to allow a tank to pass through. Even after the meetings there were over officials struggled for hours, sometimes days, to work out what could be released to the public. A meeting might continue until dawn and be followed by a one-line communiqué. And that meant trouble. For, as a general rule, the less said, the fiercer the arguing and the in-fighting. Television technicians who were allowed to film such meetings had specific instructions about who they could feature and who was to be ignored altogether. The tightest possible control was exercised over such films. And only the senior editors of the television news programmes were ever allowed access to them. During the strikes of 1980, when the authorities were falling over their own feet with anxiety, the television image began to crack. Bulletins were late, viewers were left staring at the clock. Television journalists rang up to say there would be special announcements. None came. The whole edifice of Government seemed to be crumbling.

Inside the Central Committee are the offices of the Party's theoretical journal, *Nowe Drogi*, 'New Paths'. It is about as far inside the building as an outsider will penetrate. There, in narrow, cell-like offices, with stone walls and high ceilings, the editors try to reflect their leaders' thinking.

One of their contributors, an elderly man with glasses, a rather benign figure, had managed to avoid the national disease of worrying, but only up until 1981. Since that man acted as a barometer to the mood of the building as a whole, this was cause for concern. His main worry concerned a change of leadership in the Soviet Union. In his slow, ponderous fashion he outlined the possible eventualities. The death of the Soviet leader might provide the impetus for a revolution inside Poland. The under-ground could well take advantage of the twenty-four-hour period of confusion in the Warsaw Pact that follows any Soviet leader's death. They could launch some major offensive. On the other hand, hardliners in the party might see the death as the excuse needed for a thorough crackdown. The man paused. None of the possibilities seemed to bring him any pleasure.

'You see,' he went on, 'hardline factions might want to give something to the new leadership. They might want to offer a token of their loyalty.

Did that mean Poland will have the clamps put on the moment the Soviet leadership changes?

'Not the clamps,' he said. 'But the leaders will be told to keep things quiet and calm. Not to let anyone cause trouble.'

We had moved to his flat to continue the discussion. His wife had made cakes, and there was tea. Even at the height of the crisis there was an assortment of pastries. Offering a good table was a matter of pride. The man lived in an unremarkable tenement flat, not far from the city centre. Not a top-class residence, though. Books lined the walls of the living-room. When we talked politics, his wife would make an excuse and go into the kitchen, not wishing to hear what was said. He was a good example of a loyal Party servant. He did not appear to receive much for it materially. Perhaps he jumped a few queues or had access to the Central Committee shop. But his real reward came in knowing. He knew what was going on, who spoke to whom and who had fallen out with whom. In a closed society, that knowledge was of incalculable significance. He was permitted inside the magic circle of power. He could find out almost anything.

To some extent Government in Poland was treated as a family affair. Everyone knew everyone else. To get where they were, everyone owed someone a favour. There were complex networks of patronage. Many politicians had been to school together. Many more had grown up through the rural Party networks, full of strong traditions.

'Just look at all these people at the top,' a professor at Warsaw University told me. 'Where do they come from? The big cities, Warsaw, Gdansk? No, not a bit of it. These guys come from the countryside. Little places no one has ever heard of. They grew big down there, patted each other on the back and then came up to the cities. They're country people made good. They've come a long way to get here, and they're not going to give up easily.'

The professor had been amused by my ignorance. 'Surely,' he said, 'it's obvious to anyone who's studied these things. They liked power, liked flash things around them, but kept their childhood friendships.' Sometimes they were less concerned about their policy differences than over the fact that one schoolfriend had lied to another. They were tough, but they were Slavs, and that made them volatile and emotional people. Poles often disliked their politicians. Not for their policies, though, but for much more trivial reasons: the way they spoke Polish, the schools they had or had not been to, or their level of education, which sometimes staggered even minor Party officials.

'Can you believe it?' one of them asked me in 1981, 'The vast majority of the members of the Central Committee have had no higher education. Hard enough,' he said, 'to solve the country's crisis if you were a Professor of Economics. But these people have not even been to a university to eat, let alone study.'

One senior minister felt bitter enough on retiring to refer to his colleagues as 'petty, narrow-minded opportunists. Awful men. You cannot even converse with them.' Such were the tensions between the members of that supposedly happy 'Communist family'.

The quarrelling helped officials develop their sense of self-preservation to a high degree. Once they were ministers, they received a foreign car – Peugeot was a favoured make. They had ample numbers of bodyguards, trained on the American model, and, not least, a dragon in their outer offices to order their lives and their diaries. It has to be said that, under any circumstances, a female Polish official in her mid fifties is not to be taken lightly. But these women were there to command. I remember visiting the Polish Minister of Finance, who, given the country's monumental debts, must have had the least secure job prospects of anyone in Government service. He seemed more deferential to his secretary than she to him. He was a tiny man, Marian Krzak, wearing glasses, slightly balding, a small man in a very big room. The questions had had to be submitted in advance, and he had written down the answers in English to read out. Mr Krzak had enough problems to concern him, without making an unguarded slip to the Western press. He worried, he said, about not getting enough sleep, about his never-ending files and about the fact that he was not seeing much of his family. But did he not think that people had run out of patience with the economy he was managing?

'I'm sure,' he said, and he looked down at the paper in front of him, 'that the people are aware of the need for certain sacrifices. Painful as they may be.'

He was a man without emotion. He put on no airs or graces. He presented himself as straight-forwardly as a bank-manager. A large desk, a large standard-lamp, a few differently coloured telephones were the only clues to his status.

'I'd like to come and visit your family,' I told him.

'Of course,' he answered. 'Ring my secretary, and we'll arrange it.'

Despite my attempts to make the arrangement, we could never find a convenient time.

Marian Krzak did not have an enviable job. His ministry was desperately unpopular in Government circles. How could it have been otherwise? It was, after all, an easy target. The building which housed him was unremarkable. Ordinary people knew it because the driveway provided a convenient detour from the one-way system after all the officials had gone home. And, inside, the staff were making detours of their own, trying to avoid the day when 27,000 million dollars of the West's money would have to go back.

For the most part, ministers were seen at anniversaries and May Day parades. Hats were sold and banners carried, and always, in the middle of the crowds, were the posters of Lenin and Marx. But May Day didn't necessarily mean holiday. A woman in Warsaw said that all the workers at her son's factory had been ordered to report for the celebrations as if it were a normal working day. Most of them had complied, but the moment the parade was over several had run down a side street, chucked their banners in a dustbin and rushed off home. Later, the authorities imposed stricter penalties for non-attendance. Factory managers in at least one major city, Gdansk, were warned that they would be demoted to the shop floor if they failed to turn up.

May Day 1981 was perhaps the most remarkable of them all. While the official parade took place on the main street, Marszalkowska, past the Palace of Culture, Stalin's gift, Solidarity had issued a silent message of its own. Just a block away, on the street which housed their Warsaw headquarters, members of the trade union had stretched a banner with their own May Day message in the Polish colours, red and white. It read simply: 'Free the political prisoners.'

No one tore it down. No one even defaced the accompanying posters stuck to the walls of houses in the same street. All the same, May Day or not, it was one of Solidarity's least pertinent protests. For at that time Poland had little more than half a dozen political prisoners anywhere in the country. Later there were more, but by then there was no one around to put up the banners.

Near by, the country's leaders, grim-faced and clearly under stress, marched down the street, aware that there was an alternative display. Some, perhaps, were also aware that there would not be one next year. With hindsight, the preparations to end the era of Solidarity must have already begun.

Poland seemed to have more anniversaries than any other European country. Many were connected with the Second World War, perhaps the most damaging period in the country's long history of tragedies. Often one would come across isolated candles on a pavement, or a Polish flag flying on a main street. The candles signified the anniversary of some shooting or execution. The Poles doggedly refuse to forget their dead and consider the Second World War to have taken place yesterday. Those black anniversaries gave the politicians the continuity they felt they needed. They could use them to make clear that their policies would help rid Europe of the threat of war. Thanks to Communism, there would be no more Fascist empire. But the wartime anniversaries were always open to different interpretations. And one of them developed into an almost ritual tussle between the authorities and the people. Warsaw's military cemetery was the venue. At issue, the massacre of thousands of Polish officers at Katyn Woods in 1940 or 1941. The dates are crucial, because they alone decide whether the Russians or Germans controlled the area and therefore had responsibility for the killings. That responsibility is still disputed.

The Polish authorities were understandably sensitive about the affair, and had never allowed an official memorial to the Katyn massacre. Mysteriously, though, and with clockwork regularity, a wooden cross kept appearing on the date when the massacre is widely assumed to have occurred. As soon as it was put up, the authorities pulled it down, though for the most part they had sufficient sense of public decency to wait until nightfall. On other dates in the Polish 'black calendar', visitors to the cemetery would find a cluster of candles and sprigs of green lying on the ground as if by accident. There was no name. No identification. But everyone knew that the candles were burning for Katyn.

There is a postscript to the story which is denied by officials, but widely believed by ordinary people. It is rumoured that the Soviet leader Nikita Krushchev once offered to give full information about Katyn so as to repair relations between Poles and Russians. He made the offer to the Polish leader of the sixties, Wladyslaw Gomulka, who turned it down. He told Krushchev that he did not believe he could maintain public order in Poland if the truth was revealed. Many people who accepted the story believed that an important opportunity for improving Polish–Soviet relations had been lost because of Gomulka's blindness and fear for his own position.

Given the sometimes unhappy history of relations between the two countries, some tension was understandable. Nonetheless, intelligent Poles accepted the need for a workable accommodation. A public acknowledgment of past failures and a genuine partnership of equals were the two demands that dominated. 'We don't dislike the Russians,' said a professor. 'We would just like a little more honesty about the relationship and about the past.'

The problem had as much to do with the Polish Government's credibility as anything else. The more it offered exaggerated praise to the Russians, the more the people reacted against it. The younger generation was reluctant to accept the elaborate birthday tributes to Soviet leaders presented by State television. One of them had portrayed Leonid Brezhnev as a young man in a speedboat, the wind gently ruffling his thick hair and a beaming smile on his face. Pianos, essential in such productions, played in the background.

Even Stalin found time, among his other many and varied activities, to torpedo Polish–Soviet relations. He had given the Poles a Palace of Culture, built along the lines of his outlandish constructions in Moscow. The best view of Warsaw, some used to say, was from the Palace of Culture, because then you were in the one position where you could not actually see the building.

Ordinary people had plenty of misconceptions about the Russians. Fantastic stories circulated about Soviet officials, simply because many people were prepared to believe anything about them. I once asked a miner in the southern city of Katowice what he thought.

'They take what they can get,' he said, 'like most people. They don't seem so bad. I mean the people themselves. But you know what they did in one of their mines,' he added. I didn't. 'They had a strike and the men refused to come to surface. So they brought them up and flooded the mine.'

'How do you know all this?' I asked him.

'We heard it from colleagues of ours. Sometimes Russian lorry-drivers come through, and they tell us what's going on.'

In such circumstances it was impossible to separate truth from myth, and nobody seemed to care much either way.

The Russians, of course, dominate economic and foreign policy throughout Eastern Europe. In military matters, all questions of equipment and deployment are ultimately referred to them. In Poland, there was no huge military presence. Western experts believed that only two Soviet divisions were permanently stationed in the country. Little was seen of them, and they were not encouraged to fraternize. During the Solidarity crisis, though, the Russians appeared to have extended their military communications around Warsaw. In woodland east of the capital large communication dishes began to appear above the trees. Below them Russian soldiers were sometimes seen lounging, their washing hanging from a camouflaged vehicle, their faces unshaven. A few wore just vests and trousers. There was no particular sensitivity about such installations. Westerners were only once turned away. Their presence, though, remained something of a mystery. For one week before martial law was declared they were taken down and never seen again.

It was in December 1980 that the Russians are believed to have considered intervening in Poland. Western intelligence never disclosed the full facts, but sources said that pre-battle positions had been taken up along the Polish border. Tanks and support vehicles had been fuelled and made ready. And no more than a six-hour warning could have been given of any Soviet move. The military facts were leaked later. At the time it was significant that leaders throughout the Western alliance began as if by coincidence to warn the Russians in the strongest possible terms not to intervene in Poland. Since then it has never been clear whether the Russians simply wanted to warn the Poles and the West of what they might do. There had, after all, been other warnings in the shape of massive Warsaw Pact manoeuvres.

In 1981 there was a move to depose Poland's caretaker leader, Stanislaw Kania. The attempt was led by a hardline, pro-Moscow faction in the Party's Central Committee. It failed, and the man responsible was put out to grass in the Polish embassy in East Berlin, where he failed even to attain the post of ambassador.

It was hard to disguise factional in-fighting of that kind. But it was not simply a question of quarrelling within the Party, as the Polish Communists found out. In December 1980 they and other leaders of the Eastern bloc, their defence ministers and chiefs of security were summoned to Moscow for one purpose only – to discuss the fate of Poland. A member of that Polish delegation was one of the few to relate what happened. Some months after he returned, he gave an interview to some Polish journalists about domestic politics. The interview ended, and the discussion turned to other matters. Vodka and more vodka followed. The man had been softened up, and the journalists moved in.

'What happened in December?'

'December? my God, what happened in December? What do you want me to tell you? It was dreadful. A nightmare. The Russians told us to wait outside the hall. We had to sit in an ante-room. Everyone else was let in. Can you believe that? We had to wait for hours while they discussed us. Finally, we were let in. What can I say? We were given lectures on ideological purity by the Czechs and East Germans, for God's sake. What do you think of that? How do you think we, as Poles, felt about that?'

Other sources confirmed that the meeting had indeed gone badly. The Poles were told to sort out the mess they were in, and to do it quickly. Given the troubles in the Communist Party, the lightning spread of the Solidarity doctrine and the popular support for the union, the authorities worked with remarkable speed. The most effective opposition ever mounted in an East European state was over within a year of that Moscow meeting. Small wonder that the Russians professed themselves pleased with General Jaruzelski, and decorated him to mark his birthday in 1982.

Meetings with the Russians and other Eastern bloc delegations had always been formal affairs, even without a crisis to discuss. A ministry official who had attended many of them said, 'The Russians would lay out their position before anyone else. That was for information, not discussion. Most of the officials we saw had very little room to manoeuvre. They had their instructions, and they were to tell us what to do. So the Russians would say to us, "This is our view comrades. I don't know what you think about it, but there it is. If x happens, we will do y, and so on. What do you think of that?"'

The question was normally rhetorical. And a Bulgarian or an East German would be first to get to their feet to voice approval. The Poles, it seemed, gave approval more sparingly, and took longer to do it.

'I think the Russians used to respect us Poles,' said the official. 'At least we used to get up and raise other points, at least make a semblance of discussion out of it. But we were the only ones to do that.' There was apparently no changing the Russian decision once it had been made. 'Everything was a matter of principle. Perhaps they would take time to decide on things, but, once they did, that was that. They never, never altered their position, at least with us. And they never gave up anything that was theirs.'

Among all the shortages, Russian visitors to Warsaw, official or unofficial, remained plentiful. During the day they found their way to the Soviet war memorial, a bleak obelisk on the way out to the airport, and at night they slept in unaccustomed luxury in the best hotels, those that had catered for Western tourists before the crisis. They went out in groups to the big restaurants, watched a show, clapped the singers who insisted on singing in English and Polish.

To all the official visitors Poland must have appeared a safe country. It has no land borders with the West. There seemed little danger of Western terrorism penetrating that far inside the Eastern bloc. Traditionally the security arrangements for foreigners had been relatively simple. On entering the grounds of a Western embassy there was no document check. There were no travel restrictions. For home-grown terrorism was virtually unknown in Poland. But by the time Pope John Paul visited for the second time in 1983 the Poles had woken up to the dangers of the outside world. Security men rode shotgun, American style, clinging on to the sides of cars. There appeared to be a constant lookout for snipers.

What had sharpened official awareness may have been an odd incident two years earlier. Abu Daoud, a guerrilla leader said to have masterminded the massacre of Israeli athletes at the Munich Olympic Games, had come to town. He was staying in the Victoria Intercontinental Hotel on Victory Square and was engaging in undisclosed business. Undisclosed, but likely to have touched on the buying of arms. One afternoon he made his way to the hotel coffee shop on the first floor, a favourite meeting-place for prostitutes, ordered himself a cup of coffee and settled down for a break. Not long after, a man, said to be of Middle-Eastern appearance, entered the room, took a gun from his bag and fired about six shots into the head and body of Mr Daoud. He calmly walked downstairs and disappeared into the crowd inside the main lobby.

Abu Daoud did not, however, die as he should have done with six bullets remodelling him. He lurched out of the shop, staggered downstairs into the lobby and collapsed on one of the red leather chairs next to the marble tables. From there he was taken to a military hospital and survived emergency surgery. All reports suggested he made a near-complete recovery and left the country some time later.

Polish eye-witnesses had apparently concluded that it was just another fight over a girl. That was commonplace enough. But even with all the American television networks based in the hotel and countless reporters who lived, dined and wasted time there, the story was kept secret for four days. It might have remained so but for an amateur Polish photographer whose inhibitions were overcome by the thought of hard currency and who decided to sell a photograph of the bleeding victim to an American.

The Polish police never discovered who was responsible, although the Israelis were favoured. After a few days the story was allowed to drop. It was, after all, a year when Polish officialdom had other things to worry about. But the incident served to highlight the unpredictable nature of events in Poland, for both ordinary people and officials.

Highbrow, High Class

The figure was a familiar caricature. A man who spied on his colleagues for payment and his friends for fun. 'Everyone likes something,' he said. 'I like controlling people.' He worked as a factory guard, opening workers' bags. If they arrived late he would write a report to the management. Everything by the book. 'Regulations are more important than man,' he said. 'If someone doesn't conform, he's in the dungheap.' He hated beards and tight trousers, a sign, he said, of the sort of young people who needed greater control. 'People who break laws,' he said, 'are no better than dirt. I believe in corporal punishment. Such people should be strung up and executed in public, where hundreds would see them.' His spare time gave him increased opportunity to control people. He would check on fishermen along Warsaw's Vistula River. If they had no licence he would confiscate their tackle. If they wanted it back, they had to pay a fine. Otherwise, he could buy it himself at a reduced price. He used to sit looking through the reeds, chewing a piece of grass, watching the fishermen and satisfying his warped sense of public order.

This factory guard caused something of a stir in Poland. For a Polish director made a film about him, and used his answers in an interview as the commentary. So the guard told his own story as he walked his dog, checked the factory personnel, stared out of the windows of his tenement flat and wondered why the world was so disordered. Many laughed at the film, many more were surprised that it ever got a showing. But there was criticism, too. People said the guard had been duped, that by careful editing of the film the producers had got him to confess his own sins. It hadn't been fair. At least, though, the film provoked debate. In a country where recorded speech was heavily censored, Poles relied on the arts to express openly what they could not. At times it was surprising how much could be achieved. For writers and directors seldom knew in advance about the authorities' sensitivities at any given time. Writers were like blind people parking cars. Only when they hit something did they realize they had gone too far.

In another film that was shown briefly, called *Graduation*, a director pointed up the superficiality of political education in Poland. University students doing their final exams were shown answering questions about the Communist Party. With exaggerated sincerity they would take refuge in jargon and dogma learned by rote. The film appeared to show deep cynicism among the students, and very little honesty in the exams. Some students would emerge into corridors laughing about what they had said. 'How did it go?' asked one. 'Cool,' said another, 'but I waffled.' A third student was shown trying to explain in an interview with his teacher what he understood to be the role of a member of the Communist Party. 'A Party member is a model citizen. He has integrity and high aspirations. He must be frank, loyal to others and true to ideals.' The director did not disguise the fact that the student was biting his lip, trying not to laugh.

Many of the films in that category seldom saw daylight. They would sit for years in the rambling offices of Film Polski, trodden on by Warsaw's endemic population of cockroaches and occasionally brought out to be shown to select audiences. They were often condemned on grounds of 'pessimism'. Particularly in the fifties, there was no room for artistic melancholy. Communism was supposed to inspire joy and hope. Since all art was judged to be political, films had to show the way forward. Directors and actors were charged with that duty.

But in the seventies, now viewed as a period of great liberalism and luxury, the State felt able to give the people more of what they wanted. Orthodox ideology sometimes made way for entertainment. Hard currency was used to buy foreign films and television serials. The American police series *Kojak* got a showing, though the subtitles left out some of the finer points. 'Who loves ya, baby?' was translated simply as 'Hi'. The British series *The Saint* was transmitted, as was *I Claudius*, which kept people off the streets of Warsaw week after week. But by the eighties the hard currency needed to buy Western films ran out, and the programme planners turned for their nightly inspiration back to the East. There was the long-running and popular series about love between a Polish and a Russian soldier; the Russian was the female. There were the successful children's programmes and the football matches. It was hard to go wrong there.

With the financial stringency came investigation and the mud-slinging. Poles were anxious to find out why the money in television had disappeared. Not only was there no cash to buy films from abroad, but Polish film-makers could barely afford to put film in their own cameras. Those who felt most aggrieved did not have to look far to find a culprit. Closeted away in his modern tower-block beside a tramline in the middle of a residential suburb was none other than the head of State television, friend of the powerful and one of the last of Poland's big spenders, Jan Szczepanski. Thick-lipped and bespectacled, he became a natural public enemy. In one of his final projects before being indicted on charges of corruption he built a small replica of Edwardian London in the shadow of his headquarters. It was intended for a production of Sherlock Holmes. When finished, it remained a grotesque memorial to his days of high spending. Rained on in summer, snowed on in winter, it got tattier as the years went by. Szczepanski's alleged sin included banking money abroad, collecting pornographic films, misusing privileges and embezzling funds. When a Warsaw court finally sentenced him, the prosecution listed seven cars, a helicopter, two executive jets and a sixteen-room palace with full-time prostitutes in attendance as evidence of his corruption. Clearly, he had known how to enjoy himself.

Szczepanski's fall, it was said, was symptomatic of the larger rottenness within much of the body politic. He never appeared contrite, though. During his trial he would sit nonchalantly sipping tea as the prosecution discussed his alleged misdemeanours. His place in State television was taken by a rapid succession of similarly unpopular leaders, whose main qualification appeared to be blind allegiance to Marxism. In the end, a senior Party official told me that television broadcasts, in particular the news, had become an insult to the people of Poland and would never convince anyone of anything. 'They will have to drop their primitive approach,' he said.

No one could accuse Polish television journalists of being primitive themselves. They were sophisticated, knowledgeable people. They knew what the West said about the rest of the world and what it said about them. But they clustered for their ten-thirty daily news meeting knowing exactly what was expected of them. Some would wear suits, others leather jackets. To look at, it could have been a news conference anywhere in the world. To listen to, it was a news conference right next door to the Soviet Union.

During the Solidarity period a senior editor of the news programme was asked why it had devoted almost no time to a Solidarity demonstration. His reply was direct. 'Sometimes,' he said, 'one has to weigh the benefits of objectivity against the damage to our relations with the Soviet Union.' Said in the middle of the television building it seemed so natural. Realpolitik. It was central to the philosophy of Poland's propaganda. Worry about the neighbours first, then worry about yourselves. The propaganda – and that is their word – was mouthed from the television screen, voiced by politicians, shouted down from street posters. It was repetitive and powerful. After a while it became easy to believe, almost comforting. A Polish journalist once told me of a visit to Moscow, where he had asked his host 'Why don't you report plane crashes or other disasters?'

'We don't want to upset people,' replied the Russian. 'That's not our function at all. People don't need to know about that sort of thing. It's our problem, not theirs.'

But on the night Pope John Paul II was shot it was a Polish problem, and that night ideology was taken out of the Polish television building and dumped. On hearing the news editors promptly scrapped the minutely censored bulletin they had spent the day preparing and substituted live transmission from Rome. Those who were not saying a special mass in the churches that night, and most of the population seemed to be, were glued to their television and praised the network highly. It was a pity, they said, that it took a monumental catastrophe before the journalists of Polish television news could shine.

It was during martial law that Polish television took its steepest popularity dive. Many actors refused point-blank to work for the new military commissars. The newsreaders who appeared nightly in reserve uniform were dubbed 'the lowest rank in the Army'. A number of freelance technicians and cameramen withdrew their labour. Some found it almost impossible to find any work at all, but preferred poverty to compromise. It was not long before they had compiled a list of 'collaborators', who came to be ignored by their friends and colleagues.

One actor who spoke out in favour of martial law was quickly and publicly shown the error of his ways. Early in 1982 he arrived at Warsaw's Wielki Theatre to act in an innocuous historical production, but he was the only person in the building who was unaware of the humiliation he was to suffer. Members of the actors' union had organized a special evening for him. They had invited their friends and colleagues and members of the Western press corps and told them what to do. When the actor appeared on stage, he was applauded so loudly that nothing he said could be heard. It did not take long for him to realize what was going on. He held up his hand in a gesture of resignation, shrugged his shoulders and stood lamely in the middle of the stage waiting for the clapping to die down. It didn't. He tried talking to other members of the cast, but they just smiled at him. He then tried saying his lines, gave up and walked off stage. The moment he disappeared the audience fell silent. The play was able to continue. The man appeared again. The same thing happened. In the end his appearance became a token affair. In any case, no one missed his part. For the audience that evening had not come to see the play but to take part in the professional execution of an actor. It had been a clever ploy. By applauding, the audience could not be accused of disorderly behaviour. No one could call the police and have the theatre closed. Who could complain about people clapping?

There was a similar punishment for a writer who chose to support the military takeover. He returned to his flat after a short outing, to find copies of his books piled high on his staircase, outside in the street, in his courtyard, everywhere he looked.

Overnight he and his work had become unacceptable to the public. They had chosen the most direct way of communicating their feelings.

For the Poles set specific standards for their writers and actors, who were expected to conform. People waited for them to lead by example. One famous actor told me, 'If you respect certain principles in life, then you don't have to change anything in your work. We won't perform for radio and television during martial law because what we do doesn't remain our property.' He was an abrasive man. Cool, elegant, late for his appointment and not apologetic about being so. His fame had brought him instant recognition, but no great material benefits. He drove a green Polski Fiat and ignored the adulation that came his way on the streets. 'Of course I was a member of Solidarity,' he told me. 'Wasn't everyone? But it wasn't a good time for actors. During that period people just wanted comedy or entertainment. There was little appetite for serious drama. They had their minds on other things.'

The man had not wanted to work at all under martial law, but said he had been persuaded that it suited the public interest. 'Now they come to see serious drama because there's a message in it. Reality gets reflected in art.'

He was dismissive about his films. The best ones were shot in about six weeks. As for the present, he had just taken part in a pointless but highly satisfying exercise. He had acted in a film that would never be shown. The censors had passed the original script, but the final cut, he said, would never be acceptable. The actor seemed neither surprised nor unhappy. He looked around the restaurant where we were sitting, laid down his fork and began talking about something else. His main worry was not about politics. He had the artist's perennial concern for the state of his profession.

'The problem is there's no competition,' he said. 'Anyone who gets into acting school is automatically assured of a job. Every little town has its theatre, so they're always looking for people. It's a seller's market.' He favoured a system where actors were paid a small annual retainer plus a supplement when they were actually working.

He was a big man, broad-shouldered with a large face, much more emotional in his films than in real life. Now he came over as nervous and aggressive. He did not want to be recognized; he had his mind on other things. A waiter who came up to congratulate him on a recent film received a mere nod of the head.

'Look here,' he said, when the man had gone away, 'we can resist some of what the martial law authorities do. We can win some of the battles. They're weak. We're useful to them. There won't be a return to the fifties. It's not like Gomulka. They know that the intellectuals won't just follow them as they did in the past.'

The actor was part of a glittering international set, its talent recognized around the world. None was more fêted than the director Andrzej Wajda, who was fired from his post as director of the Film X unit in Warsaw in 1982. No other moves signalled so clearly the authorities' wish to stamp their point of view on the arts. Wajda's sacking was a warning to other directors that nobody, however well known, could do as they pleased in Poland. For Wajda himself, the move marked the end of an era. For more than thirty years he had balanced precariously between what he wanted and what the State would allow. During that period he had brought Poland more hard currency and more international prestige than most other figures in the arts world. But that, said the authorities, was not the point.

He had been closely involved with Solidarity, to the extent of directing a dramatized documentary of the strikes in the Lenin shipyard – *Man of Iron*. Wajda had identified closely with the workers. He had gone round factories talking about the film, answering questions. It had given him the status, almost, of an official chronicler. 'You could see,' he said once, 'the scale of the revolution. The workers had taken over the Polish flag. No longer was it simply the property of the State. It was theirs. They had made it a symbol of their movement.'

Wajda didn't stand on ceremony. He once rang me up to ask if he could borrow a video recorder. Warsaw really was that small a city. He lived in a fashionable residential area in Zoliborz, where the rich and famous spent their money. Some houses were built like Swiss chalets. Kitchens and furniture came from the West, washing-machines from West Germany, fridges from Italy. This was one set that was never poor. But during the crisis of the eighties, many tried to hide their wealth. BMWs and Mercedes saloons would disappear into garages, and the wife's runabout, the Polski Fiat, would be left out in the drive. Fur coats might get worn to private receptions, but not to theatres or concerts where people would gawk or mutter enviously to themselves.

But money and art did not go together often in Poland. Artists were still thought to be poor, even if they weren't. 'Arts' meant activity, scores of people writing away below the surface of everyday life, unknown and often unread. It was a live world, and if the authorities had restricted literature in other East European countries, in Poland they had made writers and artists even more determined. Many intellectuals still found it difficult to get their work recognized, but the late seventies and eighties gave them something else. They regained the moral authority they had enjoyed before the war and had lost in the Stalinist era.

In the fifties a number of outstanding writers had reflected the official line either out of conviction or in the hope of an easier life. This was no longer the case. By 1981 some writers were saying you could not collaborate and be a good author. The two did not go together. The brotherhood of Polish writers was closely knit, and the Writer's Union was popular and well patronized. It was located just opposite Warsaw's Castle Square, where many of the riots against martial law had begun and ended. The Union's canteen was often crowded and there was food to spare. Sometimes members were allowed to fill their own containers with food in a makeshift take-away service.

The Union possessed unusual cohesion and inspired loyalty. One elderly writer used to talk with intense admiration of the Union's president, Szczepanski, who had been freely elected in January 1981.

'He's enormously popular and has great authority,' the writer said, 'and I'll tell you why. He never compromised. He did a lot to get young writers accepted. He would argue on their behalf. After martial law he would visit the Minister of the Interior and try to get people released. Of course, his own tragedy was that he had no time to write. Not that he was a great writer, you know, but underestimated.'

It was, said the writer, a cynical union. It contained fewer pro-Establishment figures and had a more independent character than even the student bodies. The writers, he said, were 'the nation's conscience'. Szczepanski's authority may have even served to persuade some writers not to support the State, even if they might have done so from conviction.

'One of them,' the old writer said, 'decided to do nothing but keep a low profile. His views were known, but he never collaborated. Why? Because he would have been ashamed to meet Szczepanski in the corridor.'

Solidarity did much to reinforce the position of writers and intellectuals in Polish society. They felt free enough to say more and write more than at any time since the Second World War. Their representatives signed a cultural agreement with the union, and helped to set up a Cultural Commission. And when the Writers' Union held its Congress in 1981, the class and cultural barriers were bridged. Zbigniew Bujak, head of Solidarity's Warsaw branch, a shop steward from the Ursus tractor factory and a former paratrooper, got up in front of the cream of Poland's intelligentsia to thank them for their assistance.

'We thought he was marvellous,' said the old writer. 'He spoke well, had good ideas. Everyone was very impressed.'

The old writer led a mysterious, twilight existence, and there were days and weeks when I did not see him. Occasionally he would telephone and announce simply, 'I'm coming round.' We would meet on the staircase outside my office. From there you could look out and see the primary school children playing in their courtyard. A reminder of blissful ignorance. The man was always in a hurry. He always had news. There was a confidential document, a letter from one faction to another, a hint of some complex power-struggle way below the surface.

'I can't tell you the full story,' he would say, 'but I'll get it to you when I can.'

The intellectuals of Poland considered it their duty to follow every political twist the Government made. No detail was too small for attention, no overheard conversation too insignificant. They were an essential element in the grapevine, because they invariably knew someone who had been to school with someone else who was now in the upper levels of the Communist hierarchy. In the days when Party men were being sacked daily, the intellectuals would know with exceptional accuracy who was hanging on and who was going to go. The thirst for knowledge and information had become addictive. One writer used to spend his days intriguing with his colleagues before rushing home from work to listen to foreign radio transmissions. He had to know.

In the absence of the extinct landed gentry, the intellectuals formed part of the upper class. But the country also had its nouveau riche, who could open plenty of doors by throwing dollars at them. They belonged to the ranks of diplomats, businessmen and airline representatives who had been posted abroad by the State. Returning to Poland, some brought with them their cars, their cash and a new kind of condescension towards their own countrymen. The children of this monied class became known as 'banana children'. Since a banana in Poland is a lot rarer than a silver spoon, being a 'banana child' meant having considerable privileges. They, like their parents, were not averse to using the black market to change their hard currency. I remember the son of a prominent official looking with incredulity at a friend who declined his offer to exchange dollars at a special rate.

'What's the matter with you?' he asked. 'Everyone does it, even my parents.'

He was right. Almost everyone did do it.

The 'banana children' had exaggerated ideas of their own importance. Often they were wildly materialistic. One young blood thought nothing of paying five hundred dollars for a car radio, 'as long as it was the best'. He and his friend would come into my flat and look disdainfully at the stereo or television set.

'That's an old model,' one of them commented, evidently disappointed at my poor taste. 'You can get a much better one than that. I could probably get hold of it myself if you want.'

Invariably they drank to excess; rarely would they leave a party without drinking everything in the house. The grandson of one prominent politician made a habit of insulting policemen, sometimes throwing a punch or two at them, getting locked up and then being released through the good offices of his family. While ordinary couples might wait as long as fifteen years for a flat, the *jeunesse d'orée* would move in with each other whenever the urge took them. Some would move in and stay there, because they could afford to sit at home and do nothing. In one instance a girl of twenty was given a flat with panoramic views over Gdansk because her father was the architect who designed the building. No one questioned the privilege. As long as the flat was kept registered in his name, the State was pleased to look the other way.

These upper-class kids often gave parties. Alcohol and plates of cold meat would appear as if by magic. No one appeared to have done much queuing. Often when they got tired of dancing, the children would have their pranks. One night a young man closely connected with Poland's film-star set picked up two prostitutes at one of the big hotels and took them out into the suburbs. After haggling over the prices with them he then announced that his pet dog was going to come along and watch the proceedings. The ladies began screaming and insisted on being driven back into the city centre. The youth thought the whole affair hilarious.

Such children never had to worry much about holidays. If they didn't go abroad or to their parent's country retreat, there were other options. The parents might well belong to a union, an institute or an association, and that meant it would have its own holiday home. Often it would be a stylish guesthouse-cum-pension by the side of a lake in quiet country, or even in the mountains. Rarely would there be a sign outside to show the building's purpose. The accommodation was not free, but the prices were heavily subsidized. Patrons arrived with the latest skiing equipment or with immaculate riding kit. They may not have had vast everyday wardrobes, but they had the right garment for the right occasion. Everything had to be just so. At one I visited in the south, meals were formal affairs, the atmosphere restrained and rarified. In the dining-room they talked in whispers, acknow-

ledging fellow guests with a brief formal nod or bow. No one ran
or talked loudly in the corridors. It was very much like an English
public school.

In the main, such privileged people were violently nationalistic,
against the East and the West at the same time. Some found it
offensive if you called Poland a Communist state. 'The word is
Socialist,' said one wealthy youngster, pouting stupidly.
Sometimes they had taken over the battles where their fathers had
left off. To many, the Second World War was yesterday. Whole
evenings were spent arguing passionately about how the West had
sold Poland short.

'You didn't even begin the war on the right date,' one of them
told me. 'You declared war on September the third, not September the first when we were attacked. Maybe you couldn't fulfil
your treaty with us, but you didn't even try.'

The wartime generation had evidently bequeathed to its children the sense of disappointment with the West that had lingered
since the early days of the Second World War. 'You see, we
thought you were right in with us,' one intellectual told us. 'Our
newspapers lied. Even in the early days of the war they said you
were bombing Berlin. We thought we'd be liberated in a matter of
months. Imagine our feelings when that didn't happen.'

But the attitude to the West was full of inconsistencies. Most of
them tended to separate Western Europe, which they said had
been against them, from America, where most of their relatives
had gone after the war. At one time America was good even when
it was bad. And when the American ambassador held a special
church service to pray for the hostages in the US embassy in
Teheran, the Poles turned out in scores.

Solidarity served to narrow the gap between the generations,
but it could not eradicate snobbery. For young people, 'snob'
meant driving through Warsaw in an open car with a glamorous
partner and an Alsatian in the back. For the old, it meant reading
or translating Shakespeare, and reliving the past. I remember
visiting one old lady who held her own salons once a week.
Through age and infirmity the number who attended was constantly dwindling. From her window she could see the Palace of

Culture, looking like some exaggerated wedding cake. She referred to it as 'that Bolshevik sceptre', and turned her chairs away from the light so as not to see it. Like all cultured people of her age she spoke fluent French and enjoyed using it. But she had the normal Polish preoccupations.

'I blame the West for our position,' she told me once. 'Churchill was not wholly honourable, but the main culprit was Roosevelt at Yalta and Teheran.' She paused to let me digest that, and then went to make tea.

'I know you English like it with milk,' she added. When she came back she began pouring out the tea and took advantage of her home ground.

'You know,' she said, and looked at me, 'or perhaps you don't, but the Russians once told Chancellor Schmidt of West Germany that if he left NATO for ten years he could have East Germany back again.' She had simply heard it, she said in answer to my query, and she believed it to be true. 'It fits the pattern of international intriguing that goes on these days,' she said. 'Nothing can go right while Poland remains between Russia and Germany. The danger will come,' she added, almost as an afterthought, 'when the two countries get together as they did once before.'

She came from a land-owning family, but everything had been confiscated after the war. 'We had nothing. I got work as a weaver. No, of course I didn't want to emigrate. I'm a Pole and a patriot. Where should I go? I have emigrated inside the country. I take no notice of the politicians. All right, I enjoy crossing the border out of Poland. I feel the freedom the moment I'm out. But I come back here. This is my place.'

It was easy to see her as a staid old woman with fixed preoccupations, living in a pre-war Poland that no longer existed. But it was not like that. Certainly, her class was important to her: 'Of course it matters how you speak, who your parents are, where you went to school.' But she had modern ideas as well.

'Money is not important. Those who have it simply look to their own interests. Some of us are very poor, but we still try to support the underground.'

'What about young people?'

'I think they're wonderful, very patriotic. Lech Walesa was a tough man who knew what he wanted. You see, it doesn't matter if a person is a peasant, as long as he's cultured.'

'Are you an optimist or a pessimist?'

'I'm an optimist. In the end, you know, Communism will collapse from inside.'

She had brought a little comfort with her into old age. The pictures were antique. The Solidarity badges were new. There was fine china in a glass case, books published in the West and a radio that told her what the West was saying. And if age had brought her nothing else, it had brought certainties. For her the colours of life had become sharper. Black was utterly black, and white was pristine. People were good or bad, patriotic or unpatriotic. We shook hands formally.

Although linked to class, culture had a wide appeal in Poland. There were yearly Chopin piano competitions which were discussed with as much enthusiasm as baseball in America and cricket in England. In 1981 the crowds even smashed the glass doors of the concert hall to get inside. There was always controversy over the result. People used to say it had been fixed, that someone had won it because of his country, that one player was too flamboyant or another too conservative. The subject would be passionately aired in homes and coffee bars throughout the country.

For music teaching was taken seriously in schools, and some families would pay for private tuition. One teacher became a legend. Her idea was to show what she called the 'full musical experience'. She would arrive without warning at her pupil's flat, looking flushed and excited, and announce that they were all going to a concert 'this minute'. Children, she believed, could not be taught early enough. Pregnant mothers were told to play symphonies to their distended stomachs in the hope of inspiring the yet unborn child. Babies would be encouraged to grip solid objects to make their hands more flexible. She had boundless energy, living in a tiny flat at the top of a block just outside Warsaw. The main room was dominated by a grand piano. Around it would congregate a steady stream of visitors. Madame Sophie took the pain out of learning. If a pupil could not get the piece right, she would play it herself. To make it easy, piano keys were colour-coded. Counters were placed on strategic keys. She never insisted on anyone being bright or even having talent. She took them all – the prodigies and the slow learners.

Among her major discoveries she counted the son of a farm labourer. Madame Sophie never distinguished between her pupils in terms of background or wealth. Whoever they were, she encouraged them to play annually in a public concert. The venue was always the grandest available. One year a castle outside Warsaw, the next the famous Lazienki Palace set on a lake in the capital's most impressive park. Candelabra would be placed on the piano. Each child would have a bouquet. No one would go home without having had a unique sense of occasion. In a world of shortages and stress, Madame Sophie introduced a little grace and elegance for the children of Warsaw, and they loved her for it.

Regrettably, though, she had less joy in her own private life. To say she was accident prone would be an understatement. Minor and major catastrophes would stalk her through the city and strike when she was feeling low. The day after martial law was announced she arrived at the flat of a friend, flustered and showing obvious signs of anxiety. Small wonder, thought the friend, at that moment thirty-five million people were exhibiting similar symptoms. She offered Madame Sophie a drink, and they sat down.

'Well, what do you think?' asked the friend. But Madame Sophie had other things on her mind. The husband of a close friend had taken a lover and left his family, and that was the reason for her shock.

'The worst thing,' she said, 'is that he was such a good lover, and there are few enough of those.'

That was the last in a long series of mishaps: some months earlier Madame Sophie had borrowed a car and had knocked a man down while speeding through Warsaw. The court had wanted to take away her licence, but had agreed to let her keep it because driving was essential in her job. The good luck could not last. Madame Sophie had consulted her horoscope to discover when would be the best time to buy a new car. She had already waited two years, and now she felt she could choose her time. Accordingly she chose a Thursday, went to the local licensing authority, filled in the forms and was walking overjoyed down the steps when she tripped over and broke her ankle.

At home there were trials by the score. She had once gone away with her husband in an effort to escape a party being given by her daughter. The girl had intended to take over the flat for a Saturday evening and fill it with friends, borrowed alcohol and loud music. Madame Sophie, tolerant as she was, felt the need to escape. She returned on the Sunday to find one more unkind cut. Her best blouse, a present from a relative in Switzerland left hanging in the bathroom, had been stolen. In the West you could always go out and buy another one, but in the East such relatively small incidents gave cause for anguish for days afterwards. So it was with Madame Sophie.

Her daughter had rebelled against music, and took no part in the concerts. On the other hand, she had distinguished herself as a mountaineer, and although most of her time was spent climbing in the southern Tatra Mountains she had once scaled the gates of Warsaw University in full gear to collect some possessions left by a friend. It was, by all accounts, an unusual family.

For Madame Sophie, the 'full musical experience' meant more than just music teaching. She possessed a tame piano-tuner who was equally eccentric. On one occasion he spent six hours tuning a piano he had hired out to a Western family. He then insisted on coming to tune it each week, and took over the home in the process. He would stroll around flats, entering bathrooms and bedrooms without any regard for who might be in them, dressed or undressed. He would answer the telephone and use it as if it were his own. He would leaf through private papers and make himself coffee. On one occasion Madame Sophie had to be told to remove him forcibly from a household before the owner had him ejected. She led him away rather as someone might remove a rogue dog. He was completely untouched by the trouble he had caused, only ready to create more elsewhere.

The musical set included more than musicians. Disc jockeys had come into vogue in the late seventies, and none more so than Wojciech Mann. A rotund figure with glasses, permanently smiling, he continually amazed his friends and acquaintances by squeezing his frame into a baby Fiat. He was a man of great charm. He had spent much time in the United States, had a wide knowledge of music and presented both radio and television programmes. Occasionally he would write a song himself. He tried to be dismissive about his own compositions, but didn't quite succeed. He would beam from ear to ear, unable to hide his own pride at the songs. One of them, a jumpy little number with a title something like 'Never Say Die', had been written in English and was apparently doing well in the Polish hit parade.

Mann spent much of his time on East European pop. At one stage he presented and co-linked a programme between Warsaw and other Eastern bloc capitals. But his popularity came from the fact that he tried to be original and sometimes step out of line. During a Communist Party Congress in the summer of 1981 Mann had made a habit of playing Western songs that used what he called 'dirty words'.

'No one noticed,' he said, 'and I did it as a sort of irreverent joke. Maybe some of the kids liked it.'

At any rate, it went against the trend. Normally during the Communist Party's political festivals people were supposed to be on their best behaviour. Cinema, radio and television would be under special scrutiny for their coverage of politics, and were careful not to transgress. During the seventies the authorities are said to have ordered a cinema showing *Gone with the Wind* to close down during a Party Congress. Apparently they were worried about the possible association of thought.

Wojciech Mann was not a particular fan of the authorities, and he pushed them as far as he could without losing his job. It may only have been his immense popularity that kept him employed for so long. People enjoyed the relaxed, conversational style, the unhurried delivery, the impression of spontaneity that was so different from other broadcasters. He was one of the few presenters who was entrusted with handling a live radio phone-in. Mann said he tried to talk about politics and current affairs, but it was not always easy. People had their names and telephone numbers taken, and were rung back by the radio station before they could participate. That meant there was little chance of anyone making an unguarded comment. Everyone knew they would be held responsible for what they said. As Mann put it, 'No one was going to push it.'

He had no illusions about the fickle nature of his popularity. He knew that in those days many people spoke contemptuously of those who worked in television, and that sooner or later he would suffer by association. But he believed he could still put the medium to good use. He was in his thirties and had not been much affected by his fame. He enjoyed telling bawdy jokes, and he was the chief source for a story that circulated like lightning through Warsaw during 1981.

'A man went into a travel agent,' he told me, 'and found the most appropriate travel poster of all time. It read, "Visit the Soviet Union before the Soviet Union Visits You."'

Heard in a crowded Warsaw hotel, where people talked of little except possible Soviet intervention, it certainly had a poignant flavour to it.

Mann was still laughing at the joke as we finished our meal together, weighed down by a plate of *Kolduny*, ravioli in soup and Chateaubriand. We said our farewells, and he wandered off back into the city. I never saw him after that, but all the reports said he left Poland for good after martial law and went to live in the United States. He will have been sadly missed by a great many of his countrymen.

Mann would not have enjoyed the description 'entertainer', but he belonged to that world. Poland, it seemed, had an inexhaustible supply of entertainers, ranging from the internationally known to the incompetent and embarrassing. You could see them all in Warsaw. Among the most famous were the Mazowsze dancers and singers, a group of men and women who performed in their national costume, who sang beautifully and yet kept their act simple. They tended to be booked by Western embassies and businesses. It was traditional Polish entertainment, if you can say that anything was traditional in a country that has been partitioned, swallowed up and desecrated as many times as Poland. The country's traditions have become highly adaptable.

There were plenty of compères to direct the entertainment. They were sometimes hired out by State agencies to conduct anything from children's parties to a Christmas ball at a factory. The patter was quick, the joke innocent if not childish, and some of the acts they brought with them would have won points only for trying. There were magicians who could draw rabbits out of hats, and there were those who could not. And when a half-suffocated rabbit did appear they probably got greater applause than their more adept colleagues. Polish audiences always loved a trier.

In one nightclub in Warsaw's old city, a man and a woman used to dance and mime dressed in English thirties costumes with straw boaters. Sometimes they would dance the Charleston. The Polish audiences thought it very funny. It was the nearest thing to burlesque they could see publicly. Few acts ended without a striptease, usually in two parts. The lady, often beautiful, would remove her upper clothing in the first act and the lower half in the second. The suspense was killing. Even small villages would stage a striptease. Poles were never prudish. Even State institutions would produce nude calendars.

At the other end of the scale there was no halting the progress of the arts. And as the crisis of the eighties intensified artistic inventiveness came to the surface. Hence the now-famous production of *Murder in the Cathedral* produced in Krakow's Wawel Cathedral. The play was even staged during martial law, when its heavy symbolism was most appreciated by audiences. Intellectuals would plead with their friends and colleagues to go to Krakow and see it, above all to gauge the effect it was having on ordinary people. Lines like 'will no one rid me of this meddlesome priest?' translated directly into the dramatic context of everyday Polish life and acquired unusual significance. Poles were only too familiar with struggles between Church and State. Some saw the stage production merely as an up-to-date documentary. 'This,' said one intellectual, 'was the reason for theatre continuing in Poland. It had to be seen to be believed.'

The authorities could have taken the play off, but they did not. They might have reasoned that the play acted as an effective safety-valve for artistic and intellectual resentment. Whether or not that was the official view, actors and intellectuals continued their struggle to find some room for manoeuvre. There were successes and failures and moments of absurdity. Many recalled that when General Jaruzelski once appeared before the Writers' Union saying that he needed its help there had been laughter among some of the members. The two sides seemed to have so little common ground to build on.

Among the intellectuals who fell foul of the State there was one who did so spectacularly. Zdzislaw Najder was once recognized in Poland as one of its foremost scholars and academics, a world authority on Joseph Conrad. Najder was a kindly, grey-haired figure who spent his last few years in Poland working for a literary magazine. He had been responsible for commissioning essays.

'You could guess what the censor would pass,' he once said. 'It became predictable, depending on the political season. In the sixties for instance, Polish–Soviet relations were pretty good, so you could talk about them.'

Najder had lectured abroad, mainly in England and the United States, and in the summer of 1981 he applied for documents to travel back to Oxford. In Poland all passports have to be returned after the visit for which they are issued. Each subsequent departure from the country requires a further application. Najder, who had been closely involved with Solidarity, had some delay in getting the required permission to leave, but it eventually arrived. After brief farewells with some friends outside his flat behind Warsaw University he drove away towards the East German border and never came back.

'I had an inkling I wouldn't return,' he remembers. 'At least, I thought it was a possibility.'

Najder took up his research in England, and remained abroad when martial law was declared in Poland. He does not believe he was on the first list of internees, but he felt that a return to his country then would have been unwise. Later events were to prove him right. While still in Poland, Najder had been offered the job of

Director of Polish Language Broadcasting at Radio Free Europe, the American-run station that transmits exclusively to the Eastern bloc. Najder had hesitated, but now, with tanks on the streets of Warsaw, he accepted the post. Not without severe reservations. On taking up his position he broadcast to Poland, and ended his talk on a personal note.

'I very much apologize,' he said, 'to members of my family, to friends and acquaintances for whom my appointment may bring consequences.'

Najder knew the risks. After all, Radio Free Europe had for years been a constant irritant to the Polish Government. Najder said he felt he could help his country by joining it. The Polish authorities did not agree. He was tried *in absentia* on charges of working for US Intelligence both in Poland and abroad. The case was heard by the District Military Court in Warsaw, but the verdict had been strongly hinted at by the Polish press. Throughout the trial State newspapers had effectively been authorized to convict Najder and detail such of his alleged intelligence activities as the State thought necessary. Not only was Najder pilloried in the press. Moscow Radio accused him of recruiting CIA agents from Polish intellectuals and of investigating military objectives near Warsaw and in the Polish–Soviet frontier area. And, together with other intellectuals, he was singled out for derision in that special Eastern bloc propaganda device, the political poster. On it was a list of those sons of Poland who, it was suggested, had worked against the interests of their native country. The poster was displayed, among other places, at Warsaw Airport.

Najder was right in believing his new job would cause a stir back in Poland. For several days after the news reached Warsaw intellectuals talked about little else. Opinions were divided, but most agreed that it was a major surprise.

'I would have expected it of almost anyone else,' said one student, 'but Najder was the most unlikely choice in the world.'

'Have you heard about Dr Najder?' people would whisper. 'And working for that station, of all things.'

Najder was certainly not considered the most natural candidate for the job. Many people were critical of Radio Free Europe's broadcasts and what they called their 'propaganda slant'. One clergyman commented, 'Sometimes it's a bit like hearing our side in reverse. It's good to have, but we don't believe everything we hear. Somewhere in between ours and theirs is the truth.' By this time Najder had, in the official view, gone over to 'theirs'.

Despite the surprise, though, few if any of Najder's friends lost their affection for him. Messages were sent out to him secretly, offering support and best wishes. Najder himself had been surprised at some of the people who refused to forget him. One lady, frightened of being overheard, whispered to me in her flat, 'If you see Zdzis, give him our best wishes and tell him we're thinking of him.' The police did not forget Najder either. Even during his time in Poland he had been under occasional surveillance. The State had intercepted a letter between London and Warsaw which indicated his involvement in the political underground.

'That was a major nuisance,' Najder once said.

'Did the police call you in?'

'No. Perhaps they didn't want to draw attention to us. They didn't want to create any martyrs.'

Najder's group was known as PPN, the League for National Independence. It was a loose grouping which remained anonymous throughout its life. Founded in 1976, it published its first manifesto and went on to issue political and economic statements. From typescripts came photocopies, but the financing remained haphazard. Like other underground groups, PPN had strict rules. Its members were allowed to meet only in pairs. Najder smiled.

'It depended on the weather. Sometimes we met inside, sometimes outside. I discussed most of my business in Warsaw's Bielany Park and on the slopes of the Citadel. Also at the Krokodyl Café in the old town. Not downstairs where they have the cabaret, but above that in the café. It's dark and cavernous, and the tables are not too close together. It's not easy to be overheard.'

Najder had owned a simple country villa by a lake outside the capital, and had soon noticed the attention of certain unannounced visitors.

'They built a shack,' he said, 'about a hundred and fifty metres from the house, just the other side of a fence. It was like a beach house. They would park their cars outside. Sometimes we would pass one of them and say hello, but they always looked away.'

'What did they do?'

'They used to talk to local people about me and any foreign guests I had. I think they were hoping to see much more than they did. After all, they were aiming to discover a nest of spies.'

Najder had belonged to a circle of intellectuals who had advised Solidarity on an infrequent and informal basis.

'I wanted to make the best of the union, and I simply thought there was nothing better we could do.' Najder paused for thought. 'There were of course things that the union did badly. If you have a spontaneous mass movement you can't expect too much thinking. It either walks or it thinks. It can't do both.'

For Najder the crisis had passed in frenetic activity. Always in a hurry somewhere, he and dozens like him turned their academic minds to politics. Like all of them, he grew daily more tired. He became thinner and found it hard to relax. No one with imagination could have failed to be caught up in the fast-moving events of 1981.

'As far as writers were concerned,' he said, 'we were liberated but ashamed at the same time. We could do things we'd never been able to do. Doors that had been bolted suddenly opened because of Solidarity, but we were ashamed that it took the workers to do it. We hadn't done it by ourselves. The workers hadn't been afraid to speak the truth. They behaved better than we did.'

Najder said he was not surprised by his sentence, simply disturbed and offended. It was, he said, the first time a man who had never been in Government service and had never come within a mile of any State or military secret had been given such a penalty.

The Polish State, it is true, offered no details of Najder's alleged crimes. They did not say what information he had passed on, nor did they detail the methods he might have used for his espionage. They simply convicted him. No Polish official ever communicated the court's verdict to him. No letter was ever dispatched. It was not as if the authorities were ignorant of where he could be found. Najder remained convinced that it was a warning to other intellectuals. And a number of Poles outside the country and even some inside are reported to have written in protest to the Polish Government at the decision of the judge. For Zdzislaw Najder, tried *in absentia*, had been found guilty and sentenced to death.

Najder's sentence was extreme, but life was never easy for Polish intellectuals. Some eighteen months earlier, five of his closest colleagues in the Writers' Union had found themselves with an urgent and unexpected task. They had woken up to the cold sunshine of 13 December 1981 to find that many of their colleagues had been taken away to internment camps during the night. It was even difficult to contact each other. Telephones were cut, and there was considerable panic in the capital. Nevertheless they met around lunchtime that day and agreed that their first priority was the immediate release of those colleagues. Who better to help, they thought, than the Roman Catholic Primate, Cardinal Glemp? They hurried to his residence just beside the old town.

The Primate was out of Warsaw, but he returned late that afternoon and agreed to see the writers. All were known and respected academics. The Archbishop did not stand on ceremony, nor did he give them the reception they had expected.

'We were amazed,' one of them told me later. 'His first reaction was to rail against Solidarity. He kept saying to us, "Why didn't they listen to me? I warned them this could happen." He behaved a bit like a jilted lover. We left after a while, and he said he'd do what he could to help, but we were still very surprised. It threw us.'

The five men went home aware that one battle over the trade union had finished and another with the authorities was about to begin. The Writers' Union was suspended along with all the others, but could never settle down after the freedom it had enjoyed in the Solidarity period. There was a succession of secret but short discussions between intellectuals and the Government. They all ended without progress. I was visited in 1982 by one of the country's leading literary critics, a thin, ascetic man, his English immaculate, his manners faultless.

'It is very sad,' he told me, 'but of course we cannot say how it will be in the future. We all have hope, but the signs are not good.'

He shrugged his shoulders and checked that his cuffs were an inch below the sleeves of his blazer. He buttoned it, straightened his tie and walked away.

In August 1983 the Polish authorities banned the Writers' Union after failing to agree on conditions for its reinstatement.

Some of the intellectuals gave up writing. Some of them, ironically, got their academic jobs back. One of the most notorious and outspoken returned to Warsaw University, where, he told me, he 'got a great kick out of the situation. It's really interesting,' he added with relish. One or two ended up working for a small newspaper with a highly limited circulation that had been in operation since the fifties. The authorities never paid it much attention. Censorship was described as dilatory. The name of the publication was *Blind Cooperative*, and it was produced in braille.

The Professionals

Even in the industrial suburbs of Warsaw, the snow made a difference. It disguised the rough edges of the buildings, collecting on factories and chimneys. The caretakers and the teachers had arrived at the school soon after dawn. It was the best-looking building in the district. There was a large playground and a wire fence around it. And in the distance, along a half-completed road, the snow driving against their faces, the children of the People's Republic could be seen coming to learn what the State had to tell them. This was the first shift. The shortage of classrooms and teachers meant that some children would arrive at midday, others in the afternoon. During the winter months there were those who trudged to school in the darkness of the early evening.

Inside the building was the antiseptic warmth of classrooms and corridors, and a gym lesson that showed up some surprising deficiencies.

'All the children are tired,' said the teacher. 'Many of them don't get enough to eat at home or don't get the right things. They simply don't have the energy they used to have, frankly.' She added, 'I'm afraid for these young people. I don't know what sort of world they'll have to grow up in.'

It was the head teacher who had more surprises. She was a woman in her late fifties, by nature a cold woman, but she tried to be kindly. Admittedly, she had had little to smile about. 'For twenty years,' she told me, 'I lied to the children, mainly about history. We were told what to tell them, and we did. There was no other way. But not anymore,' she went on, 'not now that there's Solidarity.' She turned away from me and looked out of the window.

'Did you regret telling lies to the children?'

'Most of all I regretted telling lies to adults, and I was found out. It was an adult education class. We were talking about the Second World War and about the uprising in 1944. Suddenly, an elderly man got up and said to me, "Look, ma'am, I know you have to say these things, but I was there, me. I know what happened, and I could tell you, and it would take days and nights to tell you, and you still wouldn't have the time." Do you know, I felt so ashamed I didn't know how to continue the class.'

'If Solidarity ever disappears, would you go back to the old days?'

'No, I couldn't do that again. I couldn't go back even if they made me.'

I asked one teacher what they did for the poorer children.

'We try to give them something extra,' she said. 'Of course, they get milk from us, and some of them wouldn't get it otherwise.'

They had brought in an English teacher on her day off, a silent, hesitant lady. She spoke English with quiet authority, excellent grammar and pronunciation. For a teacher she had a soft voice, softer on this occasion as she was unsure of her audience.

'I have two children myself,' she confided. 'I wish I knew what sort of country Poland will be when they grow up.'

So many fears in one school. So many worried teachers. As I left the school some of the children waved. The snow had been cleared from the path. The early shift would be going home in a couple of hours. I never returned after martial law but I have often wondered if the old teachers are still employed and, if so, what they now tell their children. Perhaps they have been able to compromise. A friend of mine related how in the sixties a Warsaw teacher had taught her class two versions of modern history. 'This is the one you'll need for your exams,' she would say, 'and this is what really happened.' Apparently the pupils spent much time discussing both variants, and went away taking the woman's strictures to heart. 'For heaven's sake,' she would tell them all, 'remember which story is which.'

Soon after the military takeover a number of parents reported that specific school textbooks had been withdrawn and others with a more marked ideological slant substituted. All the same, the clock was not easily reversed. At one school in Warsaw children marched round their playground in silent protest at the sacking of a teacher. At another a military commissar had visited to give political instruction and found himself being taught a lesson by the children.

'Men of Solidarity,' he told them, 'were criminals and opposed the will of the State.'

'That's not true,' one child blurted out. 'My father was in Solidarity, and he wasn't a criminal.'

The child was immediately ordered out of the classroom by the officer, but refused to go. The officer turned to the teacher.

'Tell him to leave the class,' he instructed. As she spoke, the entire class got to its feet and walked out into the playground.

From all over Poland came the stories of classroom disobedience. They were impossible to check. A good many may have been exaggerated, but it would be surprising and out of character if there had been no resistance to the new military decrees. In general, ordinary Poles believed the stories because they wanted to. Some of them became classics, like the closing of an entire school because the teachers had allowed the singing of the famous Solidarity song 'Let Poland be Poland'.

The guiding hand of the State in education was not new. It had simply receded during the Solidarity period, under the pressure of a semi-pluralist society. A young teacher in an adult education class recalled how she had marked a set of papers, sent them up to her supervisor for approval and been ordered into his office to explain what she had done.

'Why have you given Kowalski such a bad mark?' she was asked.

'Because he did bad work,' she replied.

'But don't you know who he is?' came the anguished response. 'Don't you know who his father is? You simply can't do that.'

But while some children profited from their parents' position, others suffered from it. A Warsaw mother told how her daughter had returned one evening from school crying, 'Why didn't you tell me Daddy was sacked for being in Solidarity?' The mother was stunned. She had purposely not told her daughter, nor indeed anyone else, about the dismissal. But the information had nonetheless been passed on by the authorities to the school, as a matter of routine, for inclusion in the child's personal file.

There was political influence, too, on the admissions procedure to the universities, but it came in an unexpected way. Children from worker or peasant families were granted extra admission points when the results of their school exams were assessed. They might get an extra twenty marks because they came from a poor background. That meant, though, that university classes were sometimes filled by students who were not academically fit for them. Other students would express dismay that their classes were being held up endlessly because there were 'idiots in them who couldn't keep up and couldn't understand the subjects under discussion'.

'They were even enrolled in medical schools,' said one student incredulously. 'Many were so bad that they had to be dropped after the first year, but by then the damage to everyone else had been done.'

There were constant hiccups in the education system, exacerbated by the shortage of textbooks and other materials. Bookshops in Warsaw and the main cities used to carry posters urging students not to hold on to textbooks after they had finished with them. Sometimes, though, the campaign was taken to excess. In one celebrated incident a young child was detained by police on charges of 'speculation' after he tried to sell his old textbooks for the same price as the new ones he needed.

It is not known how many students arrived at university through their parents' influence. But the widespread belief was that the sons and daughters of high-ranking officials never went without higher education if they wanted it, and sometimes claimed the qualification without actually attending the courses. This allegation was levelled against the former leader Edward Gierek and his family when his successors finally began dissecting his ten-year rule. If he was not personally involved in such transgressions, there are suggestions that some of his subordinates may have been. Education carried a distinct cachet in Poland, where politicians, in the words of one Party official, were frequently chosen not for their own abilities but for their ability to say yes to the King. Exposure to good books and a fine education were not considered prerequisites. And yet it still meant something in Polish society to say you had been to Warsaw or Poznan University. That was one more way of obtaining class in what was designed as a classless society.

Many students remained close in later life. They chased the same jobs, sometimes even dropped out together. Among some young people that was considered daring and even stylish. I knew one student who put off writing his final thesis for three years and then decided to forget about it altogether. Many people were scandalized by his casual attitude, but some secretly admired him for it. It meant being different – something that came naturally to the Poles.

But the students, who might have been expected to lead Poland's revolution, lagged far behind the ordinary workers. They watched the strikes and demonstrations, but offered little tangible support. In fact, at one time there was more discontent in the police force than in the student halls of residence. All the same, they would show their spirit in other ways. In November 1982 a Western television team stood outside the main gate of Warsaw University to quiz students about their attitude to the new Soviet leader, Yuri Andropov. Many refused to answer in English, but a small number had no compunction in making some highly controversial comments.

'No change,' said one man. 'They're all the same there.'

'No good,' said another. 'We remember him. He was Soviet ambassador to Budapest during the Hungarian uprising.'

Only one student had second thoughts. Having said his piece, he walked down the street, turned, and came back again.

'I would prefer you not to show the interview with me,' he said.

Other students praised the new leader.

'Things will move quickly,' one commented. 'Brezhnev was too old.'

But, whatever their opinions, it seemed remarkable that in a Soviet bloc country under martial law they were prepared to stand in front of a Western camera and comment on a highly sensitive political issue. It is almost a cliché to say that it could only have happened in Poland.

Not all the students of the seventies and eighties finished their studies and reported for work. A small number decided to go missing. Since everyone, including those with full-time jobs, moonlighted, they were easily swallowed up into the backstreet economy. Often they worked from hand to mouth, running errands, painting houses, translating, even typing.

'With my qualifications,' said an English graduate, 'I could have become a teacher. I didn't want that, so I dropped out. If I'd said "Yes" they could have sent me to a place I'd never heard of and told me, "Here you are, teach the farmhands English." No, thanks.'

But ignoring the moral requirement to work involved considerable risks. Anyone stopped by the police and found to be unemployed could find himself the object of unwelcome official attention. The Polish authorities were sensitive about what all the Eastern bloc countries liked to call 'parasitism'.

Polish students could not avoid exposure to Western problems. In the late seventies nearly all the major universities had a drug problem. Alcoholism was common, and vandalism among young people on the increase. In the late seventies football trains were being torn apart in the same way they were in Britain. Hopes evaporated, frustration set in. There were many teachers who knew what was expected of them, but still fought to give their students maximum independence.

Shortly before he was sacked, a senior member of the staff of Warsaw University told me: 'Universities have to be independent and represent all groups. They have to give people the instruments they will need for the next twenty years.' He crouched low over his desk as if emphasizing some important academic detail.

'If there's something you don't understand, please stop me,' he said. I sat up involuntarily. He was the teacher.

'Are you an optimist?' The question rolled off the tongue in the Poland of the early eighties.

'Look, people either think of an intellectual as a messiah or they blame him for everything. I have no choice but to be optimistic.'

He worked from an anteroom just off a large lecture hall. Around the walls were the portraits of previous rectors. At the time he did not mention he had been sacked, though he must have known about it, for the news broke in Warsaw a few days later. And that made his declared optimism all the more impressive.

In winter the University looks bleak enough. White gates, old grey buildings. The students are even more sceptical than their counterparts in the West. On their left as they walk in they pass a nondescript concrete wall. A time capsule is cemented inside it. The Solidarity students' union put it there to tell the story of their movement and the ones before it. It is still there, though the present University generation may not know about it.

Warsaw University has not changed dramatically since martial law, however, though the rules that govern it have. There are still controversial teachers, and they lecture in a controversial way. As one Warsaw professor put it, 'The present regulations are draconian, but in reality there's not very much difference. It's less a question of what rules there are, than who enforces them.'

The best proof of that argument lies with the small but hugely popular band of defence lawyers, who built their reputations in the political trials of the fifties and sixties. Their courtroom campaigns became legend. Jan Olszewski, Tadeusz Devirion, Aniella Steinberg – all had fought the State, had won infrequently and had lost with dignity. There was nothing more Polish than that.

'How do you think we survived so long?' one lawyer asked me. 'Why are we not in prison along with the people we tried to defend? The State could certainly have done it. There's only one reason.' He smiled. 'The authorities never knew when they might need our services themselves. The pendulum was always swinging. One day they'd be on top, the next they would be down. They never knew. To keep us free was part of their own insurance for the future.'

As a rule of thumb that was not bad. And even at the height of the trials in 1982 lawyers received little more than hints of disciplinary measures. 'We regarded that as an award,' said one of them. 'Sometimes the reprimand would take place in the court itself.' One famous lawyer was attacked by a judge for saying in open court that communication in Poland had been reduced to the level of tribal drums. He refused to withdraw the comment, despite demands to do so from the bench.

The defence lawyers carried out their tasks with little or no publicity and little or no thanks. But the work was varied. Sometimes they would deal with the State's enemies, real or imagined, who could not afford to pay. Occasionally they dealt with the State's embarrassments – prostitutes who offered them payment in kind or even in hard currency. The clients would come and go under surprising circumstances. On one occasion a dissident had been drinking with his lawyer in a Warsaw coffee bar when the police burst in. They ordered him to stand up, handcuffed him and marched him out without saying a word to the lawyer. 'See you in five years' time,' said the dissident nonchalantly, as the other patrons looked up at him in amazement. The lawyer considered that a reasonable estimate.

In Warsaw there were little more than twenty lawyers who took part in the political trials. Their names were never published, but were listed at a church in the old town which acted as an unofficial information point. In 1982 families of those detained under martial law regulations would try to make their first contact there. Once instructed, the lawyers, who worked all hours, would set out for the internment camps.

'What do you think of your clients?' I asked one lawyer, in his early thirties.

'Well, I was defending some of the workers from the Ursus tractor factory near Warsaw. And they are fantastic, very intelligent people. Some of the best sections of Polish society. And they used to tell amazing stories. They were talking about the industrial plan and saying they had more than exceeded production targets despite what the authorities were saying. But where were all the goods going? They weren't going to Poland. Where, then? This is what everybody was asking. They really were amazing people.'

'And the judges?'

'The majority are good. They have integrity and they try to reduce sentences. That is, they give far less than the prosecutors demand. But in some cases they have a direct line to the Ministry of the Interior, I know that from my contacts. And in some of the Solidarity cases, I believe, the judges were consulting directly with one of the deputy prime ministers.'

The lawyer had done what doctors try not to do. He had become involved. He had made up his mind who was good and who was bad, not on the basis of the fact but as a general principle. He thought and spoke in long sections, fluent and coherent. A slim man with longish fair hair and a long, aquiline nose. In other times he might have been a cavalry officer. Now he just had his cause and his family, and being Polish the cause came first.

I went back with him to his home, another nondescript block near a park. How did they find their way home in the dark? All the streets and all the houses in that area looked the same. There were no lawyer's tomes on his bookshelves, in fact not many tomes at all. His wife seemed older, but then she didn't have the Cause. She had put the children to bed, and apologized for cooking spaghetti, but there was nothing else. He wanted to talk, and said he was writing a book as well. All the trials he had attended would be documented and published abroad. The material would be sent out with the help of a friendly embassy. He didn't specify which. For a young man he had a chilling view of the world.

'Poland,' he said, 'was just one element in a large superpower game. Which element? Well, we could be turned into a vast military zone, ensuring that Moscow's supply routes stayed open.'

'Would people accept it?'

'Well, the Church might be a problem,' he said.

The lawyer found it easy to fantasize. He could have gone on far into the night, but the curfew was approaching. A friend and I got up to leave, and he offered to show us to the front door. We were going on to an all-night party from curfew start to curfew's end – one of the few benefits that martial law had brought with it. As we got into the car park, the young lawyer decided to come as well.

'I'll tell my wife,' he said and ran back upstairs. The minutes went by and there was no sign of him. Only five minutes left before the streets would be closed. He arrived smiling and out of breath.

'Tonight,' he had told his wife, 'I go drinking, tomorrow back to the defendants in the internment camps.' Her resistance appeared to have been only token.

Forty years older than the young man and about five miles away, another lawyer was sitting drinking medicine, fighting a cold. She was Aniella Steinberg, ensconced in a small flat near the city centre. She was older than all the buildings round her. She had seen Poland in so many different complexions, before and during Communism, before and after the German occupation, before and after Solidarity. To her it had all meant work. Every change in the system had brought her more clients, more prisoners and fresh definitions of guilt.

'Are you sure you've shut the door?' she asked me. I said I was. That seemed enough to establish my credentials, and she gestured me to a chair.

There was only one room: a bed in the corner, a large chair and a table piled with papers. An ancient radio sat on a shelf. There were other visitors, there always were. The State would have classed them as dissidents or undesirables, some worth screening, others not. The old lady was too old for the security services to contemplate any action against her, but she believed they followed her activities carefully. Her small flat had become a focal point for the Solidarity underground. Messages would arrive by telephone, messengers would come on foot. Her room was a clearing-house for those who sought a lawyer anywhere in the country. Mrs Steinberg would assess the case and try to find one to take it on. While she worked, a helper made tea and offered cakes: no one in Poland would have dreamt of ignoring the niceties. Some visitors came just to share in the action. Being close to her, they felt involved in the cases she handled. I remember her as a powerful woman.

'What do you want to know?' she had asked directly. She didn't want a long preamble. There was no time for one. She was neither warm nor cold, simply direct, aware that she had much to do and that she was playing in extra time. I doubt if she ever thought about duty or dedication. I doubt if she patted herself on the back at the end of the day. She did her work because it needed to be done. It had been like that since the end of the war. She was expert and influential, and the State will not miss her when she goes. But as the crisis of the seventies and eighties intensified, the Polish Government began to lose the country's intellectuals, and began to mind about it.

In 1981 they started to leave Poland in droves. And the following year the State released some startling statistics. Nearly a fifth of all Poles who had travelled abroad during the previous twelve months had failed to return home. The situation had become critical, and laughable at the same time. The famous Stefan Batory cruise liner was going to the United States full of passengers with return tickets, and coming home almost empty. If you went for a walk in Warsaw late at night scores of people could be found standing in the darkness outside embassies and consulates, staking a place in the queue for visas. Some even slept in their cars by the roadside.

Ironically, they were leaving at a time of almost unprecedented freedom and relaxation. Yet there was also social strife and anxiety. And in the absence of the free elections, the free passports and the pluralist Arcadia that everyone could only talk about and imagine, they decided after all to vote with their feet. In fact, leaving the country became a daily topic of conversation. For most it was the only time they had ever contemplated such a move.

'Many of my friends are going,' a neighbour told me. 'Oh, they have young children, they're fed up with all the trouble here and they've got relatives in the States.' Casual conversations in restaurants and cafés revealed dozens of people who were filling in forms and applying to emigrate. The manager of an hotel in Gdansk said he intended to go to America as soon as possible. His wife and family were selling their possessions wholesale. It was not soon enough. Martial law got in the way, and when I last visited his hotel he was still there hovering in the dining-room, trying to make excuses for the menu.

There were those who could not think of leaving. Soldiers, for instance, who before martial law belonged to the organization that carried more prestige than almost any other in Poland. Even when the military takeover was announced, people still referred to the troops as 'our boys' and reserved their anger for the police. Housewives would frequently take the soldiers tea in glasses as they stood on the street corners in freezing temperatures. After a while, as it happened, they were ordered to turn down such kindnesses. It appeared that one unsuspecting soldier had been given poison.

Professional soldiers were under strict political control. All officers had to be members of the Communist Party or former members of the Communist Youth Movement. But the bulk of the forces were conscripts doing military service. And by 1981 that was causing the rest of the Warsaw Pact serious anxiety. The raw recruits were joining in their thousands with several months' membership of Solidarity behind them. Had the Government waited another year to stop the movement, it might have had a predominantly Solidarity army. As it was, soldiers had to be subjected to rigorous political indoctrination during the martial law period to ensure their loyalty and compliance. Satirical comics, printed hurriedly in black and white on rough paper, were circulated in the barracks. They showed a trade union that wouldn't agree to anything, didn't want to work and set out to cause trouble whenever possible. The sketches were evidence of considerable forethought on the part of the Government. One cartoon showed a group of workers sitting playing cards. The sign above their heads read, 'We are Solidarity, we demand everything.'

But according to one soldier the State had decided that the best policy of all was to keep the troops tired and therefore compliant.

'We were dog-tired,' he told me one weekend while on home leave. 'We were kept in tents all night. We were cold and the food was poor. For breakfast there was watery soup and lard. For lunch meat and thick soup or salad, and for dinner more watery soup. We had no inclination and no time to think about what we were doing.'

'What did you think of General Jaruzelski?'

'You wouldn't want to know that. When they announced on television that some people had been killed in the Wujek mine down south, some soldiers looked at each other in horror and disbelief. I heard one story that a recruit got up and shot his commanding officer. Everyone talked about it, but we didn't know if it was true.'

The soldiers were less than happy about their new relationship with the police, and during the first days of martial law fights broke out at some of the city checkpoints.

'Some of us were armed with live bullets,' the soldier said. 'Others had blanks. In general, both sorts of ammunition would be divided up within each patrol. We were told if we shot someone we'd be OK. As for the attitude of some of the senior officers, it was "Now we've got guns let's sort out this Solidarity union."'

In the early days of the crisis there had been regular briefings for the troops, but these quickly tailed off. In any case, they contained little more than the official public communiqués. But there were rumours of troops being disciplined for refusing to obey orders. One soldier is said to have been executed for disobedience, though that may well have been the story put about by the officers simply to deter such action. Whatever the case, a doctor in Warsaw reported that the parents of a soldier had been sent a telegram a few days before Christmas 1981. It read simply, 'Your son has died. You can collect his body.'

On the streets the soldiers behaved with civility. Many showed a remarkable lack of interest in what they were doing. In one part of Warsaw it was enough to hold up a laundry ticket as evidence of official permission to move into a restricted sector. I was stopped once by a conscript who insisted on checking the boot of the car and then examining my passport.

'Ah, English,' he said, more to himself than to me. 'I have relatives in England. Maybe I'll see them in five years' time when they open the border. Maybe I'll see you there, too.' He smiled, and waved me on.

Some of the soldiers showed a touching naivety. A three-man patrol had stopped to help a woman push her car out of the snow in a northern suburb of Warsaw. Not knowing what to do with their guns they placed them on the back seat and put their full weight behind the car. The woman got into the driver's seat and revved the engine. Suddenly the car cleared the snowdrift and shot off down the road, the woman waving madly and shouting her thanks out of the window. It was only much later that she realized she had acquired three brand-new sub-machine guns, and that three raw recruits were now in serious trouble.

It would have been surprising if the prestige of the army had not suffered during martial law, for in previous crises public disaffection had been quickly expressed by falling demand for commissions. After the 1970 shootings in Gdansk, officer recruitment had been reduced to a trickle. It had been the same in 1968 after the Soviet-led invasion of Czechoslovakia, in which the Polish forces played a brief but prominent role. But the strangest shockwave of all had been felt in the Polish army after the Arab–Israeli war of 1967, an event seemingly unconnected with domestic Eastern bloc issues. At the time no one outside Poland would have noticed it. No one was looking for it. A number of Polish officers, however, are said to have had a strong sympathy for Israel. They apparently admired the country's military strategy and dedication. Many of them were unwise enough to declare their feelings, and to add that they did not think much of the Arabs' performance. Not world-shattering observations, but in the Poland of the late sixties they were enough to set off a chain reaction. For the Arabs were strongly supported by Moscow, and neither the Russian nor the Polish Communists wanted any embarrassing noises of dissent originating in their own armies. Accordingly, a group of Polish officers is reported to have been asked to sign a declaration actually condemning the Israelis. Those who refused were sacked immediately. Those who signed were thrown out anyway a few months later. And it was after that particular purge that General Jaruzelski became Minister of Defence, the start of the long road that led him to the top of the Communist Party.

It was because Jaruzelski was a general, a professional soldier, that he took power with a large measure of popular support.

'If he's a soldier he can't be all that bad,' was the popular philosophy. For a long time his people gave him the benefit of the doubt.

The military was much more part of everyday life than in the West. Soldiers in uniform kept a high profile. Lorry-loads of recruits were constantly ferried through cities. Troops took over bars and got drunk in them. Military ceremony was part of Polish life. There were the distinctive two-fingered salutes and the goose-stepping. There was hardly an anniversary out of the dozens celebrated in Poland that did not have a military connotation: the Warsaw Uprising, the Liberation of the City, the Day of the Dead. But still the reputation of the military was badly dented.

Early in 1982 I watched the normal Sunday military parade in Warsaw's Victory Square. From among the spectators came a small boy, no older than ten, who began to ape the soldiers, marching behind them in mock solemnity. None of the officers seemed to notice him, and the soldiers were too intent on keeping step. But it was an act of such blatant cheek as to be almost unimaginable. The boy marched for a good three or four minutes before breaking off, joining a friend, and then sprinting into the park behind the Tomb of the Unknown Soldier, laughing uproariously. Before martial law such an act would have been unthinkable, still more so in any other Communist country. Now, it seemed, the army had been brought down to earth. To the unofficial satirists, soldiers had joined the list of available targets.

The Polish soldier also lost prestige in the rest of the Eastern bloc. Military attachés from other East European countries had no reservations about criticizing their Polish counterparts, either in private or at official functions. One Czech attaché said he had arrived in 1981 to find the situation much worse than he imagined. The Poles would have to 'do something'. The tendency was to talk of Poland as a delinquent schoolboy. He would have to try harder and be nicer to his fellows. Already he had been sent to Coventry, and ran the risk of having his satchel snatched on the way home.

Even with the Polish army under tight political control, officers frequently quarrelled with politicians. In the autumn of 1981 special army units were sent out into the provinces, allegedly to see how they could help the civilian administration by ensuring supplies and maintaining farm machinery. With hindsight, there can be little doubt that the army was making its own preparations for martial law. At the time, though, the idea of soldiers picking potatoes and helping to milk cows was no more ridiculous than any of the other ideas that were going around at the time. Nevertheless, for some people at least, the soldiers did their job only too well. In the city of Torun officers discovered examples of 'blinding incompetence and inefficiency at all levels of the civilian administration'. They did not name the Communist Party, but it was clear that that was the target. The army published its findings in its own newspaper, and the Party started to hit back.

'The local men began screaming at the army,' one state official told me, 'and after they'd screamed at the army they began screaming at their friends in the Warsaw apparatus, saying, "Get these people out of here. They're making waves, turning everything upside down." Eventually some very senior figures in the Cabinet went to Jaruzelski and said, "Call off your dogs." But he did nothing.'

So the army was used for everything. For helping people in the country, for lending credibility to the Government, for staging manoeuvres when the authorities wanted to warn Solidarity, and eventually for knocking down factory gates to allow the police to go in and round up striking workers. Perhaps the most poignant image of the army, and the most sympathetic, was provided by the Solidarity underground. Early in 1982 it released a limited series of a photograph dedicated to martial law. It showed the gun barrel of a tank pointing towards the three giant crosses outside the Lenin shipyard in Gdansk. Protruding from the barrel was a single flower. The soldiers had not wanted to remove it.

None of the professions in Poland could remain divorced from politics, though the doctors tried hard. In any case, most of them were too concerned about the disappearance of essential drugs to involve themselves in argument. In their work, even the little miracles went a long way. But by the early eighties the tragedies were multiplying, and only big miracles were worth having.

Perhaps women suffered most. Many were obliged to buy East German contraceptive pills, which they claimed put hair on their chests, or other devices available only for dollars. Doctors had little choice but to perform successive abortions, many women undergoing them as many as half a dozen times. Occasionally there was obstruction from unexpected sources. A kiosk salesman from Warsaw had spent months piercing contraceptive sheaths with a pin before selling them. His female customers became pregnant when they didn't expect to, and eventually he was hauled into court. He turned out to be an ardent Catholic who subsequently told the judge he had only been doing his duty.

I never met a happy doctor in Poland, but I saw many who were tired beyond belief and very disheartened. In Warsaw a consultant, greying and in his late thirties, spoke of the uncertainty of his professional life.

'I'll tell you what happened to me last Thursday,' he said. 'Without any warning, one of the vital machines in the hospital, that's one of the big general hospitals here, failed completely. They called the engineers, who said it was finished. It simply could not be repaired. Now, this instrument was needed to determine the potassium levels in patients' blood. Without it we simply had to guess.'

'What did you do?' I asked.

'I prayed for five thousand dollars from heaven and a machine from West Germany. But it's not just the machine. Some days you think you're going to run out of bandages or syringes, but then a supply arrives – and then something else goes missing. You never know what you're going to have in the way of equipment or supplies at any one time.'

The doctor was in a state of some agitation. On the one hand, if he spoke too frankly to me he believed he might be in trouble. If he didn't speak frankly enough, he could not get the message through to the West. In the end his feelings got the better of him. He had, after all, worked for a year in an English hospital. He knew the differences.

'In some areas,' he said, 'we're five or ten years behind the West. We don't have the equipment, so we can't employ the latest techniques. In fact, the standard of our medical care in general is falling.'

Towards the end of the seventies it became apparent that Polish doctors could not work with their hands alone. The gap between their skill and their available facilities widened.

'My son works in a hospital in Katowice,' a man had told me.

'He knows what they do. They're giving aspirin to some patients and telling them it's an antibiotic. What else can they do? Let them die without hope?'

Communism or not, there were different classes of medical treatment. Doctors who fulfilled the required number of hours in a State hospital were tacitly permitted to run small private practices. The only complaint among young doctors was that these private physicians would take hospital supplies for their own use. It is difficult to know how widespread private medicine had become by the early eighties, but Poles often said they knew of 'someone who could help out' with asthma, sinus trouble, children's problems, or whatever.' If you wanted private treatment it was not hard to find.

There were famous doctors just as there were famous hospitals. And it was not just a case of the special Government clinics so much criticized by Solidarity. One of the best orthopaedic hospitals for children in the country was in the skiing resort of Zakopane, high in the Tatra Mountains and open to everyone. In some ways it was an unfortunate location, for it was situated less than a hundred yards from the ski slopes, which most of its patients would never again enjoy. The hospital had been converted from a fine stately home with large grounds and unusually modern facilities. It looked no worse than an English cottage hospital until you reached the main dispensary. Two chemists worked there, though there was hardly work for one. Several of the shelves in the tiny room were completely empty. Others carried a motley assortment of drugs in tiny bottles, two or three to a group. On one shelf a single bottle stood entirely alone – an eloquent illustration of the acute shortages.

A consignment of Western medical aid had arrived shortly before I had. It included vitamins and antibiotics collected by a British charity. The staff eagerly stacked the shelves, the hardest work they had done for days. The vitamins would soon be gone, they said, and they would be wanting more. As for antibiotics, they were available in Poland but there was not much choice. Looking at the shelves again, there did not appear to be any choice at all.

The director of the hospital was also the chief surgeon – part

God, part entrepreneur, part diplomat, each role as important as the other. He and his wife, who assisted during the operations, had enjoyed a big, alcoholic meal the night before I met them, but they arrived early the next morning pale and ready for work.

'Come on in,' he shouted from the theatre with the air more of a showman than a consultant surgeon. He was already at the operating table. 'This is a gypsy girl,' he explained. 'Her parents brought her in because she had a congenital deformity. We operated, but the parents wouldn't follow our instructions. They took her bandages off and didn't give her any exercise. Now we have her back again. Don't worry,' he told me, 'she'll walk again in three months time.' He picked up a small hammer, struck a few uncomplaining joints sharply, and paused while the nurse wiped his forehead. He worked away for some thirty minutes, left his wife to sew up and came out looking exuberant. The first blood of the day was his.

'You know,' he said later, 'there's been a lot of talk about the sort of health service this country can afford. There's been a suggestion we should start some sort of private scheme, with people actually paying for their treatment.' I raised an eyebrow. 'No, really' he said. 'The trouble is that at the moment the country can't afford the type of health service it wants.'

We had moved into the corridors. Every so often we would pass a child and the director would pat it on the head and tell me the case history. He could not be faulted on care. He knew his patients.

'What's the biggest problem you have?' I asked.

'Time,' he answered without any hesitation. 'Operations take too long because we don't have the newest drills or scalpels or whatever. That means the patient is under anaesthetic longer, and there's more strain and more risk. Also, the patients come in too early. They're in danger of picking up some new infection even before we've started curing them of the old one. Time, time, time,' he said. 'We have to be able to do things more quickly.'

His English was fluent. He, too, had spent some time in an English hospital. The medical exchange programme, it seemed, was thorough and effective. But the West was not all good. The doctor bent down to pick up some of the medical packets which had just been delivered.

'Look at this,' he gestured. 'Just six months to go before the expiry date. Some of the drugs arrive here and they're already out of date. We have to throw them away.'

It was to be a frequent complaint. Western companies would dump old stock on the Poles in an effort to buy cheap publicity. France and Italy, they said, were the worst offenders.

By 1982 foreign aid was threatening to become enmeshed in the nationwide chaos. Convoys of lorries were entering the country with only vague ideas of their ultimate destinations. Sometimes they travelled directly to hospitals, but other times to churches or to the Ministry of Health. No one could give an accurate estimate of the amount of foreign aid arriving in the country. For that reason, it was impossible for doctors to plan in advance. Most of them worked on the assumption that they lived in the worst of all possible worlds and had nothing to look forward to.

In some ways, the aid brought more problems than it solved. Its arrival signalled the birth of a new middle-man mafia, a group of smooth-talking provincial con-men, dressed either in imitation-leather jackets or light-blue suits. Some would freelance either for the local authority or for the Church, pushing the aid through their own channels. On occasions Polish food would be substituted for Western products. Some goods would go missing altogether. One member of this mafia used to live in the northern provinces, but travelled frequently to Warsaw. He had a grey moustache, a dirty complexion with long sideboards, a day's beard, a thin nose, a foxlike leer and big yellow teeth. He walked jauntily on pigeon toes. He often carried a big black hold-all, stuffed with hams and salamis. Judging by his figure, he never ate them. He worried and sweated instead, and his wallet grew fat. His efforts meant that aid organizations had to waste much valuable time checking parcels to try to stop the wholesale looting. 'As if,' said one of the organizers, 'we don't have enough to do already.'

There certainly was enough to do, particularly in the hospitals, and too few people to do it. Nurses were in critically short supply, and patients told of having to make beds and serve meals as soon as they recovered sufficiently from their operations. One lady who went into hospital for an abdominal operation came out with heart trouble. She said she had been obliged to help in the wards and wash linen. A young mother had had the misfortune to give birth on what was called a 'Free Saturday', when staff levels were cut back even more than usual. Her baby was wrapped in a cloth and placed on a window-sill. She herself had to lie on a stretcher in a corridor. There were no clean sheets and no evening meal. There was no one on duty who could have discharged her. Outside, her distraught husband had to make do with gesturing at the window and shouting, as men were never allowed into maternity hospitals. Some of the mothers had walkie-talkies, but that was small comfort.

Nurses often had to moonlight to survive. One girl with four years' nursing experience was still earning the minimum salary – around thirty pounds a month – during the late seventies. She supplemented her income by turning up at the notorious Bristol Hotel discotheque in Warsaw. There she became involved in quite a different profession. 'I used to come to meet men,' she told me once. 'I came twice a week. Once I'd do it for money and once for love. What the hell, at the end of the month I'd doubled my salary.' She never stayed talking for long, but would spend the evening groping among the strobe-lit bodies for a suitable candidate. Often they were Arabs, often they had dollars. She and the other ladies with her would begin the evening by pricing themselves around a hundred dollars, but as time wore on they assimilated their clients' culture and agreed to bargain. Outside the building were the taxi drivers in a large huddle and the pimps, sometimes one and the same, muttering and plotting to each other until the early hours of the morning. Infrequently the police would move them on, but generally they seemed to have few problems. Some of the girls would take their catches to the big hotels. They spoke good English and had plenty of quick repartee. One night I overheard a Western businessman say to a girl, 'Nice coat.'

'That's nothing,' she replied. 'What's inside the coat is even nicer.'

'How did you get into the business?' I asked her.

She didn't smile. 'I used to be an economics student,' she said. 'Look around you,' she laughed suddenly. 'How do you think I got into it?'

There was a queen amongst these ladies, a black-haired lady called Irena who seldom dined alone. Her catch-phrase was 'A little massage, darling?' as her arm wound its way through yours and her long eyelashes came close enough to brush your nose. She wasn't all heart as her skimpy outfits proved, but she certainly had charm. Irena fell in love once with an American businessman, whom she took to Katowice for the weekend to meet her parents. Her labours had enabled her to buy a silver-brown Mercedes coupé. Once cushioned inside she gave her customer full attention, for judging by the way she drove she never gave any to the traffic lights. But her success brought problems as well as pleasure. Her car tyres were continually being slashed in the primitive backstreet battles that dragged on between prostitutes and their minders. As her car was being jacked up by the repair man for the second time in a week, I asked her who she thought was responsible.

'It is the pimps of these scrubbers,' she said in impeccable colloquial English, with a gesture towards a small group of girls standing in a doorway. 'They are all the same.'

There were rumours that the prostitutes reported to the police on their clients, but no one ever proved it. There was proof, however, that the ears of the police extended into the main hotels and into the bedrooms – an exercise that must have required a sizeable investment in time and manpower. A Western colleague who finished a phone conversation with another hotel guest discovered that he could not break the connection. Not only that, but his receiver was locked on to a microphone in his friend's room that was giving him wall-to-wall sound. He could hear people talking with crystal clarity. He could even hear a drink being poured. At times the sound was punctuated with the angry invective of the eavesdropper, who was trying vainly to switch him out.

Unquestionably, the police had the worst image of any professional group in Poland, and they knew it. Some were even concerned by it. In the late seventies, a rare private meeting took place between a woman journalist and a group of Warsaw detectives. She had been specifically invited because they wanted to improve their public reputation. She herself was sceptical about their chances, but took the questions nonetheless.

'We're fed up with always being the bad guys,' one of them told her. 'What can we do about it?'

'Why are we so unpopular?' another asked. 'Doesn't the public want law and order? We're not as bad as some of the others.'

As far as she remembers, the journalist suggested a more open approach. Frankly, she had not believed they would take much notice, but the expression of concern surprised her.

Normally, the police forces of the Eastern bloc tried to avoid Western publicity, but, again with their image in mind, Warsaw's police chiefs agreed to let me visit their headquarters. It was 1981, and officialdom was falling over itself to appear liberal and open. I could hardly have been shown anything less sensitive: a roomful of recruits practising traffic signals in front of a full-length mirror. It was hard to know who among us was more embarrassed. Later we visited a former palace to review, as it turned out, police successes. A kindly commander told me, 'We have just captured a criminal who had stolen a consignment of jewellery and bric-à-brac, and here it is.' The swag was carefully laid out on a green, glazed table. Two other detectives came in. They seemed pleased with what they found. But there was some confusion as well.

'Is the crime rate going up?' I asked.

'No,' said the senior officer. 'It's actually gone down.'

'The Government surveys say it's on the increase.'

'Well, we can only speak for our sector.'

Officials were to claim later that the crime rate had risen sharply during the Solidarity period; even if that were true, the police evidently had no wish to appear inefficient.

I was taken to look over a cell. I was the only inmate. The room had been freshly painted and cleared. The local head of the station spoke about the duty of citizens and people's militias and their traditions of service.

'Why do you need to carry guns?' I asked.

'We're a paramilitary force,' he replied. 'Our police perform a different function to yours.'

He was proud of his station, proud of the vast collection of police emblems and badges that filled the entire wall. He was a big man in his fifties, athletic, with dents and bumps on his face that suggested plenty of rich and varied experience.

The Polish police were widely believed to enjoy exceptional privileges, among them freer-than-normal access to flats and, more importantly, a working life that could be as short as fifteen years. After that period it was said that any officer could retire on full pension, but was free to take up other employment if he or she wished. It must have been difficult for them to return to civilian life, though. The police had more power than the soldiers, and were feared even by some politicians. One man with relatives in the force in Gdansk told me, 'Those people, they always knew what was going to happen. They used to say to me, "In two months Solidarity won't exist. Just wait and see." And, you know, they were right.'

The criminal investigation departments were kept separate from the riot units and the political security. Residents of Gdansk told how people were drafted into the riot squads, sometimes in the middle of the night, without any warning. Senior uniformed officers would apparently march into a flat, identify their recruit and take him away to join his unit, waiting only for him to pack a suitcase. People said it made no difference whether the chosen candidate was willing or not.

The police were taught a variety of skills. One member of parliament told me how a unit specially trained in karate had been used to break a Solidarity strike in the city of Bydgoszcz. They were apparently good actors as well, trained, some said, to impersonate anyone. They were unpredictable, as likely to stop and check your identity papers as to offer you a lift home on a cold night. The police provided the final and most conclusive warning of martial law. Just a few days before the Emergency, they had landed their commandos by helicopter on the roof of the Warsaw Fire School, which had been taken over by striking students. At the same time ground units broke down the front gate. It was a spectacular operation: minutely rehearsed, expertly carried out. It was the first time Poland had seen anything like it in years.

Despite the cold, the incident brought dozens of spectators into the streets. Families clustered at the windows of nearby flats, passing cars slowed down to catch a glimpse of what was going on. At the time it seemed macabre. A grey building occupied by students with flags and posters. Fun-seeking Warsaw residents tramping around in the sludge outside, while the police prepared to smash the strike and make their own declaration of martial law. I went to look at the school the day after it was stormed. It was a cold, damp, depressing evening, and some people still stood around looking at the building as if a final firecracker might go off and keep the spectacle alive.

So when the authorities were to say later, 'We gave you all ample warning of what was going to happen,' they were right. They did. But the riot units pulled out leaving the traffic police sitting in their dilapidated blue vans, looking about as sinister as dustmen on a local round.

The police, however, were not the only professional body to be scorned. For a time staff of the airline L O T, became the butt of satire and mockery. The airline itself was variously nicknamed 'LOT of trouble' and 'Land on Tempelhof', the West Berlin airfield favoured by Polish hijackers. But the airline staff were professionals who lived with risk, greater risk than their Western counterparts. Most of the pilots, it seemed, had received their training from the air force; some, in fact, from the Royal Air Force. The stewardesses sometimes had minimal schooling, often no more than six weeks. Students often did the job in their university vacations. It was certainly popular. The hardest thing to cope with was, apparently, fear of flying.

'We don't mind the old planes,' I was told. 'Some of them have been flying for twenty years or more, so they seem reliable. It's the new jets that we worry about. Some have rivets missing from the wings.'

If the regime of Edward Gierek had had its way, some of the Soviet aircraft would have been scrapped in favour of the American planes. A senior pilot in LOT told me how a contract to buy planes from the US had almost gone through.

'We had the instruction manuals printed in Polish,' he said. 'We were all ready to fly to the States for training. Then suddenly it all fell through. There was no explanation. After that we got new Soviet aircraft. At the time it seemed to us that Moscow had vetoed the proposed deal on political grounds.'

The pilot had waited until the birth of Solidarity to say what he felt about the airlines. He was not alone in that. Now he sat in the dark air-crews' common room at Warsaw airport, lamenting the fact that he could not have the aeroplanes he wanted.

'We've demanded publicly the best equipment available,' he said. 'Everyone knows what that means. It means American aircraft, and it makes sense. They use far less fuel, so in the long run they're cheaper to fly.'

His English was precise but uncolloquial. It was control-tower terminology, the lingua franca of pilots the world over. It came with the sun-tan. As he spoke, about a hundred airline personnel were staging the first strike in the airline's history, in the history of any Eastern bloc airline. The pilot said they had plenty to complain about, not least a sensational transaction that he himself had leaked to the world's press. For months he and his colleagues had turned a blind eye as bags were brought aboard their aircraft on flights to Beirut and other Arab destinations. 'Don't look in the bags,' they had been told. 'Don't worry about them. They'll be collected at the other end.' The bags had never gone through customs. They had been taken up the steps of the plane and handed to the pilots just before take-off. At the other end, unidentified figures in plain clothes had come aboard even before the planes had finally parked and taken the bags without explanation. On one occasion the aircraft crew had looked inside, and had found guns and ammunition. That was the day they decided to blow the story to the world. The statement, painstakingly worked and reworked by the airline's Solidarity branch, said that action of this kind violated all rules of flying safety and would no longer be tolerated.

'How could we ever hope to carry passengers safely?' the pilot asked me. 'It had to stop.'

I shook hands with the man. He handed me a visiting card. Those were the days when we all thought a new-found contact would last for ever. Outside in the sunshine, a spokesman for the airline's union was telling a foreign interviewer: 'We've been on our knees. Now we're standing up. And even if it all comes to an end no one will forget that here in Poland we did it by ourselves.'

Working to Rules

On the corner of Warsaw's Constitution Square is a two-tier coffee shop. The cakes, cocktails and ice-creams sparkle from refrigerated cases. But the coffee is terrible. If you go upstairs you can sit in a gallery and look down into the main restaurant and outside to the street. The patrons there often talk wistfully of the past, when the establishment was under the old management. The old manager went to jail for corruption, but is sadly missed.

'The place just isn't as good without him,' said one man. 'At one time they sold the best things in Warsaw. Not any more.'

They still sell them if you are prepared to wait. For these days it takes almost as long as a short prison sentence to buy a cake. The procedure is designed to take the maximum time. Instead of having one shop assistant selling a cake and taking your money, no less than four women are involved in each transaction. It means that in a queue of twenty people you are liable to wait upwards of forty minutes.

The process goes like this. One shop assistant takes your cake down and puts it on paper, sliding it across to her colleague. The colleague weighs it and passes it along to another. A third lady simply wraps it, and a cashier takes your money and gives the change. It is one of the most annoying examples of commercial obstructiveness that has ever been designed. The employees are there not just because they are needed, but because the firm's director is told how many people to employ. As one State economist put it, 'In the West you have unemployment outside the shops and factories. In Poland we have it inside, holding a broom and doing nothing.'

A friend called at Warsaw's main post office late one night, thinking rightly that the queue would have subsided. The queue had disappeared, and no fewer than three assistants could be seen behind the counter. My friend leaned against it waiting to be asked what she wanted. But the question never came. One assistant was seated, and engaged in an operation that involved no small physical risk. She had taken off one of her stockings and was attacking her toenails with a large pair of kitchen scissors. She was oblivious to the waiting customer – likewise her two colleagues.

'My husband has got another woman,' said one to her friend.

'Chuck him out then,' came the response. 'I wouldn't put up with that.'

'I tried to chuck him out, but he had nowhere else to go.'

My friend interjected their short, staccato sentences, crisply lamented the birth of the three women and wished them considerable misfortune in the other world.

'What are you getting so nervous about?' asked one of the sales girls. 'Can't you wait a moment?'

And yet day and night private enterprise flourished behind the scenes. One old man plied his trade in the capital long after most people had gone to sleep. He was known simply as Stefan, and lived at the top of a tenement block not far from the University. He was especially liked by insomniac students who had learned his ways over many years. Knock once on his door and there would be no answer, knock twice and the muffled voice would shout, 'Go away. Stop all that noise.' Keep on knocking, and Stefan would finally open the door, the most reluctant, it seemed, of all Warsaw's private marketeers. It was difficult not to laugh when you saw him. A small, round, unshaven head, a string vest and a pair of pyjama trousers.

'What do you want?' he used to ask, and ushered the visitor into his room. He must have had some charm locked away, for as often as not a young blonde would be half asleep under an eiderdown on the one sofa that acted as a bed.

'My fiancée,' he would say gruffly, gesturing towards her. There would be no introductions. Stefan would shuffle over to a table behind a curtain and unlock the door with a key from around his neck. He would produce a half-bottle of vodka or some cigarettes, name his price and the deal would be clinched. Stefan made a reasonable living. He charged fifty per cent on top of the normal retail price. Once he had your money you would be shown the door, treated a bit like a necessary evil.

Early in 1980 the business came to a full stop. A friend who banged so loudly he woke up half the block received no answer at all. He had taken a couple of girlfriends round late one night in the hope of getting a drink. Then a woman leaned out of another door and shouted, 'Go to hell, all of you. The fun is over. Stefan is dead. Whores, prostitutes, leave us in peace and get out of here.' Stefan had indeed died, and a small but important social service in the capital had gone with him.

But there were others who traded at night. As one resident put it: 'In the fifties we thought that a knocking in the middle of the night meant the police. Now it's the woman from the private market selling meat.' In the early eighties groups of women used to descend on the capital selling meat privately, sometimes at astronomical prices. Not that anyone complained about cost. Most thought they were lucky to get it at any price, and particularly without having to get up at four o'clock in the morning to queue outside a shop that would not open until half-past eight. The ladies of the countryside brought eggs, chickens and vegetables, whatever they could carry. In a small way they plugged some of the gaping holes in the official supply system.

During the eighties, night-time commercial activity increased perceptibly. At midnight it was common to see people hanging around outside electrical shops in Warsaw. They were not buying or selling, they were just 'guarding the list'. No shop selling washing-machines or fridges had any hope of satisfying its customers, but they all put their names on a list. And unless that list was tended and the names regularly checked you had no chance of staying on it. So it was not unusual for people to leave a dinner party in the early hours of the morning and go off to 'list duties'. Often they would strike up friendships standing on a freezing street holding a couple of pieces of frozen paper. No one even ventured to suggest that this was the most refined sort of lunacy ever devised. They all accepted it as normal.

So great was the desperation to acquire goods that no one played truant with the street duty. But having a name on a list was not the final guarantee of obtaining a product. When it finally arrived in the shop it was advisable to tip the store manager or offer him some other mark of gratitude: a bribe, and a highly necessary one. If you forgot it, anything might happen. The refrigerator might go elsewhere or get lost in the delivery. It was a haphazard, chancy business. The fact is that shop assistants who worked for the State had only two concerns, and only one of them mattered. Making a profit for themselves and, far less importantly, making one for the State. Since most things were in short supply it wasn't difficult to achieve both aims. I remember entering an electrical shop near the main city gaol on Rakowiecka Street and asking for a fan heater. The woman had one, but it had already been promised to another client. I suggested that this might not be normal shopping practice and asked if there was a heater for sale or not. The lady hesitated.

'Well,' she said, 'I can let you have this one, but I'll have to charge you a little extra. You see, when the next lot come in they'll be more expensive.'

I paid the extra and was glad to have the heater. It was a lucky find. It was ironic, though, that such petty corruption should be taking place just across from the city's prison.

It was in the late seventies that foreign companies began to see opportunities in Poland. Just because the country was bankrupt, it did not mean that the Poles had no money. Car firms like BMW and Datsun would offer discounts on vehicles bound for Poland, and the American hamburger company McDonald's even went to Warsaw to discuss the possibility of opening restaurants. Wrangler and Levi-Strauss wanted to clothe the People's Republic in denim. The schemes were almost endless. To test the water a Japanese car firm decided to hold a sales drive at the Intraco Trade Centre in Warsaw, a mini skyscraper just north of the city centre. They brought in four hundred cars, priced them all around four thousand dollars and waited to see what happened. The stampede did not take long to begin. Before the first day was out someone had established the first twenty-four-hour list and the race was on. The sight of scores of Poles turning up at the building clutching thousands of dollars in their hand was, to say the least, a surprise. If any nationals of the other Eastern bloc countries had seen it they would have been profoundly shocked. Capitalism in all its basic simplicity was alive on the streets of Warsaw. And the cars sold out within a week.

The car business was arguably the most highly prized in Poland. Cars were the ultimate symbol of status and achievement. It didn't matter if the car was a shabby rust-heap with a two-stroke engine expelling toxic blue fumes. The fumes seldom killed anyone, and if the car moved that was enough. I knew one man who so loved his vehicle that he used to take out the battery in winter and put it in the oven to warm it up.

A large slice of private enterprise operated on Sunday morning in a field on the outskirts of Warsaw. Scores of vehicles were paraded there, the prices marked on the windscreens. In winter the owners had to sit inside to keep warm. It was an odd weekly ritual where a peasant in dirty brown overalls and an old muddy cap could be sitting at the wheel of a bright-red Mercedes. The peasant would bargain furiously and come away with enough money to take his family on holiday to Spain. Most cars fetched many times the equivalent of their new price in the West. In a society full of acute shortages, they found their own value.

'I think a car is more important than a house,' said a university professor.

'He means it, too,' his wife added. They had come to sell their car because they expected their first child. Until then they had virtually lived in the vehicle.

It was in 1980 that a car industry chief in Warsaw had the idea of transporting new cars by barge. Accordingly the first consignment was made ready, loaded on to flat barges and towed out into the Vistula River. If you had blinked and turned away, however, you might have missed it. For as the current caught the barges they sank like submarines and millions of zlotys worth of brand-new East European cars were on their way to the bottom of the river. It was then, however, that Polish ingenuity came into its own. The State had the cars lifted out, cleaned them, removed the old cans and, rumour had it, sold the evil-smelling hulks at a profit on the black market.

Repairing cars was also a profitable line. First on the scene after any accident was the State insurance agent. He would estimate the cost of repairs and submit a written report. But only the naive would expect the work to be done at that price. Among them I count myself. My car needed a front section, and I visited a private garage set back from one of the main roads to the south of Warsaw. Polish friends had insisted on a private garage. They had heard far too many stories of State mechanics removing new parts and putting in old ones. The manager of the garage looked at the insurance estimate, and then at me, with amusement and contempt.

'How long have you been in Poland?' he asked. I told him.

'Then you should know how we work,' he replied. There was silence. We looked at each other without much enthusiasm.

'This,' said the manager, holding up the insurance slip, 'is an impossibility. I could just about paint your car for this amount, without even touching the damage. Go and ask anyone else. They'll tell you exactly the same thing.'

I might have fared better as a Pole, but as a foreigner I was a perfect target. I had foreign currency, which he wanted, and an urgent repair job, which he knew I wanted. We settled for a price fifty per cent above the insurance estimate. Even so he kept some of the new parts and repaired the old ones. He had his price and the State had its. The two never came near each other. Only when I collected the car did the manager show some professionalism.

'What do you think of it?' he asked anxiously. I had to admit he had done a beautiful job.

'Ha, you see!' he said, as if he had scored a moral triumph in addition to a financial one. 'You see how well we work.'

'Perhaps,' I said, 'you could put some oil in the engine for me.'

'Haven't got any,' he replied. 'You'll have to buy it for dollars in town.' He shut the door of his office. His part of the business was over.

Nonetheless, the work had been as good as, if not better than, in the West. A Polish friend explained.

'You see, after the war they had no parts. They simply had to repair things if they went wrong. Sometimes they would make new parts themselves. I used to see cars wrapped round lamp-posts taken down and rebuilt from scratch. Now it's just the same again. They've made a virtue out of necessity.'

It was not just cars that the Poles rebuilt. They could repair radios and televisions however sophisticated the model and from whatever country it originated. I owned a washing-machine made in Western Europe which regularly went wrong. A Polish technician used to visit the flat and fashion new parts out of paper clips.

You could always tell a private petrol station from one owned by the State. If it looked closed, it was probably open if you offered money. Pretty girls would only have to smile to get extra rations or to persuade the garage owner not to stamp the ration book. In the State garages they closed at exactly the appointed time, but during the day they provided the venue for all kinds of black-market activity, from queue jumping to cut-price petrol. I remember arriving in the city of Lublin at the height of the petrol shortage in 1981. Only two garages were open in the city, and the queues both stretched for a mile and a half. At the pumps themselves business was proceeding at a snail's pace. Garage attendants were being bribed to let people fill litre cans and jump the queues. A group of vigilantes had been formed from among the drivers to prevent that happening. For once, the pump attendant's greed was moderated by the prospect of being beaten up by the drivers. Nonetheless a few slipped round the back of the garage to try to avoid detection. I remember a woman telling an attendant: 'Let me have some petrol and I'll give you extra money, even dollars.'

'Can't do it,' came the reply. 'It's too risky.'

'If you don't do it,' she said, 'I'll tell the other drivers exactly what you've been doing up till now. I've been watching you for the last twenty minutes, and it would make quite an interesting story.'

The lady got her petrol poured hurriedly into a can.

By the late seventies the authorities calculated that a third of all garages and restaurants were in private hands. It was not hard to see why. Family businesses would stay open later and work harder, and there would be less absenteeism. In State factories they used to have a saying: 'Whether you're lying down or standing up you'll still get your five thousand.' Not so in the private businesses, which even received limited tax incentives from the State.

In Warsaw there were dozens of private boutiques, tailors and dressmakers. There were even private toy firms. Just below my office was a tiny shop which made dolls and puppets and baby-shoes shaped like dogs' heads. Each article was beautifully fashioned with unusual attention to detail. Two old women owned the shop. They rowed incessantly. The last time I visited they were having a heated argument because one had arrived late.

'There was no transport. I couldn't make it earlier.'

'That's simply not good enough,' the other replied.

'Well, that's just too bad.' And so it went on. The customers queuing for Christmas presents waited, too embarrassed to know whether to stay or go. It was Christmas 1981, just a few days after the military takeover, so spirits were low and arguments at work frequent.

Next door to the puppet shop was a private bakery, where over the years the state of the doughnut reflected the economic decline. When I arrived in Poland they were sugar-coated, moist and full of jam. They first lost the sugar, then they became smaller and harder, and finally they lost most of the jam. It was a small shop with two employees and just two rooms. But the local people knew a good bakery when they saw it. People would come in off the street to eat a cream slice or a chocolate biscuit, standing by the side of the queue next to the green walls and enjoying the dry warmth.

The people who appeared to do least for their money were the property owners, who let flats and houses both to Poles and foreigners. One man owned a string of houses in Warsaw, all of them palatial. He did not advertise his wealth, nor the mink farm he ran on the proceeds. But if you were looking for a house the chances were that the way would lead back to him. Of course, the State used to demand a share of the proceeds. The Government Accommodation Agency, aptly named PUMA, used to insist on inspecting all buildings let to foreigners. The bigger the house, the higher PUMA's percentage. One trick favoured by many landlords was to artificially lower the height of the room and thereby classify it as a box cupboard unfit for human habitation. The Government inspector would arrive to make his assessment, and the false ceiling would be removed after he had gone. By and large, the house-owners were wheeler-dealers who could get hold of anything that was needed. They always knew someone who could find coal or paint or cement, particularly at a time when such goods had all but disappeared on the open market. These articles became the 'jewels' of the modern Polish state, rarer and infinitely more useful than diamonds. Thieves would steal such jewels in preference to any others. Rarely did they bother with money or gold; instead, they stole food from the back seats of cars and hijacked meat lorries. If they broke into a flat they would as soon steal from the fridge as from the safe.

This was of course the riskier kind of private enterprise, but common enough, and the 1980s brought petty corruption out on to the streets. Touts used to hang around the big hotels trying to change money on the black market. Sometimes unsuspecting tourists would be tempted into a corner only to learn that the Polish hand was quicker than the Western eye. They would receive a wad of Polish currency in exchange for pounds and dollars. By the time they had discovered it was half the agreed amount their moneychanger would be two blocks away.

The conmen and women, though, came in all sizes. I remember meeting an old lady in the beautiful market square of Krakow. She looked poor but angelic, the product, I believed, of a bygone age. Someone who talked intelligently about the old days and a woman of pride. I was to be disappointed. Looking up at me with clear blue eyes and an innocent smile, she asked me if I would like to change my hard currency for her Polish zlotys. Nowhere and no one, it seemed, was sacred.

The most refined form of private enterprise is farming. Eighty per cent of Poland's agriculture is in private hands, despite the collectivizing zeal that swept through Eastern Europe in the 1950s. But it has been a mixed blessing. The State accepted the free ownership of land, but did little to finance it. The bulk of its investment went into the twenty per cent of Polish agriculture that was under State control. If it was a choice between food and ideology, successive Communist administrations chose ideology. The result was a mass of economic contradictions, none of which helped to transfer food from the field into the stomach. Early in 1981 a group of peasant farmers had talked about those contradictions. They had gone to a field outside a northern city where the State buyer was supposed to meet them. The horse-drawn carts carried meat, eggs, milk and butter, commodities that had all but disappeared from the big city shops. They made up a convoy with at least three generations represented in each cart, grandparents, parents and tiny children. And they had waited in the field for four hours, waited until it was clear the State did not want their produce.

'How could it not want these things?' they asked. 'We know that the city people have nothing to eat, but what can we do? We take it home, eat what we can ourselves and give the rest to the pigs, and all the time the State is saying to us "OK, have your farmers' union say what you want, but we won't buy your produce." '

By then, though, farmers did not even want the State's money. It no longer bought anything they wanted. Farmers would arrange barter deals with the local authorities. Meat in exchange for coal, milk for foodstuffs.

'What use is money,' one of them asked, 'when there's nothing in the shops to buy?'

Ironically, the State still subsidized farm prices to the extent that at least some peasant farmers found they could make a profit by buying milk in a shop and selling it back to the State. There was very little evidence of economic common sense. At the height of the 1981 crisis one State economist felt moved to say, 'Far from having a five-year plan, the authorities don't even appear to have a five-week plan.'

I got to know one farmer who lived about thirty miles outside Lublin and was a respected member of the Communist Party. He owned greenhouses by the dozen, grew tomatoes and flowers and did not think much of the policies of his government.

'I tell you,' he said, sitting down in the large farmhouse kitchen, taking off his Western-style cowboy hat and throwing it on a peg, 'I tell you, the policies have been disastrous. Last year the buyers told me, "We don't want your tomatoes, we've got too many." All right, so what could I do? I threw some of them away. And then I discovered that they'd imported tomatoes from Albania. "For God's sake," I said to them, "what is going on?"'

He lived in a building without luxury. There was mud in the house, almost as much as there was outside. His children came shyly into the kitchen and were told to shake hands politely. The farmer grinned.

'We have an old saying,' he said. 'A guest in your home is a God in your home. That's how it is here.' To prove it, the whisky bottle came down from the cupboard shelf. 'Last time I offered this to my workers,' he said, 'they got so drunk they threatened to march on Moscow.' He roared with laughter.

'People think I'm a rich man in a Communist State, plus I'm a member of the Party, and they ask how the two go together. Well, I work for what I have. I was up at four-thirty this morning.' He poured me some more whisky. His wife brought biscuits and coffees. It was still morning.

'And I'll tell you something else,' he went on. 'I have to make a contract to sell pigs to the State. Now, if I want to sell one more pig than the contract allows I have to fill in enough forms to keep me in paper for a year. I had to make a personal application to sell one more pig. The authorities told me the countryside was overproducing. That's ridiculous. You know that as well as I do.'

The farmer kept close contacts with the rest of the community. On the main road you could ask for him by name and anyone would tell you his address. The tragedy, he said, was that food and grain were being hoarded by some of the farmers.

'Some of my friends have been storing grain for a couple of years. They just don't know what to do with it, and don't think it's worth selling. The trouble is, we need economic reform. They've promised reforms, but they're still all on paper. And they can't force people to sell if they don't want to.'

Two elderly neighbours arrived at this point, and when two or more Poles are gathered together the talk turns naturally to politics. There was more coffee on the table, and the level of whisky had sunk dramatically.

'The problem was the seventies,' the farmer said, 'but there's no point putting the leaders on trial.'

'Why not?' asked his friend. 'They were all guilty, even those in power now. Some of them were around during the seventies as well. They're responsible for the mistakes, all of them.'

The farmer shook his head. 'It wouldn't help,' he said. 'What would help now would be if the Government allowed more criticism. Then they might change some of the policies.'

The conversation turned to the quarrels between town and country.

'They've always been squabbling,' the farmer said. 'The town blames us for not producing enough, but it doesn't produce the tractors or the machinery that we need. The fact is that industry just doesn't want to produce things for the countryside. They want to build ships or steel. They're not that interested in tractors and combine harvesters.'

The conversation might have gone on all day had I not offered to leave. The farmer donned his boots and went off to the greenhouse to fetch some tomatoes and strawberries. No one, he said, could leave without taking something with them. As he leaned on the gate he lamented the farmers' loss of status.

'It's different in the West,' he said. 'There a farmer is somebody. I remember travelling once on a ferry to Sweden and people asked me 'What do you do?' When I told them they looked at me with respect. They thought I was an important man. But not here. People blame me for everything.'

I drove off past his fields full of Colorado beetle. There was not a drop of insecticide anywhere in the region. 'How do you live with Colorado beetle,' I had asked him. He had shrugged his shoulders, as if to say 'How indeed?'

The road back to Lublin widened suddenly. There were factories on either side of the road. It was the two o'clock shift, and people were streaming from the bus stops or getting on to bicycles. In front of them most would have a few hours of queuing for the evening meal. The farmers wanted to get them back to the land, to a cleaner climate and a life without crowds. And none of them, it seemed, wanted to go.

The other Eastern European countries often did their best to ridicule the Polish worker. Not for his zealousness, but for the fact that he or she seldom appeared to work at all. By 1981 the joke going around East Berlin was that three Poles had met at work to discuss their future. It was heavy irony rather than comedy, as one East German was forced to explain to me.

'It's a comedy on two levels,' he explained laboriously. 'Polish workers do not work, and they have no future.'

To some extent the Poles had become the laughing-stock of the Eastern bloc, but there was a serious reason for it. Contracts with other Eastern bloc countries were not being honoured, deliveries of coal and steel were late, and shipments were held up because of strikes along the Baltic coast. In addition, Poland's near-bankruptcy had caused a worldwide lack of confidence in East European economies. It became fashionable to blame the Poles for everything.

The Poles themselves knew a lot about work and also how to avoid it. There were numerous different levels of activity. There was the 'Italian' strike, for instance, where office workers used to take long lunches and leave their jackets slung over the back of their chair, implying they were still at work. There was the selective strike. Workers would down tools in one department for ten minutes and the action would then spread to another. Workers at the Lenin shipyard in Gdansk favoured that ploy. So effective was it that the management was unable to identify either the strikers or their leaders. There was time-wasting: going to see the management at regular intervals to lodge a complaint or enquire about a petition. If enough workers went along each time, production could be halted altogether.

At the height of Poland's economic crisis in 1981 it was estimated that no more than fifty per cent of Polish industry was operating in any way at all. And whereas that was a catastrophe for the State, it brought some unexpected benefits to ordinary people. Since industry was no longer needing electricity there was now enough to go round the country's domestic users, and the power cuts ceased. People could once again take their coats off in theatres, put away the candles that littered their apartments and use lifts without the fear of spending the evening in them. There was still the yearly overhaul of the city's central-heating system to be coped with, though. During the summer months, that would necessitate water supplies being turned off at random. The more enterprising inhabitants of Warsaw used to keep their baths permanently full.

For a while the power and energy shortages had made a mockery out of some businesses. I remember congratulating a friend on being employed by a computer firm.

'It's no reason for congratulation,' he said. 'It's the most boring job in the world.'

'Why? It sounds quite high-powered to me. What do you have to do?'

'I'm employed in a room with four women and we count papers and make mathematical calculations.'

'I thought the computer was supposed to do that?'

'Ha! It's too expensive for them to use the computer for more than an hour a day. It's much cheaper to hire us to do the computer's work for it.'

My friend had delighted in explaining his office routine. The woman at the adjoining desk would arrive punctually at eight-thirty and would immediately have breakfast. The kettle would be heated and a sandwich brought from home noisily consumed. That took half an hour, with a further ten minutes for washing up. Then came serious discussion. Shopping first, then last night's television. As she talked she would do her make-up, cosmetics on the table and a small mirror perched on a book. Soon it was time to stop talking about shopping and go and do it. The woman disappeared. Inquirers were told she was in another part of the building and expected back at any moment. The pattern was more or less similar for the others. In fact, so little work was done in the office that the firm was often obliged to call all five of them back on Saturdays and Sundays to do overtime. It was a great system and they loved it, and were very much in favour of the Government that let it operate so smoothly.

I came across another kind of inefficiency in Warsaw. It was early in December 1982, and my taxi had been late. I arrived at the railway station with only a few minutes to spare. No time to haggle with anyone, and I was therefore running a major risk. The haggle came at the ticket counter, as the State's bureaucracy swung into action and the ticket clerk, an elderly woman who seemed to have been born sitting down, shook her grey head over my passport and currency vouchers. She looked through the glass and said in a bored voice, 'I can't do it.'

'What do you mean you can't do it?'

'What I said. You need a special currency-exchange receipt to buy a ticket.'

'But I've always bought tickets with this one.'

'Not now. Go to the Victoria Hotel.'

'I can't. I haven't got time. The train leaves in a few minutes.'

The queue had lengthened. Behind me people were trying to look over my shoulder, nudge me, get the foreign idiot out of the way and launch into their own arguments. There were only two choices: miss the train or make a fuss and still miss the train.

'I'm not going,' I said. 'You'll have to do it. I haven't any more time.' She leafed through my papers and reached for a ticket from the rack beside her.

'All right,' she said suddenly. There was the vaguest crease of a smile. 'I like your accent,' she said. 'You can have it.' Bureaucracy surmounted, the problem melted away. The first obstacle of the night was passed and the State employees had made me a final gesture. Reduced to basics, it resembled two fingers in the air, and translated into English it said, 'I'm the one in charge and I make the rules.'

The train pulled into the station full of passengers from Moscow. I was in a compartment with a Polish businessman. He looked at me with some disdain. I wasn't the travelling companion he wanted. As the train moved away from the platform on its way west, he made for the corridor and found a carriage attendant.

'I want to change compartments,' he told the man.

'You can't do that,' replied the conductor. 'You're in C9. That's what your ticket says.'

'I know, but there's a colleague of mine just further down the car and an empty seat beside him. 'Why can't I sit there?'

'What's the point of having a number on your ticket?' asked the attendant, who had clearly never been told that the customer is always right.

'You sit in the seat you're given.'

They closed the door of my compartment as the argument continued. Voices were raised above the clatter of the wheels, and then silence. The businessman came back into my compartment, removed his bag, scowled at me and went off furiously down the carriage. I left it a few seconds and looked out. No blood anywhere and no sign of the attendant. He was in his own compartment as I walked in to ask for mineral water. He looked up, his eyes alight, grinning.

'That showed him,' he said pointing down the carriage the way the businessman had gone. 'I showed him. Let him go in the end, but I showed him.' He gave me a large wink and sat down, still grinning, on his bed. Bureaucracy, it seemed, had triumphed twice in one night. Obstacles had been successfully erected and then removed. The citizen had been shown his limitations. The result: time wasted and tempers frayed. And the journey had just started.

There is a fast four-lane highway that takes you down from Warsaw right into the heart of the industrial south, where steam trains rattle along, their headlights leering out of the semi-permanent fog. The pollution in the region was so bad that night fell earlier there than in any other part of the country. On bad days they said you could taste the acid on your own chin. In winter the snow was grey by the time it reached the ground. It fell on roads criss-crossed with cracks and potholes, on tramlines that resembled small trenches. A prime example of industrial devastation.

The men who lived here did not look like an industrial élite. But that is how the State portrayed the miners. They came up from the pits exhausted, some with their gas masks hanging out of their containers, their feet wrapped in dusters inside Wellington boots. Yet such men began to discover in the early eighties that they had considerable economic muscle. And although the men of the Baltic shipyards accused them of joining the movement late, they entered it with a full commitment.

I visited a colliery early in 1981 expecting to find a director, a few union men and some hangers-on who would tell me the Government line. But times had changed rapidly. The director wanted to see a number of policy changes at central level. The trade unionists, one from Solidarity, the other from a Communist union, spent the discussion arguing amongst themselves, while the workers who took us to the coal-face accused the government point-blank of falsifying coal statistics.

'We've been asking ourselves where all the coal has been going. Maybe they've stored it, maybe it's gone to the Russians. Who knows?'

Part of the journey underground was by railway, part of it on foot, past wooden struts many of which were broken.

'Why are all these supports broken?' I asked.

'It's not important,' a miner replied. 'They come round on Wednesdays and repair them.'

'Today is Monday.'

He laughed.

At the coal-face the man warned us all to stand back. The dangerous part, he said, was when the mechanical digger moved in and the roof was lowered to a new height. When they talk of danger in Polish mines, you listen. Too many fatal accidents have occurred in recent years for there to be much sense of security below ground.

'It's one of the issues Solidarity has raised,' said one of the miners. 'In the past far too much coal has been dug far too quickly.'

Back on the surface you could see the miners' flats close by. Many of the men would be getting ready for the night shift. In one flat I found a miner watching television with his family after the evening meal.

'It's all I do in my spare time,' he told me. He produced a long-service medal with his name engraved on it. There was a smile of pride briefly exchanged with his wife. 'They asked me to join the Communist Party after I got this,' he said. 'They thought it would be a good example, but I didn't want to. I joined Solidarity instead.' His children came in from the bedroom. He and his wife shared the living-room and made a bed for themselves out of the sofa. On the wall was a picture of a house beside a lake. There were mountains in the background. A little reminder of a land a long way from Katowice.

'Look at my daughter,' said the man. He lifted her chin. The girl sniffed a bit and coughed. 'She has asthma, had it since she was little, and you know what the doctor said to me? He said move out of the city, for God's sake, move away. How can I move, I asked him. I'm a miner. I've got nowhere else to go. All the children are the same,' he added. 'You won't find one that doesn't have asthma or a throat infection.'

Financially the man was well off. Sometimes he earned as much as three times the national average. 'It's fine,' he said, 'when there's something to buy.' Later, when food rationing was brought in, the coal-face workers were allowed more to eat than almost anyone else in the country. The allocation showed where the State's priorities lay.

The miners scored on holidays as well. There were guest-houses for them and their families, special gymnasiums and rehabilitation centres. The cynics said that the Government was simply trying to buy the men's loyalty and cooperation. If that was the case the operation was largely unsuccessful. The men were mainly of Silesian origin, obstinate, slow to anger, but once roused difficult to fight off.

In 1981 there were moves to have Katowice declared a disaster area because of the threat from pollution. People were dying because of the wholesale expulsion of industrial fumes into the atmosphere. According to figures issued by the national news agency, infant mortality was two hundred per cent above the national average. In addition, more than half the food on sale was polluted beyond accepted international standards. Doctors in the area blamed the breakneck industrial expansion of the fifties that was carried out without thought, they said, for human or animal life.

In Warsaw a panel of doctors denied the agency figures and said pollution was no worse there than in any other major industrial city. They were monitoring the fact and were taking preventative measures.

'What about the food pollution and the infant mortality rate?' I had asked one of them.

'You know what the press writes,' he said, 'OK, so they're an official news agency, but they're after a story just as you are. The facts are there – the city is no worse than any of the others.'

The miners of Katowice never looked like angry young men, not like their counterparts in Gdansk. As one of them said to me, 'We'll fight if we have to, but surely this country has had enough of industrial unrest.' He may have been echoing a popular enough sentiment. All the same, the miners were watched carefully. A woman diplomat who parked her car outside the office of a colliery director found that her licence number had been noted and conclusions drawn. An article appeared in the Warsaw daily newspaper pointing out the interest of Western 'centres' in Poland's economy, and implying that this interest was developing into interference. 'Hence,' the article said, 'the protracted visit by a member of the Western diplomatic community to one of our mines.'

The West worried a lot about Polish industry. In 1982 a major consortium pulled out of the construction of an air terminal in the centre of Warsaw amid mutual recriminations and threats. The Western group said the Poles had defaulted on payment three months in a row, and they felt they could no longer take the risk of continuing investment. Would the Poles be able to finish the building on their own, the company was asked? They doubted it. And there the terminal remains. A jagged, boxlike sculpture on the Warsaw skyline, a tribute to wasted money and misplaced aspirations. The investors blamed the Polish subcontractors. The Poles blamed the West for not submitting final drawings on time. Whatever the case, the builders stumbled from one setback to another. On one occasion half the glass in the building had to be removed and replaced because, it was said, the wrong specifications had been supplied.

Other international projects suffered. The building of a PVC plant in the central city of Woclawek had been beset by difficulties from the outset. The work was hopelessly delayed, and each side blamed the other. Only the English workers seemed to derive some benefit. A number acquired Polish wives, who, if they didn't marry for love, married for a British passport. Such was the reputation of Polish womankind in the region that wives left behind in England would ring up the company management asking what their husbands were doing in their free time. The answer was probably 'Not a lot'. The workers I saw were mostly adding up their profits on pocket calculators, eating sausages and chips in their canteen and watching outdated films such as *Last Train from Gun Hill*.

For a time at least British diplomats reaped the dubious rewards of the business chaos. In the words of one of their staff, 'We're in the debt-collection business.' British firms were owed sums ranging from five hundred pounds to more than a million. Polish ministers were asking the West for more. In addition, the Government complained of Western interference when the bankers showed reluctance in digging further into their pockets. Why should the West lend money to Poland, was the question many officials were asked. And the answer remained standard. 'Because Poland is of vital importance to the security of Europe as a whole, and it should be in the interest of every peace-loving nation to stabilize the Polish situation.'

The talk of stabilizing had some urgency. At one ministry in Warsaw a contact revealed that studies had been ordered to determine the biological minimum on which people could survive. It mattered little that in some parts of Poland there were queues for meat that would not have been consumed in the West. Some of it came from animals killed in roadside accidents or from those who had died sick. Veterinary surgeons were said to have passed the meat as fit for human consumption. And still the crowds kept on coming. In some cities there had been hunger marches. At a rally in Lodz, women had told Solidarity shop stewards, 'My child has not seen butter for two months. What am I supposed to give him? Water? Putty?' The Solidarity men had looked on in amazement and tried to calm the feelings of the crowds. But neither they nor the Government had answers.

The people who suffered most were undoubtedly the unemployed. The Government described them in statistics as 'looking for work or between jobs'. But the numbers in those categories rose steadily through 1981. Many of them lounged aimlessly around the 'employment centres' scattered around the capital. They used to go in, scan the job advertisements, go out, talk, drink and glare at passers-by. Sometimes fights would break out. If you had to visit it was advisable to make it quick. Rarely did the State allow the men unemployment benefit for more than three months. And if they refused the jobs they were offered, they got nothing at all.

I once visited a fruit-bottling factory in the Eastern city of Chelm. The workers had gone through the almost ritual statement of dissatisfaction with the economy. 'Our patience is coming to an end' was a favourite slogan in use during 1981. And then the men and women gathered round me to ask about England. 'Do they have shortages? Is meat available to everyone? How much does food cost? What does the West think of Poland?' This last became the familiar question among ordinary Poles. They were aware that for once the Polish worker had made it to the international stage. European and American television cameras were at all the major demonstrations and meetings. People in the street knew they had a captive audience in Western homes. And the workers' opinions varied about the type of impression they wanted to convey. In some of the shopping queues people would encourage the journalists. 'Go on,' some of them used to say, 'tell the West what it's really like, and show the pictures that aren't shown here.' Others were less encouraging. 'Leave us alone,' some of them shouted. 'We're not monkeys in a cage for you to come and laugh at us.' A native Pole now living in England once appeared in a Father Christmas outfit on the main shopping street in Warsaw. He had been giving out sticks of Clacton rock and oranges. He got a mixed reaction. Someone shouted at him from a passing bus, 'Go home, we don't need your charity.' All the same, the children came, not knowing whether he was to be laughed at or pitied, and the oranges went.

But the Polish workers were not always impressed by the Western reporters they met. One of them told me, 'You're too superficial. You don't ask the right questions. You're not tough enough.' In some ways the Polish workers never really grasped the function of the Western press. Some continued to see it purely as a counter-balance to their own State-run propaganda. And they were highly suspicious. One night I had to telephone a small Solidarity branch in the south-east of the country to check a report about police beatings. I got through at around two in the morning. It had been enough to ask the Warsaw operator for the Solidarity headquarters in the town. They knew all the numbers. I told them my name.

'How do we know who you are?' a man asked at the end of the line. 'You could be anybody. Give us your number and we'll call you back.' The phone rang about twenty minutes later. My number and identity had been checked.

Security became a preoccupation in the factories. At one stoppage in the Warsaw steelworks men in their overalls had herded journalists into an anteroom while the strike meeting went on in another hall. The speeches were broadcast on the factory loudspeakers. It was an eerie setting for a strike. Against the pitch-black sky the whole factory complex of chimneys, warehouses, pipes and gangways had been lit up by arc-lights. Steam came from some of the buildings. Inside the hall, huddled together for warmth, the workers were listening to a well-known dissident appealing for moderation. By three o'clock in the morning the talking was over and the strike had been called off. Could it have been that some of them simply preferred to go home to bed and take the line of least resistance? We often wondered.

The first shift at the steelworks began at five, still in darkness. Only an electric clock by the main entrance sorted out the early from the late. And the loudspeakers thumped out old sixties' hits by the Searchers such as 'Needles and Pins' – an attempt to get the workforce in the mood. Nobody sang along. Nobody even seemed to notice. The smoke from the drains swallowed them up as they went off to their work. In the days of Solidarity you could join the men on the factory floor, interrupt them, talk about their pay and demands, talk with the Solidarity men and the others from the Communist-run branch unions. People would talk anywhere and everywhere.

Earlier in 1982 I returned to the steelworks to find the mood had changed. There was no invitation to the shop floor. I waited in the director's outer office. A man in army uniform shuffled out of one room, looked at me, asked the secretary for a cup of tea, then shuffled back and shut his door. The director came out, dressed in a smart suit. 'Excuse me,' he said, 'we'll go to the conference room.'

'I can't find the key,' said the secretary. They rummaged around in a drawer and located it. We went down the corridor past the notice-boards with all the strike posters and Solidarity emblems removed. One of the union men had not turned up. We discovered him later standing out in the hallway, too shy to knock on the door and come in. The director smiled comfortingly and asked what he could do for me.

'How much is being produced here?' I asked.

'People are working normally,' he said, 'and that's the difference. Just because there was a military takeover they didn't stop having different ideas, but they did start to work.'

'Why then is there such a deep economic crisis in this country?' He smiled again. His advisers stared at me, their expressions noncommittal.

'I can't speak for the Government. Here at least work discipline has improved and we're now fully independent and self-financing. You know, we have to make a profit, and if we don't they could even shut us down.' There was a noise by the door and three workers walked in nervously. 'Ah,' said the director, by way of changing the subject. 'These men are all from the shop floor, and they used to be members of Solidarity.' They shook hands formally across the table, each reciting his surname. They all wore helmets and overalls. They all had dirty hands and faces. This was their way of telling me they were the genuine article.

Together they recited their version of why Solidarity had failed. 'The union had become too political,' one of them said. 'I'm not against them interning the leaders. They were the most aggressive people, and that includes Lech Walesa. If the union comes back it should have different people at the top.'

'You see,' one of them broke in, 'we were being manipulated. Every time we had a meeting, there would be members of the dissident groups there. We tried to put our views, different views, but not strongly enough. There was always too much pressure. You understand what I mean?' The worker looked at me sharply.

'Are you members of the Communist Party?' I asked.

'Yes,' replied the self-appointed leader. 'And I know what you're going to say. You're going to make out we were forced to say what we're saying now, but that's not true. I hope you're not going to report what we are saying unfairly.'

It was an extraordinary conversation. They had much to say and many new explanations for the past. They had taken part in strikes, but only because they had been spontaneous. 'There just wasn't the time to think about them. We had confidence in our leaders. The union people, the same ones we had elected. But they led us up the creek. Now we don't have confidence in them, not all of them anyway. You see, it had all become too political. You understand me?' It was the leader speaking again. 'The trouble was there were all sorts of different people in the union. There had to be a conflict of interests. How can a steelworker and a baker want the same things?'

'Did any good come out of it all?'

'Yes, of course. Well, yes, I suppose so.' They all looked at each other, a little lost for words. 'The start of Solidarity was good,' said the leader. 'All the useless corrupt people in the State were fired. Before August 1980 there was no socialism and no democracy. But then no one could foresee what was going to happen.'

'What did you get out of it all, personally?'

'I got free Saturdays. Well, that's a bit of a problem. It just means more time spent standing in queues. I suppose we have a steelworkers' charter and a thirteen-month salary, but can the country afford it?'

'And what's changed now?'

'Transport is better. People arrive on time. Attitudes to superiors have improved. Before the military took over the managers had to stand to attention and listen to the workers. Now it's a bit the other way round. You understand me?'

We all shifted in our seats and looked at each other. No one knew quite how to follow all that. But the worker had not finished. 'The good thing now,' he said, 'is that we know where we stand. We have firm ground under our feet. There's more of a sense of security. And, you know,' he waved his hands as if to pull the punchline out of thin air, 'women feel more secure. For the first time they're now wearing jewellery openly, on the streets.'

I got up to leave. We shook hands again. The workers looked down at the table. We all seemed glad that the conversation had ended. Outside it was as if the previous eighteen months had not existed. The factory had been militarized overnight. That meant no one could strike or resign. Any violation of the rules would be handled by military courts, and the penalties would be severe. The free, independent and self-governing trade unions had had their assets seized. The director had sole power to shorten or extend the working hours at will. Three men had been given suspended sentences for taking part in strikes: one was interned, and the former director of the plant forcibly retired. Special kiosks had been set up for the workers where they could buy products in short supply, like cigarettes. Officials claimed there were no special regulations against wearing trade union badges, but in practice if union activity was illegal then displaying union emblems would be illegal as well.

Half-way across the city there was different but related activity. The grey, concrete offices that had once housed the Communist trade union branch were open and full of life. I went up to a first-floor office and saw a secretary.

'Why all the bustle?' I asked. 'I thought trade unions were still banned.'

'That is of course true,' she replied. 'But people are not working. They're simply holding meetings to prepare for the time when they will be able to work again.' The men were downstairs in their canteen, and they confirmed the story. 'There's much to prepare for,' one of them said, 'and we shall have to be ready.'

Some eighteen months previously, a representative of that same union had welcomed the arrival of Solidarity. 'We've always wanted competition,' he had said. 'Now we can fight and put our own campaign across. It will be good for both of us.' As predictions went I suppose that one was no more inaccurate than the others that had circulated in Poland. But it was more memorable.

Down the street from that union building some of the pre-war blocks were still standing, with wartime bullet-holes etched into the cracked stone. No one had thought of repairing the walls, and they certainly did not intend to do so now. The Poles remember every conflict they have ever been involved in. They translated them into anniversaries. And now the workers, like the soldiers, had another anniversary all their own.

In the Name of the Father

The priest could not have been more than thirty-five, with thin black hair and tired eyes. It was ten o'clock at night. Far too late for him. He would have to be up again at dawn the next morning. He knocked on the door and pushed it open. Inside a dog rushed towards him barking. 'Jesus Christ be praised,' he shouted over the noise of the yapping. Inside the room there was light from a single bulb, and a middle-aged woman and her daughter came forward to greet him. Only now could you see he was carrying a cardboard box. He put it down and looked up at the woman. 'Maria, how are you?' he asked suddenly, generating cheer. He seemed to have acquired new energy. 'And the children,' he asked quickly, 'how are the children?'

'You know how it is, Father,' she sighed. 'But they are well.' The priest strode through into an adjoining bedroom. The light was on. Two small figures, bedraggled from sleep, their faces still dirty, turned over in the bed, grinning. He bent down towards them, put a hand through their hair.

'Are you good children?' he asked. 'Have you been good to your mother?' They smiled, too shy to answer. 'Look, I've brought something for you,' he exclaimed, and ran back into the main room to get his box. From it he pulled a few tins and packets and some sweets. One of the children took a bright packet and then put it back. They both smiled again, knowing it was good but not knowing why. The priest talked with the woman for a while, their voices low. They spoke with concern, she of the husband who had left her, the priest of how life would continue. A boy appeared through the front door, another son of the family. He smiled sheepishly at the priest. If he was surprised to see the clergyman at that hour of the night, he didn't show it.

They all stood there, suddenly not knowing what to say, the meek who had inherited nothing in the world and would leave nothing behind them when they left it. The priest drew on his reserves of cheer. He said good-night to them all, walked out into the corridor with its peeling paint and rotting wood, looked up at the moon and sighed deeply. He was silent for a moment, trying to gather his thoughts. The ground was stoney. There were potholes and ditches, but no street-lamps. It was a small shanty town of six or seven bungalows set well back from the main road where no one could see it. The priest grasped my shoulder, and I could just make out his disappointed expression. 'It's getting worse. None of them have any money,' he said. 'I don't know what they're going to do.'

The priest was not so different from anyone else who pushes a boulder up a steep slope and knows that's what he is doing. But he never lost his sense of humour and his commitment to a better Poland. His youth and intimate knowledge of local affairs made him privy to many secrets. He was part of the Church's nationwide intelligence network. Some knew from their contacts whether their telephones were monitored. Others knew when the workers were planning strikes. The Father knew when the patience of his parishioners was running out. His smile endured. The worse the situation became, the more he smiled. No one who looked at him would have believed him anything but an optimist. No one would have seen in his expression anything but hope. Perhaps I was one of the few to see him falter momentarily on a dark night in Gdansk.

He woke every morning of the year at four-thirty. His first job was to visit the sick in hospital and say prayers for them. 'There have been times when it's been so cold, and I was so tired, I thought how wonderful it would be to stay in bed.'

'And did you?'

'I couldn't. I thought about the people who might be dying, who might not like me see another day, or about the relatives of those who might have died during the night; and I thought, "You have to go. Who will comfort them if you don't?"'

'Did you ever doubt your faith?'

'A little girl died in the hospital. It was Christmas. I kept thinking, "Why this girl? Why did she have to die?" And I had to turn and say something to the parents that made sense. I came back to my room here and I felt so terrible.' The Father was not an ordinary priest. Perhaps there were no ordinary priests. If he was soft on the weak he was hard on the strong. I once heard him tell a parishioner, 'Forget about your husband. He left you, he drinks, he's no good. Forget about him. If you want to go away and make love for a week with someone else, do it. If it makes you feel happy, go and do it. But then come back and start to live properly.'

He had travelled once to the West. He spent the time living in the house of a depressed friend, trying to cheer her up. By day he saw bright lights and full shops. By night he had sat in a dingy room pushing a bottle of whisky out of his friend's reach and trying to stay awake past midnight.

'After a couple of weeks I had to go back,' he once confided.

'Why?'

'Because I was starting to take for granted the things I found in the West, the different aesthetic pleasures. I felt I could no longer see the problems of my people in perspective. I was starting to think of the West as normal.'

So the priest had gone home to the world he knew and the choices he had made. It was not easy. 'I love children,' he told me. 'I would have wanted my own children if I hadn't been a priest, a family, a house and a home like you have. But I decided to do something else.'

For him, perhaps more than for others, the withdrawal had been complete. He had come from a small country village in central Poland. His parents had not been educated. They could not understand why he wanted to leave the town and study for the priesthood. But despite the pressures he had gone. So he rarely saw his family. Their understanding of his life had grown little with the years.

When he had finished his evening rounds the Father changed from his cassock and put on a pair of cords. Sometimes he would drink vodka with friends, sometimes a lot of vodka. He had a small bedsitting-room and a large radio tuned permanently to foreign stations. He didn't like all he heard. 'Sometimes,' he told me, 'you talk sense. Other times, it's complete rubbish.' He laughed uproariously and slapped me on the back.

All the priests in his house ate their meals together in a cold dining-room on the ground floor. And sometimes the atmosphere itself would be chilly. Ironically, they did not welcome strangers instantly. Visitors had to earn their trust. The priests regarded their confidences as sacred. They might discuss them with a colleague, but not in front of a stranger. Their function was to retain information. Their fear was to give it away inadvertently. They would make constant efforts not to mention names, sometimes talking in whispers. As churchmen in an atheist state with a thousand years of Christianity behind them, they had few illusions about the world they lived in.

The Father had no outside entertainments. He rarely left Gdansk, still less travelled to Warsaw. His job was his life. But for him there was no slavish adherence to the Church hierarchy. The Bishop of Gdansk was too soft, he said. At times the Archbishop had conceded too much to the authorities. Then there was the Primate's Office in Warsaw. 'Well, some of them there are better than others.' But to him Church politics were a distant affair. At the local level he made no deals with the authorities, interceded for no one, and believed firmly in the good of one side and the evil of the other. On some evenings students came to his room to debate, on others shipyard workers would turn up and provide information. There was no time to theorize or chart broad designs for the future. Daily life made enough demands of its own. And when a woman helper cried on his shoulder and shouted out, 'Either our "friends" will come in or they will put the boot in here themselves,' he was face to face with his most acute problems – holding on to morale before it slipped away, and plucking hope from thin air.

The Father and his colleagues had all kinds of requests, the mundane and the extraordinary. Before leaving for the West a priest had received a call from someone identifying himself as 'Gdansk Security Police'.

'What can I do for you?' the priest had asked.

'We would like you to buy a book for us while you're away.'

'What book?'

'There's one which is printed by a Catholic press and we need a copy.'

'What do you think?' he asked me. 'That I'd go and buy the book for them and drop it off on my way back?'

The Father had grown sharp in a short time. He belonged, after all, to the oldest and most secret society in the world – the Roman Catholic Church. Anyone wanting assistance of any kind from him would first have to earn his trust. He would then be passed down the line to another priest, who could give him more help. The Father might not even say farewell to his visitor. He would simply push a note into his hand which read, 'The bearer is known to me and has my confidence. You can talk to him in private.'

It was a letter of that kind that had sent me late one night to the Church of the Holy Heart of Jesus in Gdynia, out along the suburban highway through Gdansk, past the Olivia Sports Hall, bumping over tracks and tramlines with only vague directions. The church was dark, the doors locked. It was impossible to see if there were lights on behind the curtains of the priest's residence. A young seminarian opened the door nervously. It was 1982 and a night-time knock on the door had acquired fresh significance. He had a mop of fair hair and wore a pullover on top of his grey shirt and collar. He would have preferred not to invite me in, but he did. I was shown into his tiny bedroom. There were sweets in a glass dish, posters of John Paul II and records and books from his first visit to Poland. A small electric fire fizzled dangerously in the corner. The young man asked me to wait. I was then shown up to the dining-room. An elderly priest held court at the end of the table, in deep but dismal conversation with a woman and her son. They had all but finished their meal. Some bread and a few slices of yellow cheese lay uneaten on the table. I was shown to a place on the left of the priest. Neither he nor his guests acknowledged me. The woman's monologue droned on under the one light-bulb. The seminarian let himself out, looking relieved. Finally the visitors got up to leave and the priest eyed me curiously. 'You're a journalist,' he told me. 'Are you properly accredited?'

'I have the proper card,' I replied, 'given by the Foreign Ministry.'

'Huh,' he responded, 'so you're half Communist then?' He raised his head, winked and tried to laugh. 'Come with me.'

He was a tall, broad man. His hand fastened on my wrist with a kindly grip. He led me through to his private sitting-room, where his humour and his hobbies were displayed. 'Look at this book,' he cried eagerly, snatching up a vast volume with gold engraving. 'Look inside, can you understand it?' I opened it up, prepared to be impressed by anything. Inside it the pages had been hollowed out and there were sweets for children. He laughed again, and another old man, tired and stooped, came in to join us as if from nowhere. The priest was a Kashubian from the north-west provinces of Poland, and devoted to Kashubian culture. Coloured pottery and pictures, models and memorabilia were scattered around the room with no attempt at order. 'Sit down, sit down,' he said. I obeyed. His friend looked across at me and shook his head – no gesture of welcome.

'What's happening in the Falklands?' he asked suddenly. 'You British. Another war, more killing – all for what?'

It was the height of the Falklands war, and the Polish media had not been favourable towards Britain. I explained why the war was being fought. The man shook his head again. The priest intervened.

'Come now, Stefan,' he said soothingly. 'The British have acted as they have always done. This is a matter of principle. They may have killed people, but they have done so in a most – er – most cultured fashion.' He winked at me again. 'Come back tomorrow,' he said, 'and we will talk more.'

I got up to leave. 'I hope I have not offended you,' said the old man, in a tone that implied he hoped he had. Outside, the city seemed to have died. Traffic had ceased. No one was out on the streets. On the road back to Gdansk only a petrol queue indicated that all was, if not right with the world, at least normal.

I was back the next morning, just an hour before mass. The Father was sitting alone at the head of the breakfast-table, eating stolidly. 'Sit down, sit down. Do you have your colleagues with you? Do they want to film?' I nodded in affirmation. 'Let them have some coffee,' he commanded, 'or are they allergic to it?'

He laughed, stood up, and walked unhurriedly to the vestry. 'Two of our priests,' he said, 'and a lay helper have been arrested. The police said they had thrown stones in a demonstration. They were nowhere near the demonstration. It was absolutely untrue.' He delved into a drawer and removed a scrap of paper. 'A telegram to the General,' he said. 'Jaruzelski, the one in Warsaw. No reply, though,' he mused. 'Totally untrue, of course, the whole thing.'

As he struggled into his surplus his gaze fell on a Polish female assistant in our group. The priest turned instantly into the guardian of Catholic morals. Had she been married in church, he wanted to know. Who had baptized her? Did she go to church regularly, and did she have anything to do with that nonsense pill? She evaded what she could and fell victim to the rest. Here and there he nodded his head, grunting sometimes, scolding occasionally.

The back-room duty over, he prepared for the front line. The signal was given to the organist. The pipes shrilled out a hymn, and the old man ambled out to his flock. He seemed not to notice the poor turn-out.

'We must pray for the press,' he told the nonplussed elderly. 'We must pray that they do their work well and carry out all that is expected of them.' The people in the pews stared back blankly. The Father said a few prayers, handed over to a deacon and walked towards me where I stood at the side of the congregation. The tight grip on my arm led me from plaque to crucifix, from stained-glass window to Solidarity flag, from a ship's anchor down to a crypt where the queue of people outnumbered the congregation above. They were nearly all women, standing quiet and smiling, waiting their turn. They had not come for a blessing. They had come for food – part of the weekly aid package allotted to them by their local parish church.

The priest took us upstairs. Each of us was presented with a religious bookmark and a Kashubian jug. In the giving and the taking was the unspoken acceptance that one kindness would sooner or later beget another.

The Polish Church, however, was never soft. Each argument

could become a battle, each issue a crusade. In the late seventies the Church had protested against plans to build a motorway beside the country's holiest shrine at Czestochowa. It was clear from the outset that there was no money to build the road, and the Church was too powerful to let it happen. But both sides launched themselves enthusiastically into a campaign of mutual antagonism until they wearied and dropped the subject. While it lasted, though, it had produced some impressive rhetoric, not least from the parish priest, who declared: 'These State officials, they're all the same. To begin with they start chucking their weight around, then when they get a bit older they come back saying, "Father forgive me, forgive me". It's always the same, you'll see.'

Not all the priests were so outspoken. Some of them, it seemed, had learned much from the Communist authorities about handling the press. My last visit to the Episcopate in Warsaw had brought me into contact with Father Peter, whom I had known for nearly three years.

'Good morning, Father,' I said. 'May I have a couple of words with you?'

'Good morning,' he replied. 'You've just had them.'

It was three days after the imposition of martial law and the Church had pulled up its drawbridge – the standard initial reaction to any momentous event. It had been the same with the birth of Solidarity. But Father Peter's abrupt greeting, just a step away from rudeness, was still a surprise.

Throughout our relationship the Father had done his best to present the view of the Church authorities in a calm, understated fashion. He was, after all, charged with containing trouble and I with revealing it. We would sit in an anteroom off the main hallway with its shining wood-block floors and the silence that seemed centuries old. In winter the windows would ice over. The Father would leave long pauses in his conversation and wide gaps in his answers. It was an atmosphere calculated to defuse controversy and numb curiosity.

The talks tended to be one-sided. Father Peter spoke impressive American, but had spent little time in the country. And yet his lack of exposure to American television networks had not impeded his general comprehension. He knew the difference between on and off the record and never lacked confidence. For that as much as for anything else the Father was a sometime guest at Western dinner parties. He was a jovial conversationalist, witty in both his native and adopted languages. On one occasion I remember him spooning out a second helping of cream pudding and declaring to the guests, 'There's nothing in the Bible that says you can't enjoy yourself.'

And yet the Father probably had little enough to enjoy. His face was grey and drawn, his black hair slicked straight back, a tough, businesslike look that had been born out of necessity. He had spent years picking his way through the minefield of Church–State relations. For Father Peter knew what was possible, never mind what was desirable. 'There's only one government possible here, we know that,' he used to say. 'No one else can form an administration. Sometimes we have to help them to stay in power. We don't want chaos any more than they do.' In one sense the Father said the Church had been fighting for the rights of Communists for more than thirty years. Cardinal Wyszinski, the post-war Primate, had even interceded for them at the Vatican. While on a visit there he had been asked why some members of the Communist Party actually went to church. He explained it was a quirk of Polish life, but was reminded forcefully that Communists were automatically subject to excommunication and could not therefore share the faith. The Cardinal protested and in fact offered to resign. But it was the Vatican that finally gave way. And Polish Communists, or so the story goes, have enjoyed a special dispensation ever since.

By all accounts they are still enjoying it. Just a few weeks after the military takeover a senior Warsaw churchman admitted to preparing the following candidates for baptism at Easter: a handful of officials from both the Government and the Communist Party, two Army officers and, because everything in Poland is possible, a Jew.

The priest himself had laughed when he told me, but more at my incredulous reaction than at anything he had said. And he wasn't the only one to speak of such things. A monk at the Holy

Shrine of Czestochowa had claimed the existence of a secret book kept by the Church authorities. In it were the names of Government officials who had had their children baptized. Sometimes Church marriages had taken place in secret. Such were the ways, he said, that the clergy served the Communist State.

The Church exercised influence rather than power, however, and even then the influence was sometimes ignored. Workers in the Lenin shipyard had remained silent in disbelief as a priest had sought to remind them of the value of work at the height of their strike in August 1980. A congregation in Warsaw cathedral had shifted uncomfortably from foot to foot, coughed, turned their heads in disgust and even in some cases walked out as the Primate of All Poland had adopted a moderate tone in talking about the Government. An intellectual who encountered Archbishop Glemp on a visit to Rome had been unable to disguise his disappointment as he recounted a conversation they had held.

'Archbishop, how do you think we can keep alive the spirit of Solidarity?'

'Do you know,' said the churchman, 'I haven't even thought about that.'

In fact the Church had been guilty of slow reactions long before then. Poland had been at least four months into the Solidarity era before the bishops gathered their strength in both hands and finally mentioned the union's name in public. Not that the clergy had refused to support the strikers in other ways. At the height of one confrontation in the southern city of Bielsko-Biala a bishop had been despatched from Warsaw to convey the Primate's good wishes and kind thoughts.

But the Church knew it faced a dilemma. The workers claimed God on their side, not that there was much competition in an atheist state, and their faith had to be admired and encouraged. And yet encouragement meant supporting a challenge to the only system that the Church believed would rule Poland. Events were moving so fast, however, that it was impossible to sit on the fence for long. Sooner or later – and it was later – a decision had to be taken. Eventually the Church came out of hiding and sat down beside Solidarity, but there was no smile on its face. It was to sit there warning, cajoling and moderating right up to the end of the union's life.

Despite their hesitation, the clergy were to provide one of the enduring sights of the entire upheaval of 1980. As the leaders of the Lenin shipyard's strike committee negotiated in Gdansk, the men lined up in two rows along the road leading to the main gate. Two priests sat on stools in the middle. And there, watched by everyone, the men knelt down beside them and confessed their sins. One of the priests even put up his hand to simulate a screen. The absolution given, the men would go back to their comrades and others would come out. They were still in their overalls, unwashed and unshaven. A revolution was beginning in the heart of the Communist bloc, and in the middle of it the revolutionaries were quietly seeking absolution just a few miles from the Soviet border. They were like soldiers preparing to do battle. The State officials were nowhere to be seen. The police had withdrawn. But over the shipyard gate still hung the ironic sign, 'We thank you for your good work.'

One of those priests was Father Jankowski, the shipyard priest, the man who was to act later as Lech Walesa's mentor. He was an imposing figure. His hair was black and his face like a bulldog's, round and upturned as if about to bite. An ample belly swelled his cassock, but he was tall and wore it well. Jankowski filled a room when he walked into it. A proud man with a confident message. The worse the situation became, the better pleased he seemed. Why? Because it meant that the population was increasingly united. The Father was not universally popular, and when you entered his office you could see why. It was crammed with imposing, dark wooden furniture, the style almost baroque. The items would have been more suited to a Bavarian castle than a priest's quarters in a Baltic port. Burlesque would be a better word than baroque. There was a vast chest, chairs with high backs and carved German inscriptions, arms that swept down to end in lion's heads with mouths where you could put your fingers. On the coffee table was a book that opened to reveal a cigarette case, and a few Western chocolates in a bowl.

Jankowski would sit at his desk. He was invariably smiling.

Perhaps it was his confidence that annoyed some of his associates. 'He had too much power over Walesa,' some would say. 'He's not to be trusted. He used the foreign aid in the wrong way.' Jankowski was not the only priest under scrutiny and suspicion. In the general climate of mistrust that pervaded Poland in the early eighties people would be suspected of corruption or even collaboration for no better reason than that they came from a different city. In those days there was very little trust in Poland. The more prominent the person, the bigger the target.

Archbishop Glemp himself cut a poor figure in the coffee-house chit-chat. 'He has big ears, he looks silly,' someone would say. To others he had no experience. 'He wasn't like the last one,' I was told. Many had forgotten that the last one was less than beloved when he took over the job. And it was only after some thirty years that he won wholehearted public approval. Glemp may have to run the same course. For many months after he had taken over a notice appeared next to the Cross in Warsaw commemorating Cardinal Wyszinski. It read simply, 'We are still waiting for your successor.'

Glemp's perceived fault, if that is what it was, consisted of not being instantly multi-dimensional. It was not enough that he could when necessary run with the hare and hunt with the hounds. He was obliged to rub down the hounds afterwards and then go off to console the hare's family. The Primate had to be all things to all Poles – possibly the hardest job on earth.

Glemp may not have possessed great vision, but he was not without humanity. One of the strangest and least-told stories about him involves a visit he is alleged to have made to a provincial town soon after the start of martial law. It was March 1982. Shipyard workers were standing trial for inciting strikes. Glemp's arrival was so sudden that the court had no time to decide whether or not to let him in. But there was instant pandemonium. While the judge called for order the people in the courtroom surged towards Glemp, trying to kiss his ring. Among them were some of the uniformed police officers. Glemp sat on a bench and order was restored. He remained there for about twenty minutes, listening to some of the defence speeches. He left saying he would not stop praying for the people while they continued to be arrested.

Glemp also visited internment camps. He appeared to have been shocked by what he saw. After one visit he asked, 'Do you think it is easy for the Primate to go to such places and administer the sacrament and give out New Year wishes? It's terribly difficult. God's peace is needed to visit imprisoned people and bring them a beam of freedom, to try to make what happened in Bethlehem happen there. We know that many of our brothers have been dismissed because they refuse to resign from a legal trade union. It doesn't happen without violating human rights, without harm, without some kind of humiliation. A man has a natural right to his conscience and views.'

According to many Poles, Glemp's fine words were not translated into deeds. Intellectuals accused him of obsessive fear of violence and civil war. 'He believed,' said one of them, 'that every conflict could immediately cause blood to be spilled on the streets, and that had to be avoided at all costs.' Glemp's caution had clearly appealed to Cardinal Wyszinski, who earmarked the Archbishop as his successor. But Glemp was not the Pope's choice, at least according to Church legend. It was believed in Warsaw that John Paul II had favoured the Archbishop of Krakow, Cardinal Nacharski. He was senior to Glemp, who at that time had still not attained the rank of Cardinal. But the Pope did not intervene. His respect for Wyszinski's wishes may have outweighed any reservations about Glemp. And as one Catholic layman put it, 'John Paul may be hard on issues, but he's soft on individuals. He would not wish to hurt a man's feelings.'

It is not known whether Glemp's feelings were hurt by having to wait a year to become a Cardinal – a long time for a Primate of All Poland to be kept waiting. But as in all good families he never mentioned it, though many other Poles did. Yet it was not always possible to patch up disagreements, particularly those inside the Polish church. Just before Christmas 1981 Glemp issued a statement, moderate and conciliatory. The bishops issued another, couched in stark terms and critical of the authorities and the imposition of martial law. In some churches the clergy read only one or the other of the statements. But in a large number both were delivered to the congregation, juxtaposed without any explanation. Worshippers were left to draw their own conclusions. It was one more exercise in reading between the lines. They had had more than thirty years' training in that. Glemp's position would have become easier without the existence of a Polish Pope. For the Pope was Primate and demi-god, patriot and guardian of all things Polish in the outside world.

No training, though, could have prepared the people for the visit of John Paul II to Poland in June 1979. Long after the press, both Western and Communist, had used up its supply of 'firsts' and superlatives, ordinary Poles still looked on it as a momentous period in their lives. For the visit all but deified the man in the eyes of his people. 'With our Pope we've become somebody again,' said one Warsaw resident. 'They don't crack jokes about us any more in America. All that's over now.'

The night before his arrival it seemed as if half Warsaw was on the streets. People strolled in the evening sunshine, smiling and gazing in awe at the wooden cross that dominated the city's Victory Square. No one had seen a giant cross in a capital square anywhere in the Eastern bloc. This meant change. It is difficult to describe how cities of grey concrete become caught up in a carnival. But yellow-and-white streamers fluttered from windows and balconies throughout Poland. There was colour and spontaneity where there had been none before. As the Pope's motorcade travelled through cities, buses and trams would stop in the middle of the road. People would descend on to the street and stand waving until the vision had passed. Lorries would be left where they stood. Normal life was suspended. And even in the places the Pope did not visit, his presence was noted and advertised. I remember travelling at night through the rural areas of southern Poland, through tiny farming communities and villages, and seeing a crucifix lit up in a window. It was in a tiny cottage, the only house for miles, and the cross could be seen some distance away over the fields. Someone in the bus said it seemed as if Christianity had been born again.

The people spent ten days of that year laughing and crying with their Pope. They sang to him and he sang along with them, tapping his feet in time to the rhythm. It was hard to know who was protecting him, the police or the scores of Catholic stewards in their pointed, coloured hats who seemed just too ready to use force to restrain over-excited visitors. But the Pope did not need protection: John Paul II was transparently the most popular person to visit Poland since the end of the Second World War. His visit caused a temporary but massive migration. It was seen most clearly on the morning of his final day in Poland. I had been woken at around five o'clock in the morning. The beginnings of daylight could be seen from the window. There was mist over the meadow where John Paul was to give his last service. But coming through the gloom was a steady stream of humanity, walking so silently that it was impossible to hear their footsteps. There were old and young, walking with the dogged determination of those who had come far. Some carried rucksacks, others just a few clothes in their hands, a basket, even a child. Some were barely able to pull themselves along, slouching from exhaustion. They were pilgrims of a kind no longer seen in the West. For ten days they were rich, armed not only with faith but with a champion as well.

It became almost a cliché, but the Poles used to say it all the same. 'Our country will never be the same after this.' No one promised them change. No one spoke of revolutions. No one hinted at the vast upheaval that was to take place just a year later. And yet Poland had been shifted into a new orbit. The limits of what was possible had suddenly been extended. The future, it seemed, could be different from the past.

I had watched the Pope's departure until the moment his plane began taxiing to the runway. There was a tent on the grass verge, inside it a makeshift field exchange providing international telephone connections. In the corner sat a female operator, crying as if the world was about to end. She was unable to watch the plane's take-off. She didn't want to glimpse the small white hand and the final pontifical wave. The noise of the jets drowned her sobbing and John Paul went back to the Vatican. A Pope, and a Polish one, had for the first time visited an Eastern bloc country. The unthinkable had happened. It was to go on happening in the months that followed.

The Poles took home their Papal souvenirs, the pictures, the cards, the badges, and they did what came naturally to them: they let them trickle onto the black market. If you left John Paul souvenirs lying around, they would soon find a new home. If you wanted to collect others you had to pay many times the original asking price. But commercialism never interfered with spiritualism. John Paul was believed by many Poles to have divine powers – a belief that strengthened during the 1980 crisis. Ordinary people believed the Pope had warned the Kremlin not to intervene. They accepted without question that he had given Moscow an ultimatum – 'Invade my country, and I will land my plane at Warsaw airport and sit there until you leave.' Without any evidence for it, that idea became almost a national refrain.

Three years later John Paul was back in Poland. The revolution had come and gone, and with it the silent expectation of a better future. He spent some of his last hours in the Tatra Mountains, where he had skied as a young man, and the people welcomed him according to their tradition. The night before his arrival beacons were lit on the top of hills and mountains. Many waited beside them until dawn. On the foothills they had laid out sheets and pillow-cases, some forming the sign of the cross. They were to be visible when he flew over the area in a special helicopter. That same night I talked by telephone to a Pole who lived in the mountains. He was tired but exhilarated. 'The Pope,' he said, 'made such beautiful speeches. He didn't disappoint us. He may not have said everything directly, but we knew what he meant.' Once again the Pope had brought Poland's emotions to the surface. There were those in the West who said he had delivered the Government a monumental kick in the backside. The Government said the visit had been a success, and denied that the Pope's statements had been political. The Vatican agreed a little too hastily with the official Polish assessment. John Paul himself said nothing.

The Pope retained his special affection for his home town of Krakow. A city with an ancient heart and a sprawling body of grey suburbs and dirty, grey industry. It was home, too, for the Catholic press. In a narrow cobbled street leading to the main square, one of the editors spoke of the man who to them was no more than a friend, the former Archbishop. People kept walking through the sparse offices. It was difficult to find a place to talk.

'He was so *sure* when he took the place, you know what I mean? The Vicar of Christ.' The man smiled as if recalling a distant event. 'We knew him as a very friendly man. And I must tell you, it seemed as if the Holy Spirit had prepared the world to welcome him.' It was Christmas 1978, and the Pope had been gone for two months. 'We shall miss him. It will be a very different Christmas without him. Every year it was his custom to invite us to the residence the day before Christmas Eve. And it wasn't just a polite exchange of greetings. We would talk about serious matters. Often the visits were in special circumstances, I mean political circumstances. But there will always be this emotional link with Krakow.' He smiled wryly and shrugged. '*Polonia semper fidelis*, "Poland always faithful",' he said, 'and it's true.'

I moved to a different office. Outside, the light was fading quickly, and the man inside was older. I only saw one-half of his face, illuminated by a fire.

'People do not expect John Paul to make universal changes. But there could be social changes here,' he said. 'The climate must change, and yet the issues are now the same as they were when he was here. The Church wants greater access to the mass media. It wants more opportunities to publish. Maybe even a mass, if not on television then at least on radio.' The man talked slowly and precisely. Doubtless he had said the same things many times before. After all, they were standard doctrine. The Church knew its place: neither commanding nor servile, simply locked in hard negotiations with the State. There were times when the two could work together, times when the pulpit rhetoric and the official atheism could be put aside. The men of the Party and the Cloth could occasionally meet and shake hands. But, in the end, both wanted a different future for Poland.

That conflict drew both the committed and the superficial. Some joined the Church simply because they enjoyed a fight. In the fifties wearing a cassock was sometimes enough to signify challenge to the State. In the eighties it was no longer necessary.

One female activist in Krakow took up the challenge, toyed with it, enjoyed it and refined her own propaganda. 'Just because the priests ask for more churches, it doesn't mean that they're the only ones who want them,' she said. 'We want them too. We demand them.'

'What if the State says it can't afford new churches because of the housing shortage?'

'This wouldn't be a problem. People would give their houses for church buildings. And most of the churches that have been illegally built, and there are a number of them, were originally private houses. This is especially so in the country. People will help to build a church and would give up their time to do it free of charge, in their free time, because there is such a need. And when we fight for more Catholic papers we do so because we want them.'

'But that's political isn't it?'

'When you live in this system anything you do or say that's independent of the State becomes political. To me the Church is more of a social organization. It helps the old people, fights alcoholism, looks after children and split families.'

'Has the Church come to terms with the Communist State?'

'Only on paper. But I don't see it really.'

'Is there anything the Church can learn from the State?'

The girl laughed, and the last time I saw her she was still laughing. She was playing political games in Gdansk, seeing how far she could go and how much she could get away with. She was having fun. All the young people said it: 'Why go abroad? It's difficult here, but it's fascinating.' *She* went abroad, however, and married a foreigner. But she will miss getting high on intrigue, rumour and risk.

In Krakow, Cardinal Macharski took charge of spiritual affairs much as the Pope had done previously. He was tough, but he had humour. After much negotiation with his assistants, I had been ushered into the weekly audience. It was held in a vast reception hall where the chosen few gathered under the unkindly gaze of previous archbishops, immortalized in unflattering oil paintings. The plaintive townspeople would gather in corners, there would be churchmen from the parish. Only this time the Cardinal had to contend with a Westerner wanting an interview.

'My English is not good enough,' he said.

'Yes it is. It sounds perfect.'

'I cannot give interviews.'

'Just one question, perhaps?'

A thin hand reached over and gripped my arm. 'You are a terrible man,' said the Cardinal, and smiled. 'But I suppose you are doing your work. I will answer one question. What is it?'

The Cardinal answered two. He spoke of solidarity with the West, of the value of those who gave aid to Poland. The act of giving honoured those who gave and those who received, he said. He went away to pray in his private chapel, and I was shown down the stone staircase and out into the courtyard. It was explained that the Archbishop had gone out of his way to accommodate me. He promised nothing in advance, and right up until the last minute could have refused to see or talk to me. This was ecclesiastical protocol. But the formality began and ended with the Cardinal. A lay assistant in the parish had invited me to dinner. He had offered the best food he had, even accommodation and help in the future. Charity flowed freely.

In the early days of martial law that charity was needed and given many times. The focal point was in Warsaw, at the old town church of St Martin's. Without any blessing from the State, the doors were opened to volunteers and families who made it their business to find out who had been detained and where they were being held. Lists of detention centres were posted on boards. Instructions were given on how to get there, what could be taken, who could be visited and when. It was makeshift but highly effective, an extraordinary operation: unofficial but tolerated. It had no power except by virtue of the information it obtained, but that was power enough. All day long the willing and the frightened passed through the church. Parcels were brought, stories were stopped. Lawyers were hired and dispatched. A new social service grew up. A self-help centre without finance or patronage, it worked because it had to.

The outer rooms were for the casual callers. People were sifted by a reception staff told only what they needed to know. In the anterooms there was more information available. Reports came in from other parts of the country. The effects of martial law were assessed, patterns and trends were noted. They took on only the volunteers they trusted, and sent them on missions that were often hopeless.

One young girl told how she had tried to organize a consignment of apples for a detention centre outside the capital. 'The farmers were so good,' she said. 'They would vie with each other to see who could give the most and best apples. One farmer would go through them, shining them on his coat and taking out the bad ones. "We can't let them eat inferior quality," he would say.' Eventually the truck was made ready for the journey and arrived at the camp. The guards refused to admit it. 'This isn't a holiday camp,' came the response. 'The food is fine as it is.' The girl remembered turning the truck and taking a final look at the camp. In a window high up someone had hung a towel with a V daubed clearly across it. She had wanted to cry.

The mobilization of social workers and parish councils took place right across the country, but received little publicity in the West and none at all in Poland. Quietly the priests and their assistants tried to fill the gap left by the State supply system. Goods were taken in and catalogued, then distributed where the need was greatest. The centre for distribution in Warsaw was a bleak church about fifteen miles outside the city. There were no signposts. Lorry drivers either knew the way or got lost. It involved turning off the main road and going half a mile down a mud track which led to a village. The houses were dirty and colourless. A railway line ran through the middle of them. Along the main street horses pulled carts loaded with coal. It seemed like the economy of the Middle Ages. The shops appeared to sell only bread, mineral water and jam. A consignment of aid had just come in from England.

The priest welcomed us with a powerful handshake. He had white hair and smiled little. It seemed there was no time for pleasantries. He led me down to the basement, where cardboard boxes had been piled up, appearing to support the entire building. There were car batteries, stacks of soap and washing-up liquid, margarine and vitamin tablets. A group of schoolchildren had been drafted in to sort through them. More precisely, they had finished their Bible class and had been told that other duties awaited them. Outside, a small red taxi-van had arrived from Gdansk. It had to be loaded and sent on its way by evening.

The priest left them all to it and made his way to the sitting-room for tea. He was prepared to be polite until he learned that my colleagues were from Polish television. 'What are you doing here?' he asked. 'You always put out such nonsense and twist everything. What's the matter with you and your so-called news programmes?'

They protested that they had nothing to do with the news, that they were merely a technical crew. The priest looked dissatisfied with their response. The atmosphere had soured. The TV men tried to joke with the priest. He glowered back. It was an unusual incident. Polish hospitality normally overcame even political boundaries. But as the crisis wore on patience and tolerance were at a premium. The hospitality became conditional.

The van was soon loaded, and the driver and his mate were anxious to leave. Petrol was hard enough to find during normal hours, even harder by night. I arranged to meet them the next day in Gdansk, but they never turned up. A colleague said the van had broken down. Apparently that was more the rule than the exception. The lifelines were snapping.

Church aid came in more than just a cardboard box. There are still a few orphanages, for instance, which are financed by the State but staffed by nuns. There is a constant tussle between the Church and the authorities over who should control them. But the State does not have the trained personnel, and the Church does. One such establishment lies in the industrial wasteland around Warsaw, reached by a wide road that winds its way over mud and potholes, past electricity pylons and small lakes where the rain collects. The children rush at visitors, holding their arms outstretched, desperate for affection. Some are sick. One girl had a bruise that they said was cancer. Others come from broken families. Sometimes a mother has more children than she can cope with or afford. A few are brought to the home, collected when wanted, dumped when inconvenient. One of the major problems, say the nuns, is alcoholism. 'A father comes home drunk and depressed and beats his children: then they come to us. A man is imprisoned or interned: his children come to us. We deal with people on the fringes of society.' The Sister stopped talking and walked past the dormitory. As she did so the power failed and we were left blinking in the dim afternoon light. 'Someone send for an electrician,' she commanded. 'Who knows,' she added, 'when he'll come, or how long the cut will last?' We went downstairs to sit in her office. The Sister did not want to say too much. She did not really know what I was. She had learnt to be careful of questions.

For she knew too many answers. She belonged to that powerful Church organization that had its informants in every parish and township in the country – and its standard-bearer in Rome.

'We don't have much hope for the future,' she said. 'These are troubled times. I try to look for optimism, but I don't find it.' She came outside to wave goodbye. The electrician had arrived, and the lights were working again. The children of Poland's poor would be able to see their way to bed.

On the whole, Poland's Roman Catholic Church devoted much time to the young people. There was, said the parish priests, a battle going on for the hearts and minds of the nation. It was not a battle they were prepared to concede. At times it looked more like a Catholic takeover. Sometimes in the early evenings you could watch the children come out of school in the suburbs of Warsaw and head for the church. The nearer Christmas came, the greater their enthusiasm. In one area the church stood out among the dormitory blocks, the one building that owed its design to a non-Communist order. I had stood inside the church and watched the children come in. Automatically they dabbed a finger in the holy water and dropped to one knee as they headed for the altar. And it was there that the entertainment awaited them. It came in the shape of a priest, young and versatile, a microphone in his hand, a sophisticated compère and showman. As the children sat silent he would act out the Bible stories, changing voices, sometimes imitating the animals, occasionally flinging a question into his audience, always keeping up the pace, never letting their attention wander. He knew all their names and what they could or couldn't do. 'Who was waiting in the barn, Stefan? Come on, you know who was there. Maria, what did the three wise men bring? That's right. Why does God love little children?' The patter was ceaseless, the results impressive. The group would go back home anxious to return again for the next instalment. From the Church's point of view, it was a simple and beneficial means of communication.

There is only one church in Eastern Europe that has managed to get a Communist government to attend a public religious ceremony, and it is unlikely to happen again. But for an hour at least on a wet night in the winter of 1980 the Polish President, some Party dignitaries and a guard of honour bowed their heads before a cross. It was a special ceremony, previously unthinkable. The commemoration of three giant crosses outside the Lenin shipyard in Gdansk. Their purpose was to honour an unknown number of workers who were shot dead by the Polish army in the riots of 1970. It had taken ten years for them to be officially recognized, ten years to shed some light on the darkness of that brief civil war. Families brought their children and sat them on their shoulders. From all over Poland modern-day pilgrims converged on the area. In the streets beside the shipyard people queued for metal replicas of the crosses made from shipyard steel, attached to cards with a prayer and a red-and-white ribbon, the colours of the Polish flag. Hot-dog vans were parked at the roadside, selling foul-tasting sausages from steaming cauldrons. The weather had been bad all day, squally and wet. Cars arrived late, planes arrived with their passengers sick and exhausted.

For the people of Gdansk it was a day filled with old memories. Young people remembered the stench of tear-gas in their houses, a stench that lingered long after the fighting was over. They recalled the drone of tanks passing their houses, the sound of army boots on the cobbles. And, whether young or old, they all remembered what a young worker had shouted at the officers who had stood ready to open fire. 'Just remember that you are Poles. One day you'll have to come out of the army and join us on this side. Just remember what you will feel then.' For the Party leaders who attended that night, it was a supreme act of penance: coming cap in hand to the workers, waiting until the union leaders had had their say, calling on people not to look at the divisions in society but to concentrate on the things that united them. It was the gesture of a leadership that by its own admission had lost the confidence of its people.

It was not a coincidence that they chose Gdansk to launch a powerful appeal for national unity. Not at a Party congress, with the posters and the slogans and the pictures of Lenin, but on a stormy night remembering a national tragedy in front of the largest crosses in Eastern Europe. Let us make sure, they were saying, that the terrible events of 1970 never happen again.

Later that night the people trooped off peacefully and sadly to their homes, aware that they had participated in something quite unique. It was, said one man, a final victory for the workers, for honesty and for Poland itself. The men who died had been heroes – the forerunners of the new labour movement. But there was one thing he stressed above everything else. 'This victory, I mean the founding of these new trade unions, this is Poland's last chance to develop and to change. If the people lose it, there will be no more opportunities, no more bright futures to think about.'

Not long after they were built the crosses became a little rusty. Not surprisingly: they are around a hundred and twenty feet high and battered by the salty wind. People still come and put flowers at the foot of them. Sometimes they are the first stop for married couples. They come straight from the church, still dressed in their finery. A few feet from the ground the word Solidarity is fashioned into the steel. These days it is probably the only place in Poland where that word is allowed to stand in public. Some Poles have their doubts about how long it will remain there. They say the authorities have begun warning that the ground under the crosses is marshy and unsafe. Perhaps, say the officials, the crosses might have to be removed to prevent them falling down and causing damage. The residents of the city smile and shake their heads knowingly.

Back to the Family

It was raining hard, and the Swiss Air flight from Moscow was on its way to a major financial loss. Only eight passengers were on board as the plane clumped on to the Warsaw runway, turned towards the terminal and stopped. A soldier waited at the bottom of the steps, beside him an air hostess and a bus. Just one passenger disembarked.

I could not remember such a cold May in Poland. But the trees were out and the gardens full of flowers. The rain collected in vast puddles on the roads, making them seem smooth where they were pitted with holes. I had been out of Poland for more than a year. The country had settled back into its Eastern orbit. General Jaruzelski had travelled to Moscow and received another medal. But the doubts were still there. After forty-eight hours in Warsaw officials were asking me, 'What do you think of the situation here? What does the West make of us now?' Inevitably, they spoke less than lovingly of the Western press.

'Why do you concentrate on illegal demonstrations?' asked one official. 'Don't you know there are far more serious problems?'

'What are they?'

'The appalling state of the economy and the total indifference of our young people. If you write about these things no one will quarrel with you. In the long term they could have very dangerous consequences for our country.'

You can still disagree amicably in Poland. And we did on many issues. But the official was courteous. And as I left his office his assistant forgot politics and began discussing the comedy programme *Not the Nine O'Clock News* that he had once seen in England.

'I liked it very much,' he said. 'Very funny sketches, very much to the point.'

I crossed the street to a block of flats I knew well. The doorman was shuffling around in the hallway doing nothing, and came forward immediately with his arm outstretched. 'You owe me money,' he smiled. 'You owe me lots of money. You don't remember, do you?' I shook my head. 'You bet me that the Pope would not come to Poland for a second visit. See, now you do remember.'

In the old days when I lived in Poland we had never spoken much together. But he ushered me into a room off the hallway where he poured the dregs from a vodka bottle into two glasses and toasted my return. There was sausage too. 'Go on, go on, eat it.' He speared a chunk with the point of his knife, laid it on a doorstep of bread and pushed it in front of me.

'You see, if you eat at the same time, you won't notice the drink.'

Odd how that philosophy had never taken root in Poland. The man began speaking of the Russians, of Solidarity, of the agreement at Yalta – all in much the same tone, spitting breadcrumbs on the floor, cursing fluently and not caring who heard him. Solidarity had gone too fast. It had all got out of hand. But who knew what would happen in the future? 'As for me,' he said, 'I'm an old fool. Broke my back lifting furniture, but they mended it.'

He wished me well. I paid his debt and left him marginally happier. After all, he had said his daily piece. We had carried out the pro forma political ritual – kicked briefly through modern history, barked at a few ghosts. He would do the same tomorrow with someone else. It beat discussing last night's television.

So after a year I was back in the Polish family. Not a harmonious institution, but never dull. Without exception its members spoke of the fatherland with considerable pride. But the father acknowledged some of them and not others. And there were those who later ran away from home and disavowed him.

Years before, the Polish family home had always left its door open. 'A guest in your home is a god in your home,' went the rural saying. But the gods would sometimes visit without invitation. In the bad old days of public corruption, now much condemned by the new government, they might come in a green uniform and peaked cap, carrying a briefcase.

'In that costume two of them arrived at a Warsaw flat. They

often travelled in pairs. Some said it was to increase the fun if things went well and to ensure safety if they didn't.

'Please come in,' said the Westerner. So they did, looking round the flat as the packers stuck clothes into cardboard boxes. The man was leaving Poland, and these were the customs officials. For a while they feigned interest in a picture and a few books, but with a bottle of whisky on the table they and the Westerner knew that that interest would pass. They sat down, talked of families and wives. Photographs, stained and dog-eared, were shown around. They told jokes and laughed until the tears rolled down their faces, and then the laughing stopped abruptly. 'My God,' said the elder of the two, 'what's the time?' He looked at his watch, but could not read it. 'Where are my glasses?' His friend seemed to be asleep. He fished in his jacket, lying in a heap on the floor.

'Three o'clock! The superior will be here any moment.' He turned to the Westerner. 'This superior, he could make trouble for us. You know, they don't understand, those people. With them it's always work, work, work. They don't realize there's a human side to the business.' The doorbell rang and another green-suited official walked in. The two juniors put on their jackets and told him how well everything had gone. He sat down, cautious, still official. As the minutes went by and the glasses were refilled, though, it appeared that he too had learned something of that human side of the business. The guests and the gods became indistinguishable.

Normal hospitality was invariably left to the women of the family. And they often appeared hardest hit by the Polish crisis. Many led lonely lives, cut off on suburban housing estates, with no greater ambition than to own a telephone. Not that everyone had to sit back and wait for one.

'The going rate,' said one housewife, 'is two leather jackets. I know a man who took the two jackets along to the supervisor's office. A few weeks later they put the phone in. If you don't have leather jackets, then you have to reckon on about three hundred dollars in cash. And, believe me, there are those who pay. Me, I wouldn't give it to them even if I had it.'

Someone laughed. 'There is another way,' said a neighbour. 'Become a first-class invalid. It means you'll get your phone, but you're probably too disabled to pick it up and use it. I knew a family who moved their sick mother-in-law into their flat so as to get the phone – and then pushed her out when they'd got it.'

The alternative was simply to queue for the public call-box. There wasn't even one per block. Often the windows were cracked or there wasn't a box at all, and everyone would listen to the conversation. 'I was standing there one night,' said the housewife, 'and there was a girl obviously talking to her boyfriend. And they were arguing away and she was saying, "I don't think we should go out any more," and a woman in front of me yelled out, "You tell him! That's right, tell him where to get off! I wouldn't take that from a man!" And then everyone joined in and there was total chaos.'

The women in the family enjoyed considerable authority. They demanded much from life because much was demanded from them. The privileges were limited. When pregnant they could stand in special food queues while other women poked their stomachs to see if they were faking with pillows. 'I was just about to be served,' said one woman, 'when the old bag across the counter jabbed me in the stomach and said, "You're not pregnant at all." I had been standing in there with all the pensioners and war heroes for hours.' Some women would get others to queue for them. At the rate of two hundred zlotys an hour you could rent a body to keep your place. But that only left you free to queue somewhere else. Nonetheless pregnant women got a larger meat ration than most people; on a par, they said, with a coalface worker.

As compensation there were always the so-called 'Houses of beauty'. They were to be found even in the smallest and most unbeautiful places. Their aim was not just smoothing wrinkles but lifting spirits as well. Behind them lay some sound psychology. A complete facial treatment cost about the same as a big bar of chocolate, and had the advantage of not being rationed. Women and sometimes men would come in from the cold and lie back for an hour, dreaming of youth or romance. The women cared greatly what their men looked like. There was a limited and short-lived craze for the Lech Walesa style. A number of men obligingly grew moustaches. Strangely, there was also a craze for the Government minister with whom Walesa negotiated in the Lenin shipyard – Mieczyslaw Jagielski. More than one female acquaintance described him as 'dishy'.

The emphasis on good looks led many women to spend hours making their own clothes. The richer ones would buy them from the stylish but expensive private boutiques. No one went out in the evening wearing their day-clothes. Going out meant dressing up. Taking a girl out meant buying flowers. 'What do you think?' said a young housewife, 'That you can just turn up empty-handed? You can bring one flower or you can bring twenty. It doesn't matter, but you've got to bring something.' Social points would be scored by turning up for a date with a car. That signified influence if not money. A girl would also expect to be entertained. There were never that many discotheques, but a serious relationship demanded more than a coffee bar.

There was one unadvertised disco, built like a cavern. It was almost on top of the railway tracks that ran along the Vistula embankment. You knocked on the door and a fat oaf would put his head out and demand a hundred zlotys. That was his tip and nothing to do with the entrance fee. However, the door opened and you could usher your guests inside.

I ushered mine in for the first and last time. As they entered a young girl was sick over their feet. The welcome didn't get much warmer. More money changed hands and we descended a circular staircase towards the source of a pungent, irritating smell. On each level there was a small bar and an equally small dance floor. Somebody was clearing up glasses. An old record was playing to nobody. The smell got worse. The fun was clearly over. In this case it had been ended by the police, who had broken up the party with tear-gas. No one seemed to know why.

But there was more conventional, family entertainment. Dinner at a big hotel would often be served up with a cabaret act – an obligatory striptease, a magician and some dancers. Each act got two goes, either to allow the performers to take off more clothes or to complete their number.

One of the better entertainments included an annual pop festival which, in November 1981, took place in the textile city of Lodz. It was an incongruous affair, following on from a series of so-called 'hunger marches' organized by the city's women. They had walked through the streets coining such slogans as 'The Government governs, the Party directs, and the nation starves.' At that time none of those slogans was accurate. The Government wavered, the Party panicked, and the nation more or less fed its stomach. But pop music was a welcome relief for all of them.

The devotees took it seriously. It was important to look the part. One corner of the hall was given over to the face-paint shop. You could have a spray job on your hair, choose your streaks or arrows or leave it to the experts – the Polish punks who could talk about 'jam sessions, peace and rock' as well as anyone. Each of them had paid the equivalent of two week's wages for a ticket. For that they could sleep in the hall and make love in it if they felt the urge – and some clearly did. One man explained simply, 'It means to us what it meant in Britain in the sixties. Freedom.'

At the back of the hall a line by the poet Czeslaw Milosz had been daubed on a streamer and stretched from one wall to another. It read 'Nurture the people, give them a clear sky.' Perhaps few even noticed it, but the organizers must have thought the sentiment worth underlining. At any rate, they all danced in a crowd with helmets and hats and hands stretched upwards in victory salutes. The next day they went back to the university sit-ins.

Large numbers of young people visited the West during the seventies, when visas were an attainable privilege. It meant they could see their own system and others in perspective. No one lay awake dreaming of Piccadilly, though. On the whole they returned home with fewer dreams, less hard currency than they had hoped for and some unpleasant nightmares about washing up in hamburger bars late at night and illegally. Poland's prodigal youth often found the West a chastening experience.

The young were not alone in wanting to return home. There

was Jas, who had lived for more than twenty-five years in England
and had kept to himself. But then in the late seventies he had
joined a club: the small band of people who decided to return to
their native Poland to die. For more than ten years he had worked
as a train driver on the London underground. His job had
consisted of sitting on the Central Line, speeding through the
darkness, and stopping when he arrived at the light. For that he
had acquired a house in the southern suburbs, asthma, and an
unquenchable desire to return to see his native country. And now
he had done it.

He sat bolt upright on his chair. He sported a moustache and a
military haircut. He wore a sports jacket and tie, and his English
had far too many colloquialisms to have been learned in a
classroom. 'We finally decided to sell up,' he said. 'We got ten
thousand quid for the house, and when you bring that kind of
money over here it's a lot.'

'Don't you mind about the different politics?'

He laughed. 'Why should I care about politics? Look, I say what
I want. I talk to my friends. I say what I feel. Besides – ' he spread
his hands – 'besides, I'm an old man. I'm not worth the trouble.
Who is going to care about me?'

The man had bought himself his flat. He had enough left over
for the luxuries that came with hard currency. 'I came back to be
with my friends and my family. England was fine. I have no
regrets. But now I have come home.'

It did not matter that the restaurant beside his flats served only
smoked salmon, hare in cream sauce and fruit cocktail. He had his
mind on other things. The flat seemed to have nothing of England
in it. The furniture was Polish, as were the pictures. He had
merely stopped off in the West, bought himself a slice of novelty
and then a return ticket.

One elderly woman told a different story. She had returned to
Poland with her husband in 1948. He had fought in the then non-
Communist army and ended the war in Britain. According to her,
he was told that if he didn't return home immediately he couldn't
return home at all.

'We came by ship and arrived in the port of Gdynia. It was all very strange. Everywhere there were people with guns, and they were asking who we were and what we had done, who did we speak to and all this sort of thing. And I found it very frightening.' She had had a daughter, but her husband had died. She could have gone back to the West, but knew no one and had nowhere to go. 'I miss the freedom of England. I miss the English customs. I miss just being able to get up and go somewhere when I feel like it.'

'Do you regret coming back?'

'Yes, I suppose I do. If we had stayed life would perhaps have been very different.' She smiled wearily and put down her teacup, the only china she possessed. She offered more cake and told her daughter to fetch it from the kitchen.

'It doesn't matter for me,' she said quietly when the girl had gone. 'But for my daughter it could have been very different. I mean really different, you understand me?' It was a statement, not a question.

It was not surprising that families were close in Poland, infinitely closer than in the West. So were friendships. Having a friend meant more than occasional outings to the cinema, a party or a joint holiday. A friend was someone who would hide you if you wanted to drop out, who would give you money if you were unemployed, who would share their flat and their food with you. Friendship was a long-term commitment. The poorer you were, the more essential it became.

It could not have been more essential than in a one-room squat on the eastern side of the Vistula, the side that looks towards the Soviet Union. It was not a typical room. No one would suggest that there were many Poles living in such squalor. But it represented the point where the system broke down. And whatever the Government said about welfare for all, Poland had its own socially deprived and could not cope with them.

It was November 1981, and I had obtained the family's address from a local Solidarity branch. The union was trying to help, but the problem was immense. For in this one room lived two adults and their five children. The age range was nine months to fifty years.

It was difficult for the family to welcome visitors. The room was no more than a hundred and fifty square feet. On one wall a dirty sink, beside it a table and two chairs. In another corner some of the mattresses had been piled up on a shelf. Others were already on the floor. A pram stood in the centre of the room. A child barely older than the baby was changing its nappy. There was a dank, clammy smell. It was warm but filthy. The children looked astonished to see a stranger. One of them lay on the mattress and hid under a blanket. For all its closeness the family could not do much together. They ate in shifts, two at a time, because there weren't enough plates for all of them. The parents could not eat until the children were in bed. There were not enough chairs to sit on. They could not go out as a family because they were all doing different things. The father was off work with chronic bronchitis and for the time being did nothing at all. The mother was a proud woman. She didn't want to complain, but life was hardly easy. 'There were some people who came to see us from the local council,' she said. 'They told us we couldn't stay here. They needed a room for people who were worse off than we were.' She did not smile at the irony.

'What can you afford to eat?'

'Meat is just not possible,' she said. 'I buy eggs for the children. They're quite cheap. Apples and bread, I don't know. Potatoes we get as well. There's not very much.' She put on her coat and scarf and went out into the snow to illustrate the point. A quarter of a mile away she arrived at a bustling private market. There was meat, but she didn't buy any. Poultry was being sold as well, for exorbitant prices. She bought her eggs and her apples and went home. On her husband's salary and an occasional handout from Solidarity there was no other menu available.

Poland's sociologists may not have seen this woman's plight, but they knew enough to be profoundly worried. Successive years of economic hardship with the prospect of many more to come were taking their toll on families. As one of them commented, 'After a while the people start to hate each other. They hate themselves, even, and lose their pride. And then they hate the Government.'

People complained most about the drudgery of queuing. It was not unusual for Polish housewives to first join a queue and then ask the people what they were queuing for. Shopping dominated conversations, the newspapers, sermons, dreams and drunken parties. As one journalist put it, 'We are forced to go out on the street, foraging like wild animals. I don't know if you can understand what that is like. A housewife has to give a dinner party. She doesn't decide in advance what she's going to give the guests. She goes out to see what she can find. It's still a matter of pride. You have to give your guests something.'

Surprisingly, perhaps, good manners and charm withstood the hardship of daily life. Women were treated with exceptional reverence. Men would raise their caps in greeting, bow low and kiss the female hand. Politeness and etiquette were of paramount importance. It was a social error to arrive late. It was considered awkward not to greet those who shared your table in a restaurant or joined you in a lift. Omit such niceties and you would instantly be exposed as a loutish foreigner.

It seemed there was only ever one foreigner who had been accepted unreservedly into Polish families. He was an Englishman called Clive Harris, a faith-healer from the London suburb of Wembley. Harris had been visiting Poland since the late seventies and was without question the country's best-known Englishman. It is not clear whether he really possessed extraordinary powers, for he refused to discuss them or indeed anything else. But his influence over the people of Poland was undoubtedly special. Whether in the capital or in the mountain villages of the south, the people queued to see him in their hundreds. In a country not normally given to hero-worship, Harris was one of the major exceptions. 'I would say to you that Clive Harris is my friend,' said one of his helpers. 'What can I tell you about him? He is just a nice, simple guy, and we love him. He doesn't want to get mixed up with politics. That's why you can't talk to him. He doesn't want anything to come between him and the healing.'

It was a winter morning in Warsaw when I first saw the 'nice guy' perform. The crowds had been building up since dawn. The venue was a monastery in the old town, where all those who wanted treatment would assemble. They brought a doctor's certificate, exchanged it for a numbered ticket, and wrote their ailment on the back of it. Then they would return to the queue. It was an extraordinary sight. The poor and sick from a Communist country standing as best they could, muffled against the cold. Some of them were supported by friends. Others sat in wheel-chairs. Those too sick to move were laid on stretchers in the chapel. An unending stream of suffering. To many of them Harris must have represented the answer to a final prayer. There were some habitués, though. Several had seen Harris before and derived some benefit. There had been no magic moment. The ailment had simply eased.

Harris entered the chapel silently and without any words of welcome. A short man, balding, wearing a light singlet and dark trousers, he went straight to work. An interpreter was at his side whispering 'head', 'heart', and so on. Babies were lifted up to him. He would bend towards a wheelchair. At one point he admini-stered to a priest. On all of them he laid his hands for no more than a few seconds. His eyes were shut, his expression serene. As he moved on down the line the treated gave way to the expectant. Sometimes, though, they would stand as if in a trance. One of Harris's assistants would guide them gently towards the door.

Harris's popularity may have owed something to the short-comings of the Polish health system, but the Poles' penchant for folklore and spiritualism may also have played a part. Many people possessed the strong desire to believe in something beyond the affairs of daily life. For that reason herbal treatments, potions and even acupuncture came into vogue. To some families in Warsaw the mention of a cold would immediately send them to their kitchen stoves, boiling assortments of herbal remedies. I was offered such a medicine and told to sip it slowly. A black liquid, it tasted much like cold coffee. I was given a further supply to take home in a bottle and drink before going to sleep. By morning my cold had improved considerably.

Polish families passed on more than just folk medicine. Popular mythology passed on from home to home and was widely believed. In Gdansk, for instance, it was said that a statue of Christ shed real blood at certain times of the year. The authorities had surrounded the base with concrete, but still the blood came through. A number of local people said they knew about it but refused to visit the spot. In Warsaw a building site is said to have been cursed by the Jews during the Nazi occupation. The land had been forcibly removed from them, their buildings razed to the ground. They had sworn that nothing would ever be built there again. The story says that successive building projects were tried, but they all resulted in failure. And today the site is apparently still wasteland.

The Jewish families were once counted among the richest and most influential in Poland, but the Nazis saw to their destruction; the entire Jewish population has now largely died out. By 1980 there cannot have been more than some three thousand Jews living in the entire country. It was odd, therefore, to talk of a Jewish question, but one existed all the same. It explains why about a hundred people gathered one morning in Warsaw outside the Ministry of Justice to protest about the role of 'Zionist Fascists'. Men with dark eyes and expressions of hatred assembled with posters and placards to hear speeches against Zionism. It was curious that such an issue should have surfaced on the street corner in Warsaw in 1981, when there were, after all, other grievances to be aired. The explanation lay not with the people, however, but with the politicians. Somewhere inside the Communist Party one of many factional disputes had burst into the open. Perhaps a Communist of Jewish origin had come under pressure from a group of opponents. Perhaps someone wanted to exploit anti-Semitist feeling for their own political ends. At any rate, they got their supporters on the streets to stir up trouble.

About this time workmen were trying to renovate Warsaw's only synagogue. The few remaining Jews preferred to worship in public and not in a private flat. Ryszard Tomasz was in charge of the work. He had already lain once in a grave, a mass trench that he and several hundred other Jews had dug early in 1944. Somehow, when the Nazis began shooting, he had fallen unhurt into the pit and managed to escape. These days he acknowledges things have improved, but the Jews are still not popular. 'Whenever things go wrong in Poland, people blame the Jews. When there's no bread in the shops or the trains don't run on time, they blame the Jews. We're the natural culprits.' Tomasz said the Polish Jews still passed on their history and religion to their families, but there was little reason for them to stay in Poland. The Jewish presence, once stronger in Poland than anywhere else in Europe, would one day disappear.

These days Warsaw's Jewish cemetery is full of crumbling gravestones, half overgrown with weeds. In winter a few scraggy trees provide nests for the rooks that squawk constantly overhead. At the entrance a keeper rushes out of a wooden hut to tell visitors to wear a hat. But there are few visitors. The names on the headstones mean little enough to Warsaw's inhabitants. To them the Star of David is the symbol of a race they won't be told about and will not see again in People's Poland. Occasionally you come across an old man singing a lament beside his family's grave, a wailing chant that he will take with him when he dies.

Across town the memorial to the Warsaw Ghetto is now surrounded by modern blocks of flats. It is not an attractive monument. Figures frozen in struggle with a different system and different politics. A few sad flowers and pieces of straw are pressed against them. In the late afternoon a handful of old men walk pensively up and down beside the monument, then sit down, rest and walk again. At times when the suburban traffic clears there is a moment or two of peace.

To underline its declared tolerance of the Jews the Polish State pays considerable sums of money to support a Jewish theatre. Most of the actors have to be taught Yiddish, but the theatre is recognized as professional. It has provided at the very least a training-ground for actors who have moved on to other theatre companies in Poland. In general it is poorly patronized, and without official finance it would have folded years ago. Foreign tourists are the mainstay. Most neither understand the Yiddish nor the translation into Polish provided on headsets. If it were not for the music it would be a highly forgettable evening in Babel. But the music rescues the performances.

Those who understand the languages say the standard of the acting is high. It is run by a cheerful, middle-aged man who sees no problems, hears no problems and has only kind words for the

State. He says there is no anti-Semitism. His theatre is proof of that. What the State pays has nothing to do with conscience money. It is an attempt to keep alive an integral part of Polish culture. The theatre draws both converts and sceptics, but it remains the only stage of its kind outside Israel, and the only one conceivable in a Soviet bloc capital.

'. . . And what if family life in Poland doesn't work out?'

'We get divorced just like you in the West. But it's hard to find somewhere else to live.'

So it was for a woman in her late thirties living on the outskirts of Poznan, in the concrete, flatland that seems to stretch for so many thousands of miles through the East. Her husband had divorced her. She was left with a bright, cheeky teenage daughter who already preferred staying home with her boyfriend to going out. She herself had acquired a man. He had attached himself at a party and had flung his arms and his emotional burdens around her neck. She had carried them partly to escape from her own.

'I never really liked him. But, you know, he was there and seemed to need me. I didn't even fancy him. But he kept on at me and in the end I let him have what he wanted.' She laughed and then shrugged her shoulders as if it was all rather trivial. 'And then he went to England and got involved with some Polish woman there. He was only away for a short time. I don't really know what happened, except I picked up the pieces. He came back saying he hadn't meant it and it was me he loved and all I wanted to do was to tell him to leave me alone.'

'Why didn't you tell him that?'

'I did, but he kept coming back saying he didn't know what he'd do without me. He had money, came from a good family. It shouldn't have been so hard for him, but it was. He still comes back and I still see him. Why? I don't know. You tell me why. Perhaps there isn't anyone else. Perhaps I've just got used to him. Who knows?'

Her moods made her very sad or very happy. There was little in between. And in the end the daughter became the dominant character, often abrasive and needlessly thoughtless in comments to strangers. Her mother became annoyed with her, but could think up no punishment. The effort was too great. Mostly mother cooked, daughter ate. She loved cooking. The sauces would compensate for the lack of substance. When I remember her I see a narrow kitchen crammed with utensils and packets, a sitting-room where unexpected guests were always bedding down on the floor, books in English and Polish. In the corridor hangs her half-length coat made of rabbit.

In January 1982 she was fired from her clerical job in a State industry. In order to live she began selling clothes, a talent she suddenly had to discover. She is back in an office now, though, and her love-life is still a problem. 'Maybe,' she says, 'I prefer living alone.'

I was back in the family for just two days. Long enough to hear that they had saved since their son's birth fifteen years ago to buy a flat for his eighteenth birthday. They had paid a small monthly sum to the post office, but they were no longer sure why they had bothered. The authorities had told them that their subscriptions had not yet purchased a full square metre of flatland, let alone a whole apartment. The son would be badly disappointed on his eighteenth birthday – and quite likely on his twenty-fifth as well.

The bad weather stayed on throughout my visit. But as I left the family the children were skate-boarding outside the flats, while others kicked around a football. Then the boys carried their satchels inside and dumped them, the girls took off their uniform brown aprons and began their homework. One of them was reciting the poem for next day's memory test.

> Day of Victory – verdant May
> The scent of lilacs in the air.
> Grandpa sits lost in thought
> Recalling days of war.
>
> How with the great Soviet army
> He marched against the foe,
> Although it seems a hundred years
> It wasn't long ago.

How he had a comrade Misha
Who in the trenches lost his life.
With more comrades like his Misha
We could fight the whole world's strife.

Day of Victory – verdant May
The lilacs cast a shadow.
Grandpa sits lost in thought,
Think along with him.

That night I drove home around one o'clock in the morning. I passed an electrical shop, and in the light from the window display you could see four deck chairs on the street and four blanketed figures in animated discussion.

I had forgotten the consumers' night-shift, keeping the list of those who had ordered electrical goods safe twenty-four hours a day until their products arrived or until they became too bored or sick to continue. It was the only reliable way of doing business.

They sat there and I drove past. They were just a hundred yards from a large luxury hotel, and just two hundred yards from the Tomb of the Unknown Soldier – who in his time had heard quite a few of those nice promises too.

Not the End

For about a mile the ground rose steadily. A few trees already showed the colours of autumn. Then there was a sudden dip and a downhill slope all the way to the border, the bridge and the river. The end of the Slav lands and the beginning of East Germany – where the Russians had put it. The car rattled, but it had made good time from Warsaw. The four hours to Poznan had been the worst, all horses and carts, unlit by night, a constant danger to the heavy east–west traffic.

'My heart was beating so loudly,' said the girl. 'When we got close to the border I felt that anyone outside the car could have heard it with no difficulty at all.' They slid into line behind a Renault. A quiet, fraternal border post, a few cars and some lorries standing unattended.

'They were going over the car in front, literally taking it apart,' she said, 'and I thought, "This is it. My turn next. Something will go wrong." I turned to my friend and said to him, "In a few minutes I don't think you'll be my friend any more."'

Her thoughts returned to the day a few weeks earlier when her passport had been born. Out of the vast bureaucracy, the dead weight of files, reports, applications and petitions the system had thrown up her name. The militia had given her the news and told her to go to the Passport Office. She had gone there hardly daring to believe it was true.

'I've come for my passport,' she told the woman in the office.

'What's your number?' The woman checked a list. 'What have you come for?' she shouted. 'We're still doing those who came way before you. Can't you see how busy we are?'

'But the militia told me to come here.'

The woman's expression changed rapidly. 'Oh, I see. I'm so sorry.' She tried to smile. If there had been a red carpet in the cupboard the girl is convinced she would have brought it out and laid it. 'Well, that puts a different complexion on the whole thing. Let me look at the list. Oh, yes. Here it is. There . . . there, it's all in order. I'm so sorry for the trouble.'

The girl sent a telegram from the first post office she passed. Her relatives in France would get a shock some hours later. She went home, hardly noticing the way. The days that followed were spent saying goodbye. 'See? We said you'd get out,' her friends told her.

'I didn't take anything with me. Nobody gave me a present. I left all the books and posters and badges . . . everything I had collected. I didn't even do the washing up. I left it for my friends and family. I think I knew I wouldn't be coming back. At least for a long time, many years, till things changed. Not the end . . . but just a long, long time to wait.'

The owners of the Renault were packing away their possessions. They were angry and annoyed. Already the customs men had lost interest in them. They started the car and moved off. The girl said, 'I opened the window and handed out my passport.'

'What happened then?'

'Nothing. I had been tricked. Nothing at all happened. No search, no questions, nothing.' She was genuinely offended. 'I could have had five printing-presses in the car and they wouldn't have found them. I was so surprised.'

The car crossed the Oder into East Germany, on to the straight roads that Hitler had built for a very different kind of world. A few hours later they drove through the final border at Helmstedt into West Germany, past the dogs, the no man's land, the tank traps, the guns, walls and cameras – the heap of sophisticated paraphernalia that lets the East sleep peacefully at night.

'We celebrated in one of those roadside cafés just inside the border. A cup of coffee – not champagne. It was so hot and I was so tired – tired psychologically, deep down inside. It was three days before I broke down – and then I couldn't stop crying.'

Six months earlier the girl had celebrated what was to be her last birthday in Warsaw. Twenty-six candles on a cake that had taken a large chunk out of the monthly sugar ration. Someone turned down the lights and lit the candles. She blew them out and everyone clapped and cheered and sang the Polish 'Happy Birthday' – 'May You Live a Hundred Years.'

And then, according to custom, they lit just one of the candles, a small, wavering flame that is left to burn to symbolize the future. She does not remember if it burned all the way. By that time the guests were caught up in the laughter and the celebrations. Most probably someone just put it out after a few minutes and threw it away.